Work and Object

Work and Object is a study of fundamental questions in the metaphysics of art, notably how works relate to the materials that constitute them. Issues about the creation of works, what is essential and inessential to their identity, their distinct kinds of properties, including aesthetic properties, their amenability to interpretation, their style, the conditions under which they can go out of existence, and their relation to perceptually indistinguishable doubles (e.g. forgeries and parodies), are raised and debated. A core theme is that works like paintings, music, literature, sculpture, architecture, films, photographs, multi-media installations, and many more besides, have fundamental features in common, as cultural artefacts, in spite of enormous surface differences. It is their nature as distinct kinds of things, grounded in distinct ontological categories, that is the subject of this enquiry. Although much of the discussion is abstract, based in analytical metaphysics, there are numerous specific applications, including a study of Jean-Paul Sartre's novel *La Nausée* and an exploration of conceptual art. Some surprising conclusions are derived, about the identity conditions of works and about the difference, often, between what a work seems to be and what it really is.

Peter Lamarque is Professor of Philosophy at the University of York. He has published extensively on the philosophy of art and the philosophy of literature. His books include *Truth, Fiction, and Literature: A Philosophical Perspective* (with Stein Haugom Olsen; Clarendon Press, 1994), *Fictional Points of View* (Cornell University Press, 1996), and *The Philosophy of Literature* (Blackwell, 2008). Among his edited books are: *Philosophy and Fiction: Essays in Literary Aesthetics* (Aberdeen University Press, 1983), *Concise Encyclopedia of Philosophy of Language* (Elsevier Press, 1997), and *Aesthetics and the Philosophy of Art: The Analytic Tradition: An Anthology* (with Stein Haugom Olsen; Wiley-Blackwell, 2003). He was Editor of *The British Journal of Aesthetics* from 1995 to 2008.

Work and Object

Explorations in the Metaphysics of Art

Peter Lamarque

OXFORD
UNIVERSITY PRESS

Great Clarendon Street, Oxford OX2 6DP
United Kingdom

Oxford University Press is a department of the University of Oxford.
It furthers the University's objective of excellence in research, scholarship,
and education by publishing worldwide. Oxford is a registered trade mark of
Oxford University Press in the UK and in certain other countries

© in this volume Peter Lamarque 2010

The moral rights of the author have been asserted

First published 2010
First published in paperback 2012

All rights reserved. No part of this publication may be reproduced,
stored in a retrieval system, or transmitted, in any form or by any means,
without the prior permission in writing of Oxford University Press,
or as expressly permitted by law, by licence or under terms agreed with the
appropriate reprographics rights organization. Enquiries concerning
reproduction outside the scope of the above should be sent to the Rights
Department, Oxford University Press, at the address above

You must not circulate this work in any other form
and you must impose this same condition on any acquirer

British Library Cataloguing in Publication Data
Data available

Library of Congress Cataloging in Publication Data
Library of Congress Control Number: 2010920509

ISBN 978–0–19–957746–0 (Hbk)
ISBN 978–0–19–965549–6 (Pbk)

Printed in the United Kingdom by
Lightning Source UK Ltd., Milton Keynes

Contents

Preface vii

1. Introduction 1
2. On Bringing a Work into Existence 33
3. Work and Object 56
4. Distinctness and Indiscernibility in the Allographic Arts 78
5. Aesthetic Essentialism 95
6. Aesthetic Empiricism 122
7. Imitating Style 139
8. Objects of Interpretation 153
9. How to Create a Fictional Character 188
10. Art, Ontology, and the End of *Nausea* 208
11. On Perceiving Conceptual Art 220

Bibliography 234

Index 245

Preface

This is a selection of papers of mine on a tightly-knit cluster of issues regarding the metaphysics and ontology of art. Most, although not all, of the papers have been published before but I have reworked them all to a greater or lesser extent. I have tried to remove repetition but some points inevitably come up more than once, fitting into slightly different contexts. Also by tolerating a degree of repetition I have made it possible for each paper to be reasonably free-standing and readable independently of the others. Although I have given some care to the order in which the papers are presented (it is not the order in which they were written) so as to allow the arguments to develop, there is no harm in dipping into the volume at any point to reflect on specific topics.

Several themes weave through the papers and it might be helpful to give a brief overview of these so as to form a general picture of the areas covered. Here are some of the issues addressed:

Issues about ontology

On the face of it pictures, novels, poems, symphonies, improvised jazz, sculptures, buildings, ballets, improvised dance, movies, conceptual art, photographs, and multi-media installations are a motley, ontologically speaking. Much philosophical ingenuity has been invested in finding unity here, notably through appeal to traditional categories like physical particulars, universals, mental entities, actions, and so forth. A central theme of the book is that such uniformity as there is lies in the idea of a 'work', while allowing that works can be particulars or types. The nature and ontology of works as cultural artefacts is explored, e.g. set against the realist paradigm of mind-independent objects; as are relations between works and 'mere objects', works and other kinds of artefacts (e.g. those defined through their function—such as tools or machines), and works and natural objects. Key theses defended on the ontology of works are: that works (including musical, pictorial, literary, sculptural, etc. works) are cultural artefacts among whose essential properties are intentional or relational properties (i.e. *what they are* as works is partially dependent on how they are *taken to be* by qualified observers); that works are distinct from the 'objects' that constitute them; that they are underdetermined by physical or notational properties; but that they are nonetheless real (not merely ideal) entities, among the 'furniture of the world' (though not of course 'natural'), publicly perceivable, and objectively characterizable.

Issues about art and aesthetic properties

No attempt is made to define 'art' and only tentative suggestions offered about how works of art can be delimited from the wider class of works (e.g. in relation to values). But some core issues in aesthetics are addressed: what aesthetic properties are (how they relate to non-aesthetic properties, how far they are intrinsically evaluative), the role they play in the identity conditions of works, the nature of forgeries and parodies, and the status of copies, performances, and variations. Key theses on aesthetic properties are: that some works possess some aesthetic properties essentially; that aesthetic properties are relational, resting partially on responses of qualified observers; that their relation to non-aesthetic properties is probably not best characterized as supervenience; that objects per se, including those that constitute works, do not possess aesthetic properties essentially; and that a case for aesthetic realism can be made.

Issues about the metaphysics and epistemology of cultural artefacts

The idea that works, perhaps all cultural artefacts, have essential properties that include intentional and relational properties is explained and defended. Works owe their existence to human acts and their continued survival to human attitudes; they have a beginning (i.e. they are not eternal, even those that are types) and they cease to exist when their essential intentional and relational properties, including generic and work-specific properties, are lost; the 'objects' that constitute them might survive even though they (the works) do not. Epistemological questions are raised. What is it to perceive, experience, and understand works as described? What are the criteria for a qualified observer on whom norms of perception, experience, and understanding are dependent? What is it to experience a work *as* a work? How, for example in the case of a painting, does that experience relate to the experience (perception) of the physical basis of the work (i.e. the paint, canvas, colours, etc.)? Does it make sense to suppose that observers might be deeply mistaken about the properties of a work (in a way that they perhaps could be with natural objects)?

Issues about meaning and interpretation

Mere objects have no intrinsic meaning; such meaning as they have they acquire through human activity and intentionality. Works, in contrast, given their essential properties, are intrinsically bearers of meaning or significance. In virtue of what? Do their meanings change as contexts of reception change or is their meaning tied to their identity? Meaning properties include what works are *of* or *about* but only some meaning properties are subject to interpretation. Key theses on these issues are: that the nature and methods of interpretation are relative to the objects of interpretation; that the debate between realists and constructivists on interpretation (whether or not interpretation can partially create the objects of interpretation) gains clarity in the light of the distinction between works, in the sense defined, and objects; that a robust, non-relativistic, view of interpretation can allow for a degree of 'construction'.

Issues about experience (and 'empiricism')

An important theme is the role of experience not only in the appreciation and evaluation of works but even in their identity conditions as works. A moderate version of 'aesthetic empiricism' is defended, according to which *there can be no aesthetic difference without a perceptual (experiential) difference*. A criterion for the role of provenance-related facts in contributing to the identity conditions of a work is proposed via the following question: *What information about a work to be aesthetically evaluated would an informed observer need in order to experience the work in a manner appropriate to the kind of work it is and sufficient to set a standard for a correct aesthetic response to that work?* Two further principles inform the discussion: (a) If there is a difference between a work and an object or 'mere real thing' then that difference must yield, or be realizable in, a difference in experience; and (b) If *a* and *b* are distinct works then the experience of *a* is different from the experience of *b*, when each is experienced correctly.

Issues about creation

What is it to create a work? What is it to create a fictional character? If works are 'cultural' or 'institutional' entities what is involved in bringing them into existence? Key theses here are: that works are the product of human agency and intention; they 'emerge' when work on them has been completed; they are completed, as opposed to abandoned, under a conception of the finished product; the creation of a completed work involves the manipulation of a 'vehicular' medium constrained by an 'artistic' medium; completing a work is not just deciding to stop—i.e. to stop manipulating the materials—but involves making that decision in the light of a conception of what has been achieved, against a background of cultural practices that determine what *can* be achieved at any time. On creating fictional characters, it is argued that they are initiated types (in Jerrold Levinson's sense), grounded in acts of story-telling, although not essentially bound to any one, even if tied to a reasonably determinate historico-cultural context; character-identity is interest-relative and a character's variant identity conditions determine which of its properties are essential; fictional characters are created just to the extent that their grounding narratives are created, narratives that afford a kind of indexicality in character identification. The literary dimension of character creation is also explored accommodating symbolic, value-laden, and interpretation-dependent factors.

Issues about style

What is style? What is it for a work to exhibit a style? It is argued that a distinction should be drawn between 'act-based' and 'feature-based' conceptions of style, the former defining style as 'a way of doing something'; that stylistic properties apply to works not objects, such that two indiscernible objects associated with distinct works might exhibit distinct styles; that discerning a work's style presupposes knowledge of the work's origins; that one consequence is that parodies and forgeries might, in spite of appearances, fail to reproduce styles (except under the more limited 'feature-based' conception).

PREFACE xi

Issues about value

What kinds of values do cultural artefacts, and works in particular, possess? In virtue of what do they acquire these values? What are the consequences of their ceasing to be valued as they were valued when created (e.g. as a result of social change)? Key theses are: that the identity of a work is intimately tied to its value, broadly conceived; that value is grounded in the experience a work affords; that where the valued experience, normatively associated with a work, is no longer achievable (either because of deterioration in the work itself or because of a loss of underlying cultural conditions) then the work's survival is put in jeopardy; that there is a high degree of normativity in judgements of a work's value (how a work is valued is linked to its aesthetic and other properties as a work, and to the experiences it affords when experienced correctly).

Applications

Throughout the book specific examples from a range of art forms are offered and discussed by way of illustrating the theses. But two papers are devoted in a more focused way to applications of the 'work'/'object' distinction: 'Art, Ontology, and the End of *Nausea*' (Chapter 10) and 'On Perceiving Conceptual Art' (Chapter 11). Both make substantial claims about the works involved. The discussion of Sartre's novel *La Nausée* interprets the final scenes in the novel as proposing a view about art ontology, consonant with Sartre's philosophical writings about the imagination. This view, it is argued, relies on something like the work/object distinction, whereby works of art are not objects of perception at all, nor strictly objects of thought (like a circle), but objects of the imagination which acquire intentional properties (e.g. aesthetic and representational properties) only as such, these properties never being inherent in the physical analogues created by the artist. This theory is expounded in detail, in a largely sympathetic spirit. The work/object distinction is also applied to conceptual art. Drawing on the principles of aesthetic empiricism, it is argued that conceptual art can only be appreciated as conceptual art (indeed as art at all) if it is associated with distinctive kinds of experience, not reducible to the experience of the 'mere real objects' which form their observable base (from urinals to lights going on and off). It is also argued that reductive accounts that try to assimilate such art into pre-existing categories—the philosophical, the literary, the visual—are inadequate.

The broader context

Many of these issues are at the forefront of current philosophical aesthetics. The metaphysics or ontology of art has been given huge impetus by the groundbreaking work of analytical philosophers like Nelson Goodman, Arthur Danto, Richard Wollheim, Joseph Margolis, Nicholas Wolterstorff, Eddy Zemach, Jerrold Levinson, Gregory Currie, David Davies, Amie Thomasson, and Nick Zangwill. There is considerably more clarity now than thirty years ago about how works of art fit into the general scheme of things. This book aims to consolidate and extend this foundational work, putting forward a distinctive set of hypotheses across a range of issues and offering a unified vision of the field. In recent years aesthetics has been brought right into the mainstream of analytic philosophy, forging deep and illuminating connections with other branches of philosophy, including metaphysics, philosophy of mind, philosophy of language, and value theory. The book builds on these connections and it is hoped will stir interest in philosophers working in these other areas: on realism, essentialism, cultural objects, interpretation, identity, the metaphysics of properties, and on artistic values. It also aims to make an impact directly on aesthetics, showing how analytical methods can be used effectively to probe enduring and difficult issues about the arts. Here in particular it builds on the work of prominent aestheticians like Frank Sibley, Kendall Walton, Malcolm Budd, Roger Scruton, Anthony Savile, Alan Goldman, Noël Carroll, and Robert Stecker, who, among many others, have shown how rigorous thinking is possible about the values of art.

I owe far more debts of gratitude for my thinking on these topics than I am able to acknowledge. I realize working through these papers that three antecedent philosophical works in particular have clearly had a profound influence on me—Arthur Danto's *The Transfiguration of the Commonplace*, Kendall Walton's 'Categories of Art', and Jerrold

Levinson's *Music, Art & Metaphysics*—and the frequent references to these throughout the book account for most of the repetitions. I thank those authors profoundly and apologize if I have too shamelessly appropriated their ideas. Apart from that, I have profited enormously from discussions of my work in a large number of locations around the world where I have been privileged to give papers, including meetings of the British Society of Aesthetics, the American Society for Aesthetic, and the Nordic Society of Aesthetics, as well as numerous philosophy departments at home and abroad. I thank all the people who contributed to those discussions.

Source of previously published chapters:

'On Bringing a Work into Existence', in Michael Krausz, Denis Dutton, and Karen Bardsley, eds., *The Idea of Creativity*, Leiden: E. J. Brill, 2009.
'Work and Object', in *Proceedings of the Aristotelian Society*, vol. cii, part 2, 2002, pp. 141–162.
'Distinctness and Indiscernibility in the Allographic Arts', in Claes Entzenberg and Simo Säätelä, eds., *Perspectives on Aesthetics, Art and Culture: Essays in Honour of Lars-Olof Åhlberg*, Stockholm: Thales, 2005.
'Aesthetic Essentialism', in Emily Brady and Jerrold Levinson, eds., *Aesthetic Concepts: Essays After Sibley*, Oxford: Oxford University Press, 2001.
'Imitating Style', in Lars-Olof Åhlberg and Tommie Zaine, eds., *Aesthetic Matters*, Uppsala: Uppsala University Press, 1994.
'Objects of Interpretation', in *Metaphilosophy*, special issue on The Philosophy of Interpretation, vol. 31, nos. 1/2, January 2000, pp. 96–124.
'How To Create a Fictional Character', in Berys Gaut and Paisley Livingston, eds., *The Creation of Art*, Cambridge: Cambridge University Press, 2003.
'On Perceiving Conceptual Art', in Peter Goldie and Elisabeth Schellekens, eds. *Philosophy and Conceptual Art*, Oxford: Oxford University Press, 2007.

I am grateful to the publishers for permission to reproduce this material.

1

Introduction

This book explores the very idea of a 'work'. What kinds of works? Things like: pictures, prints, musical works, poems, novels, dramas, films, architectural works, sculptures, dance, as well as various styles of performances, multi-media displays, installations. This is not an exhaustive list. Some but not all of these will be works of *art* in an honorific sense. Works of art will have a special place in the enquiry but will not be its sole focus. Indeed to give primary focus to the great iconic works of art—from any tradition—can lead to distortion in an ontological enquiry as such works often turn out to have properties of a peculiar and uncharacteristic kind. Value will be absolutely central to the enquiry but it would be wrong to suppose that the difference between those works that are art and those that are not rests only on their relative location on a scale of value. There is no one set of values that applies across all works, even across works in a particular medium. Criteria of value are related in a complex way to aims, genres, conventions, and practices. The difference between, say, a run-of-the-mill whodunit and *Middlemarch*, in virtue of which the latter is a work of art but not the former, is not that the former tries and fails to do what the latter does well. They are different kinds of works and in important respects are incommensurable. To count as a work at all is already to be invested with some value, to invite and have the potential to sustain a minimal degree of interest of a specific kind. That is not to say there cannot be bad works but even bad works have achieved the status of works.

Not just any scribbling can count as a picture or any stream of words a poem or any sounds a musical work, quite apart from their status as art. To count as a work the scribbles or words or sounds need to meet certain conditions, both generic and genre-specific. Much of this enquiry will be a pursuit of just such conditions, a pursuit by no means straightforward. Two tendencies in attempts to characterize works will be confronted and rejected: the tendency to suppose that inherent or formal properties alone are sufficient to determine what counts as a picture or a poem or music; and the tendency to suppose that the properties by which works are identified as works are always value-neutral.

No attempt will be made to *define* 'art', as that enterprise is commonly understood, even though some of the conclusions will be conducive to certain approaches to the definitional issue surrounding art. Finding a theory of the *work* is task enough. The term 'work' applies widely and the central connotation of *working*, as an action, should not be overlooked in this context. The idea of a purposeful activity, engaged in with some degree of effort and with some more or less determinate end in mind, crucially underpins a generic conception of 'work' covering activities as diverse as working on a building site, working at an essay, working for a living, and producing a work of art. Already such a list indicates a process/product ambiguity in the term 'work', which distinguishes, for example, 'The work took three days' and 'The work is hanging on the wall'. While it might seem obvious at first sight that philosophers of art are concerned with the product sense of 'work', in fact the process/product distinction has been deliberately blurred by those who argue that works of art, including paintings, poems, and symphonies, are, from an ontological point of view, *au fond* more like processes than particulars, perhaps *actions* or *performances* of a certain kind.[1] Even if we seek to retain the distinction we shall see that matters concerning the process of producing a work—the *means* by which it is produced—will play a central role in the identity of the work itself.

Questions about work-identity will be at the heart of the enquiry and another important distinction arises: between those factors that determine, of any work, what *kind* of work it is, and those factors that determine what *particular* work of that kind it is. In other words we need to ask in virtue of what, say, this set of sentences counts as a *novel* or a work of *history*, or these physical marks as a *picture*; but also in virtue of what the sentences count as *Middlemarch* or *The History of*

---

[1] Gregory Currie, *An Ontology of Art*, New York: St Martin's Press, 1989; David Davies, *Art as Performance*, Oxford: Blackwell, 2003.

England (think of translations or corrupted texts) or the marks count as *The Last Supper* (think of wear and tear and heavy-handed restoration). There are complex issues about work-identity and survival, from both a theoretical and practical perspective. How much restoration can a painting sustain and remain the *same work*? How far can a musical or dramatic performance deviate from the composer's or author's instructions and remain a performance of *that* work? How damaged can a sculpture become, through weathering or neglect, and remain not only the sculpture it once was but indeed a sculpture at all?

1.1. Preliminary Distinction between Work and Object

A distinction between 'work' and 'object' runs through this study and it will be helpful at this early stage to give a brief initial sketch as to what that distinction amounts to before it is further refined in pages to come. Associated with every work is what might be called its constituting medium or material. For pictures the medium includes such material as canvas, paper, paint, charcoal, as well as configurations of line and colour. For carved sculpture the material is stone, marble, wood, or broadly anything that can be carved; for cast sculpture it is bronze or iron, or other materials that can be moulded and set. For literary and musical works the constituting medium is more difficult to specify, at least without begging important questions in ontology. To say that language is the medium of the literary and sound that of the musical might be true but is not entirely illuminating. More precisely it might be supposed that word-sequences of some kind constitute literary works and sound-sequences of some kind musical works. That at least will be sufficient for the time being. Other types of works should follow this general pattern. Films are constituted by projectable images, dance by sequences of bodily movements, buildings by bricks and mortar. This is all rough-and-ready, needing considerable refinement. But it helps to yield a key question to be investigated, namely how a work and its constituting medium are related. If the medium—patches of paint, configurations of lines, pieces of bronze, sequences of words or sounds or movements—can be squeezed into a catch-all notion of 'object' then the question becomes: how does a work relate to the object that constitutes it?

The answer to be proposed and developed is that a work is not identical to its constituting object, having fundamentally different identity and survival conditions. The existence of a constituting object—a painted canvas, a piece of moulded bronze, etc.—is never sufficient for the existence of the corresponding work. Works are underdetermined by their physical or structural properties, or, put more strongly, there are possible worlds where, for any given work in this world, a structurally isomorphic object exists that is not a work at all or not that work. A work is a cultural entity whose existence depends essentially on appropriate cultural conditions. Without those conditions, which make possible the creation of the work in the first place and ensure its subsequent survival, the work would not exist even if the materials that make it do exist and exist in just that form.

The contrast between work and object is not perhaps quite as sharp as these preliminary points suggest. Works *are* objects (broadly construed) but objects of a distinct kind, cultural or 'institutional' objects. The crucial distinction is between that which depends essentially on human thought and cultural activity and that which does not. Objects, in the sense in which the term contrasts with 'works', do not depend on such thought or activity. Of course for those with anti-realist inclinations in epistemology the idea that objects of any kind should be entirely distinct from human thought is already contentious and question-begging. But, for the purposes of this enquiry, there should be no need to engage deeply with the realism/anti-realism debate in epistemology, even though there are issues to be addressed about realism in specific areas, for example, regarding aesthetic qualities and indeed works themselves.

To get a handle on the idea of objects or object-based features being independent of cultural activity, think of what it might take to describe and investigate the properties of objects in this sense. The culture-independent existence of objects is determined by the degree to which the investigation can proceed without reference to cultural practices and using only, for example, the language and methods of the physical sciences.[2] The properties of paint, colour, bronze, sounds, and movements are amenable to such description. Interestingly the properties of language seem not to be, except at the fundamental level of the production of sounds or the physical properties of inscriptions. This might be problematic for incorporating literary works in the general schema. No doubt it would be possible to contrast literary works with the bare inscriptions or sounds that underlie their linguistic realization but it might seem more useful to draw the relevant contrast between work and *text*, where a text is already identifiable in linguistic—and thus cultural—terms. This might well serve to set literary works apart, an issue that will come up as we proceed.

No argument has yet been given for why works are not identical to their constituting materials and that will call for detailed attention later. Two further points, though, need to be made on the idea, briefly sketched, that these materials (the 'objects') are distinguishable from the works they constitute in virtue of being characterizable through naturalistic (scientific) methods without reference to cultural activity. The first is that many of the materials used are themselves products of human artifice and invention, thus, arguably, not separable from human culture. The point is not the same as a general anti-realist conception that sees all objects as dependent on mental activity. Certain pigments of paint are artificially produced, bronze is an alloy, even paper and canvas require manufacturing processes. But all that the argument of independence requires is that the constituting materials are, as it were, analysable in physical or naturalistic, as opposed to cultural, terms. No essential reference to the cultural

---

[2] John R. Searle has drawn a similar distinction between 'those features we might call *intrinsic* to nature and those features that exist *relative to the intentionality of observers, users, etc*'. He goes on to describe a screwdriver drawing out these contrasting features:

It is, for example, an intrinsic feature of the object in front of me that it has a certain mass and a certain chemical composition. It is made partly of wood, the cells of which are composed of metal alloy molecules. All these features are intrinsic. But it is also true to say of the very same object that it is a screwdriver. When I describe it as a screwdriver, I am specifying a feature of the object that is observer or user relative. (*The Construction of Social Reality*, Harmondsworth: Allen Lane, 1995, pp. 9–10).

However, Searle's discussion is far more inclusive than our own and he seems not to hold that the social artefacts he describes exist as distinct entities from the objects (or activities) that ground them.

conditions required to make bronze or steel or paint is needed to give a complete physical analysis of their intrinsic natures. The underlying thought here is important for it is possible to give radically different kinds of descriptions of ostensibly (though not actually) one and the same object, either as a *work* or as a mere *object*, where cultural properties play an essential role only in the former. The fact that certain materials, for example pigments of paint, are difficult to make, requiring complex and expensive procedures, has no explanatory role in the purely physicalistic description but might be absolutely crucial in understanding the cultural significance of the artefact.

The second point concerns the limitations of what I have called physicalistic or naturalistic description. In the cases where the works are themselves physical objects, their physical properties are readily amenable to such descriptions. But not all cases do seem of this kind. We have already noted a problem about literary works. If the constituting materials of literary works are taken to be token physical marks or sounds then there is something for physics to investigate. But that seems to ignore the crucial aspect of literary works, namely that they are linguistic entities of some sort and thus, given that language is a cultural phenomenon par excellence, not describable in the vocabulary of the natural sciences. A related but not quite identical problem arises for musical works. If the constituting medium of music is taken to be token sounds (i.e. actually occurring sound waves) then indeed there could be naturalistic, culture-independent, descriptions of it. But, more plausibly, what constitutes a work of music is not a sequence of sounds in a given performance but something more abstract like a sound-sequence-type multiply realizable in different performances. Such a move can readily be applied back to literary works, identifying them not with individual token texts but with, say, sentence-sequence-types. But abstract entities like types do not seem to be the subject of empirical or naturalistic enquiry. So even then the general schema looks inadequate.

In certain respects the objection is well taken showing how difficult it is to generalize across works and how flexible a notion of 'object' is needed. But there is no call to abandon the central claim about works and objects, namely that for every work there is an underlying constituting medium, describable (broadly enough) in culture-independent terms, even if in the case of literary works we need to descend to a pre-linguistic level of mark-types and sound-types (in fact appeal to sentence-sequence-types might be sufficient on the assumption that no reference is made to any further cultural or work-specific role for those types). That the claim is sustainable for sound-types (music) is evidenced by the fact that many sound-types, some ostensibly very similar to musical ones, are instantiated in entirely natural occurrences, from birdsongs to wind or water effects. Presumably these can be studied both in their instantiated tokens and with regard to the formal or other qualities they possess as types—and this without reference to human culture.

1.2. Constraints and Desiderata

Discussions of the nature of the work have led to almost every conceivable ontological position being proposed. Works have been thought to be physical objects, abstract entities of various kinds, action-types, performance-tokens, mental states or processes, imaginary objects, and other things besides. So how should we proceed? What constraints can guide us in pursuing a theory of the work? Ontological enquiries—asking what kind of entity something is—are by their nature abstract and it would surely be unduly realist-minded to suppose there is a fact of the matter waiting to be discovered.[3] Ontology, as Quine has taught us, is largely a matter of choice, albeit not arbitrary choice. For Quine the ultimate constraint is Occam's Razor or ontological parsimony: do not multiply entities beyond necessity. The best theories, we are told, are the simplest, those with the least ontological commitments. But Quine also taught us that theories are underdetermined by the evidence so we should not expect ultimate convergence towards any single optimum theory and if that is true in science it seems all the more likely to be true in

---

[3] Amie L. Thomasson has advanced detailed arguments against the 'discovery paradigm' in the ontology of art: 'since facts about the ontology of the work of art are determined by human conceptions, the resulting facts are, as we might say, ontologically shallow—there is nothing more to discover about them than what our practices themselves determine' ('The Ontology of Art and Knowledge in Aesthetics', *Journal of Aesthetics and Art Criticism*, 63, 2005, pp. 221–229, at p. 228).

theorizing about the cultural realm. In any case, seeking simplicity and minimizing ontological commitments, while no doubt sound, are principles that apply at a very general level. What guidance can we seek for our theorizing in the specific context of works?

David Davies has proposed a 'pragmatic constraint' in precisely this area and it is a good place to start:

> Artworks must be entities that can bear the sorts of properties rightly ascribed to what are termed 'works' in our reflective and appreciative practice; that are individuated in the way such 'works' are or would be individuated, and that have the modal properties that are reasonably ascribed to 'works', in that practice.[4]

It must be right, first and foremost, to ground a theory of the work in the very practices—critical, creative, institutional—in which the individuation and appreciation of works takes place. A theory wildly at odds with the implicit norms of such practices could not command assent. In this there is a disanalogy with scientific theory or even with some philosophical theory. Assumptions governing our day-to-day commerce with the natural world and the linguistic practices associated with those assumptions have throughout the history of science been vulnerable to scientific advance: from Copernicus to Einstein, deeply held 'commonsense' beliefs about how the world is and the well-entrenched linguistic idioms that support those beliefs have been challenged and undermined. In philosophy, many would agree with Russell's claim—or at least not suppose it to be outrageous—that 'the point of philosophy is to start with something so simple as not to seem worth stating, and to end with something so paradoxical that no one will believe it'.[5]

Davies's pragmatic constraint might well be accepted by many aestheticians as a broad procedural principle but it has not stopped philosophers from pursuing the Russellian path and ending up with theories that clash, sometimes seriously, with what seem like fundamental beliefs held by practitioners of the arts. Collingwood argued that 'the work of art proper is something not seen or heard';[6] others

---

[4] David Davies, *Art as Performance*, Oxford: Blackwell, 2003, p. 18.
[5] Bertrand Russell, *Logic and Knowledge*, R. C. Marsh, ed., London: Allen and Unwin, 1956, p. 193.
[6] Collingwood, *Principles of Art*, p. 142.

have deduced that musical works are discovered not created;[7] others again (including Davies himself) that works of art like paintings are not particulars but actions or performances of some kind. It would be quite wrong of course summarily to dismiss such views because they clash with 'commonsense'. But such outcomes make one question the force or applicability of the constraint. Perhaps, as Davies reflects, practices associated with the arts are not sufficiently coherent or consistent to constrain theorizing. For this reason he introduced the terms 'rightly' and 'reasonably' into the statement of the constraint, requiring that theory should emerge only from 'rational reflection' on the practices, rather than trying to patch together an unruly motley of unreflective modes of speaking. The danger with this proviso, though, is that it could license an almost wholesale rejection of the assumptions behind such modes of speaking, following the model of the sciences.

There is a much deeper reason for trying to preserve basic beliefs about works enshrined in practices. The works and the practices are internally linked in a way that is not true of natural objects and the linguistic practices within which they are identified and described. It makes sense to say that many of our commonly held beliefs about natural objects are wrong or misplaced, that we could find out things about their intrinsic nature that deeply clashed with such beliefs. But works have no independent existence from the very practices that serve to discriminate them from other things. We could no more find out that we are massively wrong about those discriminations than we could find out that we were wrong all along about what counts as scoring a goal in soccer or how to move a castle in chess. The whole system of beliefs underlying our talk about works, performances, copies, scores, reproductions, restoring, exhibiting, appreciating, forging, and creating is not independent of the practices that define and make possible our multi-faceted commerce with works in the first place. Of course there is often little reflection on how these discriminations are made; of course there might be inconsistencies revealed under pressure of reflection; of course there are difficult and controversial cases. If none of that were true there would be no need for enquiries of this kind. But the rootedness of works in human practices must be

---

[7] A notable recent example is Julian Dodd, *Works of Music: An Essay in Ontology*, Oxford: Oxford University Press, 2007.

the starting point for—and the principal constraint on—any enquiry into the ontology of the work.[8]

Needless to say, there are different practices to take into account, some of which will be described in the coming pages. It is arguable that each of the art forms, from literature to cinema, from dance to architecture, have distinct practices associated with them. What makes something a literary work, for example, rests on complex interactions between writers, readers, critics, libraries, publishers, booksellers. The varied modes of producing and responding to works of literature, appreciating, interpreting, and evaluating their content, or marketing, cataloguing, and collecting copies of them, derive from long and evolving traditions. But nothing could *be* a literary work if it were not for activities of this kind. The discriminations that practitioners make are integrally tied up with such activities. So it is with all the arts and with works of comparable kinds.

The attempt to characterize identity and survival conditions of works—as part of a general theory of the work—might seem remote from such specific practice-based activities, but no competent exploration of the former can ignore the latter. The practices associated with works of all kinds are constituted by complex networks of beliefs, conventions, specialist terminology, and basic, often unstated, presuppositions. The ontologist looks for even more fundamental principles underlying all or most of the relevant practices and the pragmatic constraint tells him to take heed of the attributions and discriminations made within the practices and as far as possible not to conflict with them. With such in mind there seem to be a handful of very general but fundamental desiderata in exploring the 'work' which, if at all possible, should not be given up: for example, that works (of art) are public not purely mental entities; they are open to objective description; they have essential and inessential properties; they are grounded in human acts and attitudes; they are cultural, not merely natural, entities; they are created and can come into and go out of existence; they possess meaning or significance and are subject

---

[8] For pertinent observations on constraints on the ontology of art and on the importance of commonsense beliefs, see Amie L. Thomasson, 'The Ontology of Art', in Peter Kivy, ed., *Blackwell Guide to Aesthetics*, Oxford: Blackwell, 2003 and 'The Ontology of Art and Knowledge in Aesthetics'.

to interpretation; and they have intrinsic as well as instrumental value. No doubt these call for further explanation, even justification, but they provide at least an initial framework for the investigation.

1.3. Indiscernibles

An important strand in the argument that follows concerns so-called 'indiscernibles', namely pairs of items that are ostensibly indistinguishable (in outward appearance) yet purportedly are different *kinds* of entities, having different properties, including aesthetic and art-related properties. Discussion of indiscernible pairs has played a prominent role in the ontology of art, although not always to support the same conclusions. A preliminary word on the topic will help set up some of the debates to come.

As 'indiscernibles' have been the province of Arthur Danto for over forty years, we should begin with a brief reminder of his well-known examples. In his classic paper from 1964, 'The Artworld', Danto revealed the impact on him of an Andy Warhol exhibition in a New York gallery that consisted of facsimiles of Brillo boxes piled on top of one another.[9] Warhol's boxes were in fact made of plywood rather than cardboard but to all intents and purposes his boxes were visually indistinguishable from commercially manufactured Brillo boxes. Yet to Danto's satisfaction, and to that of other art critics at the time,[10] Warhol's Brillo Boxes were works of art, while the commercial ones were not. In what could the difference lie? Broadly Danto's answer is this: that Warhol's Brillo Boxes are not just physical objects but objects of a different kind, they embody a thought, express a meaning, have a content, they are about something, they are embedded in art history, while the commercial artefacts, in spite of having a function and conforming to a design, have no meaning, do not stand for anything, and have no connection with a theory of art.

---

[9] Arthur C. Danto, 'The Artworld', *Journal of Philosophy*, 61, 1964, pp. 571–584.

[10] Although, as Danto points out in a later essay, the judgement was by no means universal: see Arthur Danto, 'The Art World Revisited', in *Beyond the Brillo Box: The Visual Arts in Post-Historical Perspective*, Berkeley, CA: University of California Press, 1998, pp. 36–37.

Spurred on by the Brillo Box example and similar cases such as Marcel Duchamp's ready-mades (from fifty years earlier), Danto went on to construct his own thought-experiments involving indiscernibles, including, famously, the nine exactly alike all-red canvases,[11] each of which (in Danto's story) embodies a different work or in some cases not even a work at all, like the primed canvas by Giorgione on which, if he hadn't died young, he would have painted his unrealized masterpiece 'Conversazione Sacra'. It is all good fun. Because there is nothing, so the story goes, that allows us to distinguish the canvases visually, the question arises how it is possible for some members of a set of indiscernible objects to be artworks while others are not and how even among those that are artworks they can be different works. Danto believes that to answer such questions is to find the essence of art.

He also believes the method is entirely generalizable in philosophy. Indeed he thinks that the problem of indiscernible pairs, whose members occupy what he calls 'distinct ontological locations', is the very 'form' of philosophical questioning.[12] He gives examples from other areas of philosophy: Descartes's dream experience exactly matches waking experience, such that only an epistemological theory, not finer perceptual investigation, could discriminate between the two. Or in Kant's moral theory two actions might be exactly alike, both conforming to principle, while only one has moral worth (the other being merely prudential). Or, similarly, taking an example from Plato's Republic, the behaviour of a perfectly just man might be indistinguishable in outward appearance from the behaviour of a perfectly unjust man. Or there is Hume on causation, showing there is no discernible difference between events that are merely conjoined and those that have a genuinely causal connection. Or Wittgenstein asking what the difference is between my raising my arm and the arm rising. Danto attributes to Duchamp the parallel insight in philosophy of art that between pairs of indiscernible objects—snow shovels, urinals, combs, etc.—one might be an artwork, the other not.

On the basis of his discussion of indiscernibles Danto elaborates his subtle and influential theory of art. From his thought-experiments

---

[11] A. C. Danto, *The Transfiguration of the Commonplace*, Harvard University Press, 1981, p. 1f.

[12] A. C. Danto, *The Philosophical Disenfranchisement of Art*, New York: Columbia University Press, 1986, p. 151.

emerge a set of necessary conditions for a thing's being a work of art: mere appearance, for example, does not matter; what is crucial is that the work be about something, and subject to interpretation, it must express an attitude or point of view on its subject (which he associates with the work's style), and, importantly, it must be historically situated within a theory of art.[13] Only at a certain point in the development of art is it possible for a urinal or snow shovel to become art.

By emphasizing essential conditions for arthood, Danto is explicitly repudiating the anti-essentialist Wittgensteinian tradition that sees 'art' as a family resemblance term; and by arguing that not all art-related differences are perceptual differences he appears to reject the formalist tradition, for example of Clive Bell. Even Danto's Hegelian 'end of art' thesis, which is really a thesis about the end of art history, is inspired by the indiscernibility tests. Danto believes that art history comes to an end in the work of Andy Warhol, not only because there is nowhere else for art to go but because, in Hegelian fashion, art has finally transmuted into philosophy. As Noël Carroll puts it, summarizing Danto:

> once art has raised the problem of the nature of art in its proper philosophical form, art cannot bring the problem any closer to its solution. The problem has to be turned over to philosophers. That is, once modernism discovers the problem of indiscernibility, it has taken the problem as far as it can go. It remains to philosophy to finish the job. Nevertheless, in so far as the problem has been pushed as far as art can push it, the internal, developmental history of art terminates when modernism reaches the limits of its capacity to disclose the nature of art.[14]

There are certainly misgivings one could have about the kind of thought-experiments that Danto offers—Richard Wollheim, for one, has expressed deep misgivings[15]—but at least some of Danto's intuitions are sufficiently plausible to make us hesitate in endorsing any theory that contradicts them. In particular, as anticipated earlier, we shall be drawing out the consequences of the possibility of an object being distinct from a work even where the work shares all

---

[13] For an illuminating analysis of Danto's definition of art, see Noël Carroll, 'Essence, Expression, and History', in Mark Rollins, ed., *Danto and His Critics*, Oxford: Blackwell, 1993, p. 99ff.
[14] Carroll, 'Essence, Expression, and History', p. 93.
[15] Richard Wollheim, 'Danto's Gallery of Indiscernibles', in Rollins, ed., *Danto and His Critics*, pp. 28–38.

the material properties of the object. Duchamp's *Bottlerack* might be indistinguishable in material form from other bottleracks from the same manufacturer but is, arguably, distinct from them—and different in kind—in virtue of being a work.

Where we have to be especially careful is in the use of the term 'indiscernible'. Wollheim asks whether the indiscernibility is 'initial' or 'ultimate', in other words whether the twinned items in Danto's thought-experiments are indiscernible as the result of an initial cursory look or whether the indiscernibility persists through the most thorough and, as it were, discerning perceptual study.[16] The point is not to highlight a difference between the unaided eye and the technology of magnification for no amount of mere technological examination will reveal a difference between the red squares. Wollheim's point rather is that when all the relevant information is in about the items being perceived—including information about the artists' intentions—the items might no longer be perceptually indiscernible but indeed have come to *look* different (in a suitable context of viewing). This point will be crucial in the discussion to come. Danto's reply is to refer to his other examples of indiscernibles, such as Plato's perfectly just man alongside the perfectly unjust man, where close attention to physical properties will not reveal the relevant distinctness.[17] But it is far from clear that the comparison will meet the Wollheim objection. After all, attending to the observed behaviour of the two men might well reveal differences between them. Even where perception alone will not serve to distinguish among 'indiscernibles', Danto needs to defend, rather than assume, the analogy of pictorial art with non-perceptual cases. By emphasizing non-perceptual aspects of the differentia between art and non-art—along with his view that what makes something art, deep down, has very little to do with aesthetic qualities—Danto is in danger of being over-impressed by an eccentric range of cases (such is Wollheim's worry). Danto can poke fun, for example, at George Dickie for trying to rescue some aesthetic appreciation in the appearance of Duchamp's *Fountain*, which Danto believes, agreeing with Duchamp, is deliberately unsightly.[18] But

[16] Wollheim, 'Danto's Gallery of Indiscernibles', p. 35.
[17] Arthur Danto, 'Responses and Replies', in Rollins, ed., *Danto and His Critics*, p. 197.
[18] Arthur Danto, *Philosophical Disenfranchisement of Art*, p. 33.

Danto's insistence, like Duchamp's, that we need to move beyond aesthetics—'surfaces', he says, 'lovely or awful, are irrelevant or merely a fact'[19]—is not one of the more readily acceptable intuitions behind the indiscernibles cases. What needs examining is precisely what it is to experience a work as a work as distinct from experiencing something else that might look like, but is not identical to, that work. It might be very important that the relevant experience be an experience of aesthetic features for, as we shall see, it might be that the aesthetic character of a work is essential to that work's identity.

1.4. Aesthetics and Experience

The central role of experience in our apprehension of works is another core theme of the book and a version of 'aesthetic empiricism' will be defended. One claim of the aesthetic empiricist is that there could not be an aesthetic difference between indiscernible pairs without an experiential difference. This seems directly at odds with the use to which Danto and others have put the indiscernibles thought-experiments. If two perceptually indiscernible objects could be distinct works—as Danto believes—then it is a short step to saying that they could be truly characterizable through different aesthetic descriptions (perhaps, in the terms of Kendall Walton, when located in different artistic categories). Then it looks as if there could be an aesthetic difference without a perceptual difference and that contradicts aesthetic empiricism. However, it is important to establish just what the contribution of perception or experience is in the apprehension of aesthetic differences. Confronted with two 'indiscernible' objects with no further facts about them known, perception will not serve to discriminate between them (that is indeed why they are 'indiscernible'). It is only when there *is* a known difference between the objects, established by reference to facts such as conditions of production, intention, or artistic category, that, according to the aesthetic empiricist, there *must* be the possibility of

[19] Ibid., p. 13.

a difference of experience when the objects, now conceived as *works*, are correctly perceived.[20]

It is not just indiscernible pairs in *art* that raise issues about aesthetic appreciation. Similar examples can arise in nature, as was noted long before Danto. Immanuel Kant offers his own examples, one of which, about a 'rogue of a youth' imitating a nightingale's song, will be discussed in Chapter 6 'Aesthetic Empiricism'. Here is another of Kant's examples:

> it is of note that were we to play a trick on our lover of the beautiful, and plant in the ground artificial flowers (which can be made so as to look just like natural ones), and perch artfully carved birds on the branches of trees, and he were to find out how he had been taken in, the immediate interest which these things previously had for him would at once vanish.... The fact is that our intuition and reflection must have as their concomitant the thought that the beauty in question is nature's handiwork; and this is the sole basis of the immediate interest that is taken in it. (*Critique of Judgment*, Part I, Book II, §42)

Shakespeare raises a related point with examples of his own. Here is Portia at the beginning of Act V of *The Merchant of Venice*, speaking to Nerissa:

> The crow doth sing as sweetly as the lark,
> When neither is attended; and I think
> The nightingale, if she should sing by day,
> When every goose is cackling, would be thought
> No better a musician than the wren.
> How many things by season season'd are
> To their right praise and true perfection!
>
> [Act V, Scene I, 102–108]

---

[20] Nelson Goodman offers his own well-known but rather obscure—and controversial—formulation of a similar line, discussing his example of a Rembrandt and a perfect copy (forgery):

although I cannot tell the pictures apart merely by looking at them now, the fact that the left-hand one is the original and the right-hand one a forgery constitutes an aesthetic difference between them for me now because knowledge of this fact (1) stands as evidence that there may be a difference between them that I can learn to perceive, (2) assigns the present looking a role as training toward such a perceptual discrimination, and (3) makes consequent demands that modify and differentiate my present experience in looking at the two pictures   (*Languages of Art*, Indianapolis: Bobs-Merrill, 1968, p. 105).

For an illuminating discussion, see Robert Hopkins, 'Aesthetics, Experience, and Discrimination', *Journal of Aesthetics and Art Criticism*, 63, 2005, pp. 119–133.

Portia is elaborating on a similar analogy she had drawn a few moments earlier:

> A substitute shines brightly as a king,
> Until a king be by; and then his state
> Empties itself, as doth an inland brook
> Into the main of waters.
>
> [Act V, Scene I, 94–97]

Shakespeare, through Portia, is speaking of the context-dependence of judgements of beauty. The lark and the crow can be judged equally fine songsters, with their own very different melodies, as long as they are not heard together; and if the nightingale should sing during the day amidst the cackle of geese and other sounds we would not rate her higher than the wren. The point is not one (or not just one) of relativity for Portia introduces a normative element, insisting on 'right praise' and 'true perfection'. Our judgements of beauty demand that the proper context of perception be taken into account. The songs should be valued for what they are but, as phenomena of aesthetic interest, what they are is partially determined by the appropriate context in which they occur. The beauty of the nightingale's song is inextricably linked to the setting in which it naturally occurs. Only when indiscernible pairs are appropriately contextualized can they yield the right kinds of experiences. The king-substitute looks as good as (indistinguishable from?) the king until placed side by side with the real thing.

In Kant's example the 'lover of the beautiful' might be taken in by the artificial flowers but when the facts are revealed the aesthetic interest will 'vanish'. The experience of flowers only yields genuine aesthetic pleasure when accompanied by 'a concomitant thought that the beauty in question is nature's handiwork'. We might put it like this: it is not just the *appearance* of the flowers that is pleasurable but the appearance of the *flowers*.

The analogy with works is plain to see. Works too are subject to normative conditions of perception. Both the context of viewing and appropriate background knowledge contribute to the experience demanded by, and realizable in, a work when perceived correctly. Duchamp-style ready-mades—perhaps conceptual art in general (see Chapter 11 'On Perceiving Conceptual Art')—bring the point home forcibly for to perceive the snow shovel or the urinal merely as 'objects' is to fail to see them as *works*, and thus to fail to see the works at all.

Kant's example of the artificial flowers parallels the case of artistic forgery, which again is a topic that winds through the discussion (notably in Chapter 4 'Distinctness and Indiscernibility in the Allographic Arts', and Chapter 7 'Imitating Style'). Philosophers interested in the ontology of art have tended to focus on a rather special mode of forgery, the exact duplicate copy (hence the connection with indiscernibles). In fact the more common form of art forgery is where the forger seeks to reproduce the *style* of another artist, rather than some particular work (the much discussed examples are van Meegeren's forgeries of Vermeer—see Chapter 7). The key question in this context is not the moral (or legal) one of deceitfulness in passing off one's own work as someone else's, probably for financial gain, but whether there could be a genuine aesthetic or artistic difference between an exact copy (as in the former kind of forgery) and an original. It looks as if the distinction between work and object might be able to cast light on this question, developing the idea that, although the *objects*, as mere physical things, might be indistinguishable, the *works* are not. And do not aesthetic and artistic values reside in *works* rather than objects per se? Of course there are those—perhaps defenders of strong versions of aesthetic empiricism—who insist that if the original and copy are really indistinguishable in appearance then there can be no justification in saying that one has more *aesthetic* value than the other.

Gordon Graham has emphasized the tension between art establishment views about forgeries and about ready-mades.[21] While art museums are quick to reject forgeries when these are exposed as such, they are happy to embrace ready-mades. Is that position consistent? In the forgery case a good forgery might be indistinguishable from a work that is highly valued—why then is the forgery removed from view and thought to have no value? The ready-made case is a mirror-image of this. The ready-made is indistinguishable from an object that has no artistic value—why then should the ready-made be put on view,

---

[21] Gordon Graham, 'Aesthetic Empiricism and the Challenge of Fakes and Ready-Mades', in Matthew Kieran, ed., *Contemporary Debates in Aesthetics and the Philosophy of Art*, Oxford: Blackwell, 2006.

and highly valued, while the duplicate remains unnoticed? This looks like a problem for the aesthetic empiricist who recognizes value only in outward appearances. Would not such a person be committed to a consistent treatment of forgery and ready-made: either exhibit both or neither? David Davies has argued that the practice of the art world actually shows aesthetic empiricism to be false.[22] However, Graham, in response, is surely right to think that on its own this argument begs the question: 'The acceptance of ready-mades *presupposes* the falsehood of aesthetic empiricism, for the simple reason that, if it is true, the acceptance of ready-mades by the art world or anyone else is based on error. The existence of the practice cannot be taken as a decisive "fact" independent of the beliefs underlying it.'[23] What I hope to show in the chapters to come is that the work/object distinction can help in such disputes. To the extent that ready-mades are acceptable as works of art it is on the basis of the *kinds* of things works are (indeed what these works in particular are) and the peculiar properties they possess. Correspondingly it is just such peculiar properties that can be invoked to explain why forgeries are legitimately rejected.

1.5. Aesthetic properties

One peculiarity of works, so it will be argued, is that among their essential properties—those properties that help determine their identity—are relational and intentional properties. This implies that *what they are* as works is partially dependent on how they are *taken to be* by qualified observers. This already sets them apart from mere (culture-independent) objects that gain their identity as objects from their intrinsic properties. (Note that we often *identify* objects by appeal to relational properties—the third book on the shelf, a planet in the solar system—but that is not equivalent to having relational properties essentially.) Perhaps even more controversially it will be argued that some works have some *aesthetic* properties essentially. Thus, it might

---

[22] David Davies, 'Aesthetic Empiricism and the Philosophy of Art', *Synthesis Philosophica*, 15, 2000, 49–64.
[23] Gordon Graham, 'Aesthetic Empiricism and the Challenge of Fakes and Ready-Mades', pp. 14–15.

be that a work is essentially graceful or delicate or tragic. If aesthetic properties, as seems right, are response-dependent properties this claim might seem strange. For how could any responses to a thing be partially constitutive of that thing's identity? Are not facts about how people respond to something merely contingently related to the existence of that thing? Couldn't responses change over time? And differ for different people or different cultures? Could it really be that something might cease to exist when people stop responding to it? Again, such sceptical questioning is entirely legitimate when applied to mere objects. But works are not mere objects and it is precisely their embeddedness in cultural practices that gives them this peculiar status and at least paves the way for making sense of these seemingly bizarre consequences.

There are two kinds of relations that are problematic for aesthetic properties: their relation to non-aesthetic (e.g. physical, structural, intrinsic) properties and their relation to qualified observers. On the former relation, there is no doubt that aesthetic properties are *dependent* in some way on non-aesthetic properties, as forcibly argued by Frank Sibley, but the nature of that dependence is not clear. It seems plausible to think of aesthetic properties as *gestalt* or emergent properties that become manifest through a certain kind of attention to a thing's observable properties, more specifically its appearance, how it looks or feels. It is sometimes claimed that aesthetic properties supervene on non-aesthetic properties, in a sense spelt out in Chapter 5 'Aesthetic Essentialism'. But it is far from clear, as argued in that chapter, that the relation is best characterized as one of supervenience. What the Danto and Walton indiscernibles examples seem to show is that there is no straightforward supervenient relation between aesthetic properties and a base of physical or structural properties alone: aesthetic properties might vary against the same physical base. But once additional relational or intentional properties are built into the non-aesthetic base then the line between the supervening and the supervenient becomes blurred. The discussion intriguingly mirrors the discussion of how object-centred properties relate to work-centred properties, a topic at the very core of this book.

The relation to qualified observers has also to be handled carefully. When aesthetic properties are said to be response-dependent it cannot be that they are dependent on *any* responses. Few philosophers suppose that aesthetic descriptions are entirely subjective and much of the debate about aesthetic judgement in the eighteenth century (one thinks of Hume and Kant) rested on attempts to secure some kind of objectivity or at least inter-subjectivity in the aesthetic realm. The idea that there is degree of *normativity* in aesthetic judgement—that in certain contexts there are judgements one *ought* or ought *not* to make—has long been found appealing although its foundation has proved difficult to pin down. Postulating aesthetic *facts* as truth-makers for aesthetic judgements has seemed too strong, at least if facts are construed on the scientific model. Few have supposed there are mind-independent aesthetic facts. Yet it has not been thought inimical to defences of aesthetic *realism* that an element of response-dependence should be acknowledged.[24]

Jerrold Levinson, for example, is not untypical in defending realism by appeal to the responses of qualified observers. But it is instructive to compare Levinson's characterization of the ideal observer with David Hume's. For Levinson the observer, whose responses ground aesthetic normativity, is one 'who views a work correctly', that is, 'who properly situates a work with respect to its context of origin, including its place in the artist's oeuvre, its relation to the surrounding culture, and its connections to preceding artistic traditions'.[25] The characterization is different in subtle ways from that of Hume's 'true judges', who, it will be recalled, possess 'strong sense, united to delicate sentiment, improved by practice, perfected by comparison, and cleared of all prejudice' ('Of the Standard of Taste'). The main difference is to do with expertise. It is not that Hume's judges do not need expertise—they must be knowledgeable about art and about the artistic tradition—but the kind of expertise is rather different. For Levinson, the emphasis is on work-specific facts about provenance and art-historical context. For Hume, the emphasis is on receptivity, open-mindedness, experience, and clear-headedness. Levinson's position, unlike Hume's, is informed by the thought—so well articulated by

---

[24] For a critical survey of arguments for and against, see Nick Zangwill, 'Aesthetic Realism 1' and John W. Bender, 'Aesthetic Realism 2', both in Jerrold Levinson, ed., *Oxford Handbook of Aesthetics*, Oxford: Oxford University Press, 2003.

[25] Jerrold Levinson, 'Aesthetic Properties, Evaluative Force, and Differences of Sensibility', in Emily Brady and Jerrold Levinson, eds., *Aesthetic Concepts: Essay After Sibley*, Oxford: Oxford University Press, 2001, p. 62.

Kendall Walton—that the aesthetic properties we perceive in a work are dependent, amongst other things, on the art-historical category to which the work is correctly assigned. Once again it relies on the idea that *perception*, especially perception of aesthetic properties, is thoroughly imbued with *thought*, reinforcing the idea that how things *appear* is not independent of how they are *thought to be*, and emphasizes the role of art criticism and art history in the correct discernment of a work's aesthetic qualities.

But Levinson's defence of aesthetic realism also rests on the distinction between a descriptive core of (most) aesthetic concepts and an evaluative component. Take an aesthetic term like 'gaudy'. According to Levinson, we might 'approve a work *for* its gaudiness, . . . or *despite* its gaudiness', which, he claims, 'suggests that the essence of gaudiness is not a judgement of disapprobation on the speaker's part but instead a kind of appearance: a perceptually manifest effect one can register independently of any evaluative assessment of or attitudinal reaction to that effect.'[26] Levinson's point is that for most, although not all, aesthetic properties there is a phenomenological core, experienced by informed observers, that yields just the kind of objectivity required for a genuine aesthetic realism. He says: 'there is in regard to a given object almost always a descriptive aesthetic content such that ideal judges who would not apply to the object all and only the same aesthetic predicates—because they have, by assumption, different evaluative reactions or attitudes towards that content—can still agree on what that content is.'[27] In many ways this is attractive as a defence of realism as it is able to accommodate divergent, perhaps recalcitrant, evaluative judgements while retaining a core element of inter-subjectivity of response. That said, there are undoubtedly problems about how to characterize this core and whether it really is common to those who disagree at the level of evaluation.[28]

More interestingly the plausibility of this approach to aesthetic properties might partially rest on a blurring of the aesthetic with the art-critical, and this in spite of the phenomenological language. Art-critical judgements, of a descriptive rather than evaluative kind, lend themselves to a realist construal, to the application of truth conditions,

---

[26] Levinson, 'Aesthetic Properties, Evaluative Force, and Differences of Sensibility', p. 63.
[27] Ibid., p. 66.   [28] John W. Bender, 'Aesthetic Realism 2', pp. 93–94.

much more readily than pure aesthetic judgements. To recognize a work as baroque or romantic or symbolist requires less of an exercise of taste than do claims about its being graceful or delicate or unified. But if Ted Cohen is right there is no sharp line here.[29] Cohen famously argued, many years ago, that Sibley's distinction between aesthetic and non-aesthetic properties could admit of no principled or non-circular method of demarcation. Indeed Cohen challenged his readers to sort into aesthetic and non-aesthetic groupings a variety of terms applied to works of art, including (these are drawn from his list): allegorical, baroque, classical, derivative, didactic, geometrical, gothic, impressionist, Kafkaesque, nationalistic, painterly, realist, romantic, and symbolist. It just isn't clear, Cohen argued, whether the use of these terms rests primarily on 'taste', the Sibleyan *gestalt*, or on rule-governed conditions. Perhaps the urge towards aesthetic realism, especially in Levinson's version, which pulls apart the descriptive from the evaluative, encourages a similar blurring between, on one side, the phenomenological, i.e. purely aesthetic, and, on the other, the taxonomic or critical-cum-historical.

However, in the context of a theory of the work such a blurring need not be viewed negatively or as a weakness of this version of aesthetic realism. We have already intimated that in the case of some works there is a close, indeed essential, relation between the work and certain aesthetic properties, such that the very identity of the work is tied up with aesthetic responses to it. Now works themselves also gain their identity by being embedded in an art-historical context. Furthermore, if Walton is right, the correct perception of aesthetic properties in a work depends partially on recognition of the category of art to which the work belongs. What this all suggests is that the more we emphasize expertise in aesthetic judgement and the role of ideal observers, the less we will expect too sharp a line between aesthetic and critical-cum-historical judgements. Just as a work might be essentially classifiable as romantic or realist—to fail to classify it in those ways would be to fail to understand it—so it might be essential to discern the gaudiness or gracefulness of a work (whatever evaluation one gives these). The work, it might be said, *demands* judgements (or

---

[29] Ted Cohen, 'Aesthetic/Non-Aesthetic and the Concept of Taste: A Critique of Sibley's Position' *Theoria*, 39, 1973, pp. 113–152.

24 WORK AND OBJECT

responses) of these kinds, a demand fully acknowledged by the ideal observer. However, the possibility of locating aesthetic properties (and aesthetic responses) in a continuum with art-historical properties, and recognizing a realist element in both, only arises given the nature of works as culturally and historically embedded with at least some essential relational and intentional properties. It would seem much less plausible to make any such claims for 'mere' objects.[30]

1.6. Interpretation

If it is granted that works have relational and intentional properties as part of their very nature the question arises of exactly what properties are 'in' any individual work and which are 'imputed' to it. This brings up the vexed topic of interpretation in the arts. The emphasis in the discussion to follow is on what might be called the metaphysics of interpretation. How does interpretation relate to the different kinds of objects being interpreted (see Chapter 8 'Objects of Interpretation')? Does the mode of interpretation invited by *works* blur the distinction between what is *revealed* in interpretation and what is *constructed* in interpretation?

To get an idea of what is at stake in these questions and in the metaphysical enquiry that underlies them, let us start with a subsidiary question: what is the relation between the properties of an

---

[30] There is, however, a view about the aesthetics of the natural world that draws on parallels with the cultural embeddedness of works of art. Here is Allen Carlson explicitly drawing out the comparison:

the new paradigm for aesthetic appreciation of environments is comparable to the new paradigm for appreciation of art. The latter . . . is that of emotionally and cognitively rich engagement with a cultural artefact, intentionally created by a designing intellect, informed by both art-historical traditions and art-critical practices, and deeply embedded in a complex, many-faceted art world. The former may be characterised as emotionally and cognitively rich engagement with an environment, created by natural and cultural forces, informed by both scientific knowledge and cultural traditions, and deeply embedded in a complex, many-faceted world. (Allen Carlson, 'Environmental Aesthetics', in B. Gaut and D. M. Lopes, *Routledge Companion to Aesthetics*, London: Routledge, 2001, pp. 432–433).

On this account, of course, the difference between works and certain kinds of (natural) objects is not so great; indeed it likewise introduces a role for expertise in the appreciation of nature.

object (of any sort) and an interpretation of that object? It might seem natural to suppose that any genuine properties of an object are antecedent to any competent interpretation, indeed that the role of the latter is to disclose or bring to light the former. Interpretation, on this view, recovers such properties as are in an object but are not immediately apparent.[31] Such a conception is motivated by a realist intuition: things are as they are independently of how they are thought to be. Interpretation aims at truth. A more radical supposition, however, is that at least some of an object's properties, in some cases, are *constituted* by interpretation—they come into being only through interpretation. On this view, interpretation is constructive, helping literally to create objects of interpretation.[32] The motivating intuition here is anti-realist or constructivist. Must there be a conflict between these two intuitions? How might they apply to works?

A simple solution might be to postulate two broad species of interpretation, the truth-seeking kind that reveals hidden properties and is essentially a mode of exploration and discovery (call it revelatory interpretation) and the constructive kind that enlarges and offers new perspectives but strictly neither describes an antecedent reality nor aims at truth (call it creative interpretation).[33] To the extent that these are distinct and recognizable species, they conform to different demands we make on interpretation. Sometimes we expect interpretation to tell us what an object is really like, to show us something we have missed about the object; at other times this enquiry can seem altogether

---

[31] A clear defence of such a view is found in Robert Stecker, *Artworks: Definition, Meaning, Value*, University Park: Pennsylvania State University Press, 1997; and 'The Constructivist's Dilemma', *Journal of Aesthetics and Art Criticism* 55:1 (Winter), pp. 43–52; it is also defended in different chapters in Jerrold Levinson, *The Pleasures of Aesthetics: Philosophical Essays*, Ithaca, NY: Cornell University Press, 1996.
[32] The view is presented in Joseph Margolis, 'Reinterpreting Interpretation', in John W. Bender & H. Gene Blocker, eds., *Contemporary Philosophy of Art: Readings in Analytic Aesthetics*, Englewood Cliffs, NJ: Prentice Hall, 1993, pp. 454–470; and in *What, After All, Is a Work of Art?* University Park: Pennsylvania University Press, 1999; Michael Krausz defends a similar view in *Rightness and Reasons: Interpretation in Cultural Practices*, Ithaca, NY: Cornell University Press, 1993 and *Limits of Rightness*, Lanham, MD: Rowman & Littlefield Publishers, Inc., 2000.
[33] Some such distinction is acknowledged in Jerrold Levinson: 'Two Notions of Interpretation', in Arto Haapala and Ossi Naukkarinen eds., *Interpretation and Its Boundaries*, Helsinki: Helsinki University Press, 1999, pp. 2–21; in Eddy Zemach, *Real Beauty*, University Park, PA: Penn State University Press, 1997, p. 117; and in Peter Jones, *Philosophy and the Novel*, Oxford: Oxford University Press, 1975.

too pedestrian for we expect an interpretation to be fresh, original, and imaginative, showing us not hidden facts but new possibilities. Interpretation in musical or dramatic performance provides obvious instances of the latter.

Unfortunately distinguishing these two species of interpretation in itself does little to illuminate the problem originally posed, which is a problem about an object's properties and where, as it were, those properties reside. While it might be true that some interpretation is revelatory and some creative, it is clear, for one thing, that not any creative interpretation is as good as any other. What constrains acceptable interpretations of any kind is surely nothing other than the properties of the object itself. An object must have some properties in itself—some identity conditions—in order to be identifiable as an object of attention. We demand of creative interpretation not perhaps that it be true *of* the work but at least that it be true *to* it. Yet how are we to draw the distinction between what is revelatory and what is creative if we do not already know what properties truly belong to an object? It looks as if the realist intuition cannot simply be abandoned in favour of the anti-realist one, even in the most promising cases. But if the two species of interpretation are applicable to one and the same object then merely drawing that distinction will not tell us any more about how properties relate to interpretations.

It is arguable that the distinction between the two kinds of interpretation, with their corresponding intuitions, already presupposes a distinction between different kinds of objects and even different kinds of properties. Drawing on the distinction between work and object it seems possible—and promising—to seek to reconcile tensions in common suppositions about interpretation by finding a suitable role both for the realist intuition that objects are identifiable through their intrinsic properties independently of interpretation (even if subject to interpretation) and for a moderate version of creative interpretation allowing that some properties of some kinds of objects (works, in particular) are the product of, and are not antecedent to, interpretation.

If we think of 'ordinary' objects—plants, animals, planets, mountains, even those 'constituting' materials of paintings and sculptures that were mentioned earlier—we can give a rough-and-ready characterization of their intrinsic properties as those that belong to the object per se, apart from the relations that it stands in with other objects. These properties are not context-sensitive; being 'in' the object they persist from context to context. Some intrinsic properties are essential, without which the object would not be the object that it is; some are non-essential or contingent. Often the difference between essential and non-essential intrinsic properties is explicable in terms of determinable and determinate properties. Extended objects, like the ones mentioned, have spatial properties—size, shape, volume, and so forth—essentially but particular sizes, shapes, or volumes only contingently. Properties of objects bearing on their microstructure and the nature of their constituent elements are also intrinsic and might themselves be essential or non-essential.

'Ordinary' objects also have relational or extrinsic properties, including simple relations with other objects: next to, bigger than, owned by, parent of. They also might possess intentional properties, deriving from the attitudes, desires, thoughts, and fears they invoke in human beings: desirable, frightening, inspiring, dangerous. A subclass of intentional properties are aesthetic properties, of the kind earlier described, which can be possessed by natural objects as well as artefacts. In the case of 'ordinary' (or 'natural') objects only a small, highly restricted, class of relational or extrinsic properties are essential and almost certainly no intentional or aesthetic properties. Kripke, famously, has claimed the necessity of origins for living things, although this might be seen as a consequence of the necessity of constitution, in this case genetic structure. Normally relations that objects stand in to other objects, including the responses they invoke in people, are merely contingent. The objects could retain their identity even if those relations do not hold.

The striking contrast with cultural objects (with 'works') has been our dominant theme. Natural objects seem to allow little room for interpretation other than the strictly exploratory or scientific. Their intrinsic properties might be hard to discern and might at some level be theory-laden but the thought that the properties themselves, as opposed to the characterization of those properties, might be radically variable relative to human interpretative schemes or actually be constituted by interpretation, as claimed for cultural objects, has little intuitive appeal—except to the most extreme anti-realist. Works, however, seem altogether more intimately related to interpretation. If the argument so far is accepted, and cultural objects have intentional and relational properties as part of their identity conditions, then we might say, albeit with a hint of paradox, that works are *intrinsically* intentional and relational. But then the distinction between intrinsic and relational properties, paradigmatically attributable to natural objects, cannot apply in any straightforward way to cultural objects.

If we confront a painted configuration on a wall or a shaped piece of stone merely as physical objects we might well be able to explore their intrinsic physical properties but if we are asked to *interpret* or make sense of them we would inevitably need to know something about their origins. Without such information—and more besides—it seems that too many interpretations are compatible with the mere physical facts to make any meaningful interpretation possible. In short, only when we know we are looking at a *work*, indeed a work of a certain kind, would we know how to start the interpretative process. This encourages the thought that it is works not mere objects that are the bedrock of interpretation, at least in standard cases. We must not be blinded by the ease with which—given familiar cultural conditions—we are able to identify works as works. That should not lead us to suppose that the work simply *is* the object that we see. To recognize a work as a work—a coloured configuration as a painting (i.e. an intentional object conforming to cultural practices)—presupposes fairly complex background conditions. The only—rather special—sense in which interpretations apply directly to *objects* is the sense in which artists project an interpretation onto an object—perhaps a 'found object'—in order to render it into a work. It is in this sense, and only in this sense, that Arthur Danto sees works as functions of interpretations on objects.[34] But Danto's theory does not imply that the interpretations of art appreciators are directed at objects rather than works. We have to know both that something is a work and broadly what kind of work it is to begin interpretation.

What about the tension noted earlier between the need for identity conditions of a work to be sufficiently robust to provide a stable object of interpretation and the possibility that some properties of works are

---

[34] Arthur C. Danto, *The Philosophical Disenfranchisement of Art*, New York: Columbia University Press, 1986, p. 39.

constituted by, not antecedent to, interpretations? This of course is an instance of the familiar hermeneutic circle. But in distinguishing objects and works we now have better resources for approaching the whole question of what properties belong to a work and what properties are imputed to it through interpretation. Because works already have intentional and relational properties as part of their nature, they are, as it were, inseparable from their cultural wrappings, such that features of these 'wrappings' can be thought to 'belong to' the works themselves. Thus, properties deriving from how works are taken or thought to be can be part of the identifying conditions of works. It is perhaps here that revelatory interpretation and creative interpretation come closest together, where the former discloses properties present in a work and the latter generates such properties.

It would thus be wrong to insist on too sharp a line between, on the one side, objects, intrinsic properties, revelatory interpretation, and realist intuitions about truth, and, on the other side, works, intentional properties, creative interpretation, and anti-realist intuitions. The position is more complicated as we saw from the earlier discussion of aesthetic properties. For one thing, there is still room for realist intuitions in talking about works even if they need to be refocused. If the identifying conditions of works rest essentially on how they are thought to be then the realist divide between what something is and what it is thought to be does not immediately apply. But once a work has been accepted as such within a relevant cultural practice a kind of realism about its properties (even its aesthetic properties) is possible.

Take the often discussed example of Van Gogh's *Potato Eaters*.[35] Earlier arguments have suggested that there is nothing intrinsic to the physical marks, brush strokes, and colour configurations of the painting that determines that it is a work at all or a work of a particular kind, far less a representation. The representational properties are underdetermined by the physical facts. But once categorized as a representation, within a recognizable tradition, then certain basic facts about its depictive qualities are assumed; trivially that it depicts people sitting round a table, for example. Such a fact must be a

---

[35] This is an example discussed in Michael Krausz, *Rightness and Reasons: Interpretation in Cultural Practices*. We shall return to it in Chapter 8 'Objects of Interpretation'.

starting point for interpretation, not a product of interpretation. Of course all the interesting aspects of the painting's meanings leading to different and competing interpretations—formalist, psychoanalytical, Marxist, feminist—are still left open.[36] Even further along this line, just because certain properties of works are not obvious to any but the suitably informed does not imply they are matters of dispute or subject to mere hypothesis rather than truth or that they are not, in the relevant sense, objectively present as characterizing features of the work. The kinds of art-historical facts mentioned already have an easy realist construal. Conventional iconography in medieval painting, for example, establishes that the depiction of saints or allusions to Biblical events or other kinds of symbolism are matters of objective fact, even if accessible only through interpretation. This, of course, is revelatory, not creative, interpretation. It seems plain that we can retain realist intuitions even when talking of works and their intentional properties.

However, the anti-realist intuition that interpretation *imputes* properties, thereby helping to construct works, is of fundamental importance in thinking about works, even if it has little or no role in thinking about mere objects. Creative interpretation is rooted in artistic practice. After all, it is through a species of creative interpretation that an artist endows otherwise inert matter—paint, marble, words, sounds—with intentional properties and transforms objects into works. This is Danto's notion of the transformative power of interpretation, alluded to earlier. But creative interpretation is not restricted to artists. Critics too can have a transformative role in the appreciation of art; like artists, they too must employ the imagination in their response to art. Creative interpretation must supplement

---

[36] H. R. Graetz (*The Symbolic Language of Vincent Van Gogh*, McGraw Hill, 1963) interprets the painting in psychoanalytic terms, referring to the inner conflicts in Van Gogh's life; Albert Lubin (*Stranger on the Earth: A Psychological Biography of Vincent Van Gogh*, Holt, Rinehart, and Winston, 1972) claims the painting is about mourning; Griselda Pollock ('Van Gogh and the Poor Slaves: Images of Rural Labor as Modern Art', *Art History* 11, 1988) offers a Marxist-feminist interpretation. Is it truly a property of the work that 'the darkness and detachment of the figures express a lack of love and understanding which Vincent felt in his parents' house' (Graetz) or that 'the child represents Vincent's dead brother' (Lubin) or that the painting is 'about otherness and difference' (Pollock)? The work itself is perhaps indeterminate in these respects and we would have to follow through the interpretations carefully to see which, if any, might make any claim to truth rather than construction.

the revelatory kind. It is in the nature of the practice of art that appreciators engage imaginatively with works, projecting fruitful ways they might be seen or heard or read or performed. This is creative interpretation for it is constrained not by truth but by imaginativeness and possibility. The best creative interpretations are those that take the established aspects of works, those elements intrinsic to the works, and find new saliences for them,[37] or new ways of thinking about the work's themes, motifs, or symbolic or figurative aspects.

Does this activity genuinely add to the work or just play games with it? One reason for thinking it does expand the very conception of the work is that works, as intentional objects, bear with them the critical tradition that develops around them. This is partly a consequence of the practice of art, which invites critical engagement, but is also partly connected to the intentional nature of works, whereby, as we have seen, their identity is tied up with responses to them. Of course not any creative interpretation establishes a critical tradition. Only the best, most exciting, imaginative, or illuminating do so. But these imputations enlarge a work, they show ways in which indeterminacies can be filled out, they change the way a work is conceived, and if they become canonical there is no going back; the work grows into this new conception. What begins as a mere possibility develops into a realization and this becomes another route from 'imputed to' to 'in' or 'part of'.

We have travelled a winding path from our original conundrum about interpretation and the properties of works. Room has been found for the insights behind the two apparently irreconcilable positions: that of the realists, who hold that interpretation can only reveal pre-existent properties of works, and that of the constructivists, who hold that interpretations can help construct works. We need to preserve a fairly robust realist notion of works, even while acknowledging their grounding in cultural conditions and intentional properties. But the emphasis on the practice-dependence and intentionality of works has shown them to be crucially different from ordinary objects such

---

[37] The idea of interpretation as the assignment of saliences is developed by Michael Krausz in *Rightness and Reason: Interpretation in Cultural Practices*. Arguably this is what is going on in the interpretations of *The Potato Eaters*, mentioned in note 36.

that many common assumptions about realism do not apply. It is part of the practice involving these strange objects that, in opening up a field of possibilities, and inviting imaginative supplementation and the active search for new saliences and creative readings, there is scope in interpretation for work enlargement and creative imputation, as well as the revelation of what already exists.

2
On Bringing a Work into Existence

2.1. The Completed Work

The phrase 'completed work' has a pleasing ambiguity between process and product. When an artist's work is completed a completed work comes into existence. Completion of one kind signals completion of the other. When the (artist's) work stops the work (of art) starts. Indeed it seems a necessary condition for a work to come into existence that the work on it has been completed. The question is: what exactly occurs when a work comes into existence? If that question seems tendentious—as it will to some—then an alternative is this: what kind of change is wrought upon the world when the artist's work is completed?

It is far from clear what kind of thing a completed work is. Indeed given the diversity of the kinds of works at issue—paintings, prints, symphonies, songs, poems, novels, dramas, films, architectural works, sculptures, dance, etc.—it might seem unreasonable to expect any single or informative answer across the board. The intuitive differences between, say, sculptures and symphonies, the former apparently physical particulars, the latter apparently abstract structures, immediately suggest there is no one 'kind of thing' that a work is, thus that it is pointless proceeding. But the focus for the discussion seeks to accommodate the obvious diversity of works and, as far as possible, stay neutral on pressing issues in work ontology.

The latter might not be realistic in all cases. For example, if you hold that musical works are eternal sound-structure-types[1] then you

---

[1] As does, for example, Julian Dodd in *Works of Music: An Essay in Ontology*, Oxford: Oxford University Press, 2007.

will not be impressed by the phrase 'bringing a work into existence' for you hold that the work has always been in existence. However, you would be hard-pressed to deny that the 'composer' of the work actually worked at the composition (even if this work was a process of 'discovery') and completed it at some point. Then the question returns: what has changed in the world when the artist's work is completed? To suppose that the world was no different, in musical and artistic terms, after 1808, when Beethoven completed his Fifth Symphony—especially on the grounds that the Fifth Symphony has always existed as a sound-structure-type—is hyperbolic. The differences before and after this event are manifest and far-reaching. Perhaps, though, it might be argued, it is not the work itself that had this influence but the *discovery* of the work or the spreading *awareness* of the work. In any case, that a change was wrought upon the world when the compositional work was completed seems undeniable. So let us focus attention on that change.

The enquiry needs to be pinned down a bit more. For one thing, it does not need to be distracted with attempts to define art. Some of the works on the list will be works of art in an honorific sense, but many would not merit that title. There are paintings and poems and songs that are not normally considered *art* but are nonetheless completed works and need to be included. Questions of value, however, are inescapable in the enquiry. Michel Foucault, writing about linguistic works, nicely brings out the practical as well as theoretical problems in delimiting works, and the peculiar role of judgements of value.

What is a work? What is this curious unity which we designate as a work? . . . If an individual were not an author, could we say that what he wrote, said, left behind in his papers, or what has been collected of his remarks, could be called a 'work'? . . . Even when an individual has been accepted as an author, we must still ask whether everything that he wrote, said, or left behind is part of his work. The problem is both theoretical and technical. When undertaking the publication of Nietzsche's works, for example, where should one stop? Surely everything should be published, but what is 'everything'? Everything that Nietzsche himself published certainly. And what about the rough drafts of his works? Obviously. The plans for his aphorisms? Yes. The deleted passages and the notes at the bottom of the page? Yes. What if, within the notebook filled with aphorisms, one finds a reference, the notation of a meeting or of an address, or a laundry list: Is it a work or not? Why not? And so on, ad infinitum. How can one define a work amid the millions of traces left by someone after his death? A theory of the work does not exist . . .[2]

Foucault despairs of finding a determinate answer to the practical questions he raises for the scholarly editor. Surely he is right that there is not always a clear line round what should count as an author's 'work' worthy of preservation. He is also right that value judgements relating to an author's status can affect whether a product of a certain kind counts as a work; Nietzsche's letters are 'works' while the letters of an unsung bank clerk might not be. But we need stricter conditions on what counts as a work than the constraints imposed on a conscientious editor. That brings us back to 'completion' for the fragments and jottings that catch the eye of the editor are not 'completed works' in the sense sought.

Of course the idea of 'completion' is not itself value-free. There is an aesthetic as well as a genetic conception of completion in the context of works.[3] A work-in-progress might seem aesthetically complete—well-structured, unified, pleasing—even though for its creator it is unfinished or has even been abandoned, just as a work completed by an artist, to that artist's satisfaction, might appear aesthetically incomplete. To deem a work aesthetically incomplete is to make a judgement about it, to say that in certain respects it fails, it lacks unity, coherence, or appropriate closure. Genetic completion also involves a value judgement, this time by the artist. This is a judgement that now is the time to stop, that the work is complete. This is a decision that an artist must make. But aesthetic completeness, as we have seen, is neither necessary nor sufficient for this decision, for genetic completeness. An artist might stop working believing the work to be aesthetically complete in cases where objective critical opinion judges it aesthetically incomplete or the artist might stop working and be indifferent to aesthetic completeness. Of course there are many reasons why an artist might decide to stop work, not all

---
[2] Michel Foucault, 'What is an Author?' in William Irwin, ed., *The Death and Resurrection of the Author,* Westport, CT: Greenwood Press, 2002, p. 11.
[3] I borrow the terms from Paisley Livingston whose discussion in 'Counting Fragments, and Frenhofer's Paradox', *British Journal of Aesthetics,* vol. 39, 1999, pp. 14–23, I have found very useful.

of them resting on the belief that the work is complete. Some artists simply abandon their work. However, it would be wrong to endorse Paul Valery's often quoted saying that 'A poem is never finished, only abandoned' for the standard case remains that in which the artist decides the work is complete and therefore stops. In what follows, a 'completed work' will be one that satisfies genetic completeness, in this sense: the work is completed as a result of a decision by its creator that the work is complete.

2.2. Unfinished Works

We need a brief word here about the celebrated cases of *unfinished* works that acquire the status of *works*, indeed canonical works, even in their unfinished state. Do these constitute counterexamples to the idea that a work is brought into existence when the work on it is completed? There are many examples, including Schubert's Symphony No. 8 in B Minor (the 'Unfinished Symphony'), Mozart's Requiem, Charles Dickens's *The Mystery of Edwin Drood*, Franz Kafka's *The Castle*, Robert Louis Stevenson's *Weir of Hermiston*, among numerous others. Some, but not all, are unfinished because the author or artist died before completion. Do such cases suggest that we need a notion of *work* that is somehow independent of completion? Or that a work can be brought into existence without being completed? Caution is needed in what generalizations can be drawn.

There are a number of salient features of these well-known cases that affect how they are to be accommodated. First, in each case the artist concerned is already celebrated for other works and at least part of the fascination with the unfinished works is explained by their being the product of famous people. Unfinished works by unknown artists are much less likely to be recognized as significant in themselves. Second, there is usually enough of the work extant to make it an object of interest in its own right. Mere fragments left by an author or composer or sculptor (works that have barely got started) might fall under Foucault's general conception of a 'work', in the sense of something worth preserving just because of its provenance, but nevertheless attract little attention from an aesthetic or artistic point of view. In the kinds of cases listed, it is not just the fame of the artist that attracts attention to them but at least something approaching aesthetic completion or an integrity in the unfinished work that gives them aesthetic appeal. Schubert's symphony is often performed as it stands and the unfinished novels have been published in their unfinished state. Thirdly, efforts have been made to complete the works: Süssmayr's completion of Mozart's Requiem is an obvious example. Arguably this does bring a new (completed) work into existence in a more conventional sense.

Perhaps we need (already have) a distinct category of works— unfinished works, in their many different forms—that invite their own special modes of appreciation, related to, but not identical with, the modes associated with completed works. To hear Schubert's Unfinished Symphony is to hear it *as unfinished* with all the poignancy and curiosity that that entails. Note that there is a derivative form of genetic completion in these famous unfinished cases, for although the artist has not made the decision that these works be 'presented to an artworld public' (in George Dickie's phrase[4]) a decision has been made by others (the artist's admirers, publishers, performers, etc.) to do just that: they are presented as works for appreciation, *as if* they were completed works in their own right. They are a kind of appropriated work. To the extent that we are inclined to think of them as works of art then they are 'brought into existence', partially, of course, by the artist's own work, but partially by the decision of others that they be treated as works, indeed as a special case of 'completion' in their own category.

2.3. Creating and Bringing into Existence

Returning to the earlier discussion, we need to be a bit wary of conflating 'creation' and 'bringing into existence'. Harry Deutsch has given reasons for keeping these distinct.[5] He cites the case of painting by numbers. Those who apply the paint have brought the painting into existence but 'all the creative work has been done for

---

[4] George Dickie, 'The New Institutional Theory of Art', in P. V. Lamarque and S. H. Olsen, eds., *Aesthetics and the Philosophy of Art: The Analytic Tradition: An Anthology*, Oxford: Blackwell, 2003, p. 53.
[5] Harry Deutsch, 'The Creation Problem', *Topoi*, vol. 10, 1991, pp. 209–225.

them'. In general, '(t)he creative part of creating a painting may in fact consist of doing less than bringing the painting into existence. It may consist in devising a scheme for where on the canvas the paint should go; or it might consist merely in creatively envisaging in some detail what the painting will be like.'[6] The problem is not peculiar to painting by numbers. Arguably an analogous situation arose in Renaissance studios where a master painter would give instructions to teams of workers on what should be painted where. Creativity is credited to the master although the underlings bring the painting into existence.

It is not only creativity that is at issue in such cases. There are also issues of work-identity. When avant-garde artists do something apparently similar the question arises of what kinds of works they are creating. Thus, the conceptual artist Sol LeWitt laid down specifications for certain of his works without putting them into effect himself. One such, *Wall Drawing No. 623 Double Asymmetrical Pyramids with Colour Ink Washes Superimposed*, which has been realized (if that is the word) in a mural in the National Gallery of Canada, consists of instructions as follows: 'colour ink wash: the background is grey, blue, grey, blue; left pyramid: the apex is left—four sides: 1—red, blue, blue, red, blue; 2—yellow, blue, grey, blue; . . .' etc. But what is the work? Given that there can be different ways of realizing the work and given that LeWitt is a conceptual artist, it could be argued that the work is the *idea* rather than the painted mural itself.[7] (Even if this is right in this particular case, it should not be taken as a general endorsement of idealist theories of the work such as Collingwood's, which identify the work in every case with something mental.) Clearly to know if and when a work has come into existence we need to know what kind of work it is. But it is worth distinguishing a value-free conception of creation where it literally means bringing into the world something that did not exist before, in contrast to an honorific sense implying originality or 'creativity'.

---

[6] Deutsch, 'The Creation Problem', p. 211.

[7] The case is discussed by David Davies in *Art as Performance* (Oxford: Blackwell, 2004) who argues for the centrality of the idea in the work's identity: 'The fact that there are actual enactments of LeWitt's constraints . . . bears upon the appreciation of the work only by, as we might put it, "enlivening" the idea, supplementing the intensionality of the vehicle as verbally specified', p. 232.

2.4. Medium and Manipulation

An initial, if no doubt over-simple, description of what artists do in bringing a work into existence is that they are 'making something out of something'. In every case there seem to be 'materials' worked on, even if the materials take very different forms in different cases. A simple paradigm is that of the sculptor carving a sculpture out of stone or wood. The material is the physical material used (stone, wood) and a completed work appears after a process of carving and shaping and polishing. The sculpture is made out of the physical material. So much is obvious. Much less obvious is the relation that the work (the sculpture) has to the material out of which it is made. Indeed this is a pivotal issue in our enquiry. Is the sculpture identical with the shaped material out of which it was made or is the sculpture a distinct object, an object of a distinct kind, constituted by, but not identical with, this physical material? For those works with a similar physical base—painting, buildings, prints, even films—similar questions arise.

It is common to call the materials out of which these works are made their 'medium'; in these cases the medium is physical, including a range of familiar kinds from canvas, paper, paint, charcoal, or bronze to more exotic substances. But the idea of a medium in relation to works needs more refinement. For one thing, the medium is not always physical and there can be 'multi-media' works. To include musical and literary works we need a broader conception of 'materials' to include abstract entities such as sound-types, word-types, and structure-types. But if such entities are admitted, then the parallels with physical material return. For it still looks as if the *work* of the artist can be described as a kind of patterning, shaping, configuring, in general manipulating, of a medium running up to the production of a completed work. The musical composer tries out sequences, patterns, and juxtapositions of sound-types, along with rhythms, pitches, tones, and harmonies, until the right final structure is in place and compositional work stops. This too is a kind of manipulation of a medium, not totally dissimilar to the work of a painter or sculptor. Likewise for the author writing a sonnet or novel. The medium here is language but a process of structuring and manipulating takes place; the materials are the words, meanings, and sentence-structures afforded by the language, and in a more literary context the ideas, themes, genres, styles, character-types, plot-types on which the author is drawing. The question that we asked of the physical works is directly applicable to works of these other kinds: what is the relation between the medium manipulated into a structure and the work itself? Is the musical work identical to the sound-structure-types of which it is constituted or is it something distinct? Is the literary work identical to its constitutive word-sequence-types (its *text*) or is it distinct?

Before addressing these questions directly, more needs to be said about the crucial idea of a medium. So far a medium has been identified with the 'materials', broadly conceived, of which works are constituted. These materials are not necessarily physical—they can take the form of abstract entities—but in each case it is not implausible to describe artists (or makers of works generally) as *manipulating* a medium as an essential part of the process of making a work. Works are made out of the materials of a medium. However, within aesthetics it is now common to distinguish a medium of this kind—the kind that has been called a 'vehicular medium'[8]—with another kind, sometimes called an 'artistic' medium.[9] There is no settled view as to exactly how the latter should be defined. Perhaps, as one commentator has suggested, ' "Medium" in this sense is closer to "art form" than to "kind of stuff" '.[10] Let us say that an artistic medium involves *the conception of a work by its maker as being a work of a certain kind*.[11] The important point is the intentionality. A work's artistic medium is not determined (exclusively) by art-historical or third-person classification but by the way in which the work is conceived by the person making it. There might be cases where the artistic medium is unknown to art history (perhaps this is true of the prehistoric cave paintings), making the work virtually impossible to understand or appreciate.

The combination of vehicular and artistic medium allows for a richer understanding of what it is to make a work. For an artist is not

---

[8] Davies, *Art as Performance*, p. 56ff.
[9] The term comes from Davies, *Art as Performance*, p. 56.
[10] Jerrold Levinson, *Music, Art & Metaphysics*, Ithaca, NY: Cornell University Press, 1990, p. 29.
[11] David Davies writes: 'attention to the artistic medium of a work necessarily refers us to the intentionality of a maker who acts in light of these supposed understandings in manipulating a vehicular medium', *Art as Performance*, p. 60.

just manipulating materials but is doing so under some conception of what kind of work is aimed for. Of course it would be wrong to suppose this conception is always precise or unchanging. Artists might set out with only the vaguest conception of what they are doing and might change their minds midway. But artists rarely work randomly—Jackson Pollock's 'action paintings', for example, were far from random and issued from quite determinate conceptions of an artistic process—and, when they do, this itself helps determine the kind of work they produce. Furthermore, the way an artist conceives his work and the kind of work he conceives it to be does not take place in a cultural vacuum but against a complex cultural background of practices, conventions, established modes (accepted or reacted against), prevailing ideas, political and social currents, as well as available materials, technology, and economic circumstances. Clearly, then, completing a work is not just deciding to stop—i.e. to stop manipulating the materials—but involves making that decision in the light of a conception of what has been achieved, against a background of cultural practices that determine what is possible at a given time.

Now we can return to our questions about the relation between the materials out of which a work is made and the work itself. This closely ties in with the earlier question of what change has been wrought on the world by bringing a work into existence. I shall consider three suggestions and make a preliminary case for rejecting the first two and endorsing the third.

2.5. First Suggestion

Let us return again to the simplest case, that of the carved sculpture. Physical changes are wrought upon a physical medium. Is not the work, then, none other than the piece of stone as it appears at a certain point in time, namely when the sculptor stops work on it? On this view, the only relevant change in the world when a work 'comes into existence' is that something (the artist's activity) has stopped. The piece of stone in itself continues to exist but it is no longer being chiselled and worked. It is the same piece of stone that it was before the work stopped but now it has acquired a property it did not have before, namely *being a sculpture*. The property of being a sculpture, on this account, is not different in kind from other properties possessed by the stone: *being white, being smooth-textured, being shaped like a person, being seven feet high*. Something that previously wasn't a sculpture is now a sculpture, just as something that previously wasn't smooth is now smooth. A work comes into existence when predicates like 'is a sculpture', 'is a painting', 'is a musical work' become truly applicable to some 'material' such as a physical object or abstract entity.

This account has the appeal of simplicity but only, I suggest, because it combines truism with false analogies. It is a truism that when a work comes into existence the predicate 'is a work' is truly applicable where it was not before. A true proposition can now be formulated about something in the world that would not have been true prior to the work's coming into existence. When Michelangelo finished the Pietà it became true that the Pietà exists, something that was not true while he was still working. But that says no more than that the work was finished when the work was finished. We still don't know what difference it made to the world that 'is the Pietà' became true of a piece of marble, nor indeed how that should be construed. The proposed account is misleading in its comparison between the predicates 'is a sculpture' and 'is smooth-textured' or 'is white'. Although it might be true that the predicates are all applicable to one and the same object, the piece of marble, only the latter two predicates identify intrinsic qualities of that object. However the qualities came to be possessed by the marble, e.g. through polishing and cleaning, they remain physical qualities of the object. Exactly those same qualities could have been possessed by the object without any human intervention. Such, though, is not the case with the property *being a sculpture*. That property is essentially connected to human agency. Nothing is a sculpture—indeed nothing is a work of any kind in the sense intended—except as a product of human action. But even more than that, if we apply our earlier finding, there must be intentionality deep in the very concept of a work. A work is the product of an agent's manipulation of a medium and becomes a work, and the work that it is, only under a conception supplied by the agent. A necessary condition for a piece of marble becoming a sculpture is that it be conceived as a sculpture by its maker.[12] Without that it remains just a piece of marble.

Behind the view discussed lies an analogy that, although initially plausible, is flawed. It is an analogy with an activity like cooking. A cook will 'manipulate' the ingredients until a dish is complete. When the cooking is done new predicates are applicable to the finished product: *being a fried egg, being a sponge cake*. It is tempting to see *being a sculpture* as analogous, as the same kind of predicate. In both cases there is a process completed and the coming into existence of something that wasn't there before. But disanalogies have already been identified. *Being a fried egg* (like *being smooth-textured*) is a physical property, or strictly *being fried* is a physical property of an egg. It is defined as such independently of human intention. Most eggs are fried deliberately for human ends but that might not always be the case. There could be fried eggs—even, however improbably, sponge cakes—without human agency. More importantly, a fried egg could come into existence without being conceived as such either by its maker or by others. That is not the case with works. Paintings, sculptures, and symphonies don't happen by accident. The cooking paradigm can be put schematically. *Cooking a φ with a set ψ of ingredients is such that when ψ has reached a certain physical state s then (by skill or good luck) ψ becomes a φ just in virtue of its attaining s.* When the egg undergoes a certain physical change it becomes a fried egg. But in the case of works there is no physical state (or state of an abstract entity) the possession of which is sufficient for a work to come into existence. We cannot say that when the marble looks a certain way (e.g. resembles so-and-so, has a smooth texture, etc.) then a sculpture exists, nor can we say in the musical case that when a certain combination of notes or a certain structure has been assembled then a musical work exists. A completed work, we have seen, depends not on the state of the materials used but on a decision by the maker, and its being the work it is depends on how it is conceived by its maker.

---

[12] There might be ancient or primitive works the creators of which did not possess the concept of sculpture. We should be wary, though, of how to treat these. It might be that they have been appropriated into the sculptural tradition by those who found them. Arguably, it is those who found the works, not those who created them, who *made* them as sculptures.

These seemingly innocuous observations already have far-reaching consequences for what can count as a work. If there can be no works without human agency and intentions and no works that are not conceived as such by those who fashion them then there can be no 'found' works, nor any eternally existing works. Beethoven's Fifth Symphony cannot exist eternally as an abstract sound-structure-type, as some modern Platonists have supposed. That is not to say that there is not an abstract sound-structure-type associated with the work but, void of any agency or any conception of the work, that sound-structure-type per se could not *be* the work. Those who do wish to identify a musical work with an eternal sound-structure-type might respond by locating the required human agency in the *discovery* of the structure and the required intentionality in its becoming an object of *appreciation*. It is only when the sound-structure-type enters human consciousness, they might argue, that it becomes a *work* in the broader sense of the term but it always existed as a work in a generic sense. This, however, is already a retreat from the stronger conception of *work* mooted earlier. The fact that a composer 'discovers' a sound-structure is not the right kind of change in the world to count as completing a work in any acceptable sense.

2.6. Second Suggestion

Out of this response there can be developed another more refined version of the view that *being a painting*, *being a sculpture*, and *being a musical work* are properties that a vehicular medium—a physical object, an abstract type—acquires as a result of the work of an artist in manipulating that medium. This version has more to commend it, although ultimately it too must be rejected. A work is still essentially identified with the 'stuff' of which it is constituted but the change wrought in the world when the work comes into existence is that the constituting material acquires intentional and relational properties that previously it did not possess. To be a sculpture is to be a piece of marble (wood, etc.) shaped and configured by human agency and which has come to possess intentional properties such as *being conceived as a sculpture, being an object of appreciation, being a representation of David, being in the classical style*. The parallel now is not between *being a sculpture* and *being smooth-textured* or even *being a fried egg* but between, say, *being a sculpture* and *being elected mayor*. When Jones is elected mayor something of a different order happens to him than when he puts on weight or loses his hair. The latter are physical changes, the former changes in status. Jones's election as mayor brings with it a range of institutional powers and responsibilities. Acting as mayor, Jones can formulate and implement policies on local matters, can represent the city on official occasions, can make appointments and award prizes; in addition, certain attitudes to him as mayor will be expected, a degree of respect or deference, demanding of him an obligation to act with dignity and decorum, 'upholding the office'. Analogously, when a work comes into existence it too acquires a status conventionally defined. Certain expectations arise for works, however humble. They are open to special kinds of appraisal, they are located in traditions and styles, they invite appreciation as works of a particular kind, and they can be attributed meaning or symbolism.

The idea that works, on becoming works, acquire a distinctive status and a distinctive range of intentional properties is correct and important.[13] The analogy with an institutional role like becoming a mayor is illuminating. But how far can the analogy be pressed? Later we shall find reasons for caution. Is *being a work* a property that something can have at some times but not at others? Nelson Goodman, who invites us to ask not 'What is art?' but 'When is art?' answers in the affirmative:

an object may be a work of art at some times and not at others. Indeed, just by virtue of functioning as a symbol in a certain way does an object become, while so functioning, a work of art. The stone is normally no work of art while in the driveway but may be so when on display in an art museum. In the driveway, it usually performs no symbolic function; in the art museum it exemplifies certain of its properties—e.g. shape, color, texture. . . . On the other hand, a Rembrandt painting may cease to function as a work of art when used to replace a broken window or as a blanket.[14]

As long as an object possesses the functions of a work of art then it is art but just as Jones may retire from the office of mayor and lose

---

[13] See Ch. 3 'Work and Object'.
[14] Nelson Goodman, 'When is Art?' in David Perkins and Barbara Leondat, eds., *The Arts and Cognition*, Baltimore: Johns Hopkins University Press, 1977, p. 17.

his mayoral status so an object can cease to be art when it loses its relevant functions. According to Goodman, 'That an object functions as art at a given time, that it has the status of art at that time, and that it is art at that time may all be taken as saying the same thing—so long as we take none of these as ascribing to the object any stable status.'[15] In fact Goodman retreats from the strong position apparently defended: 'Perhaps to say that an object is art when and only when it so functions is to overstate the case or to speak elliptically. The Rembrandt painting remains a work of art, as it remains a painting, while functioning only as a blanket.'[16] The point is that it does not so easily lose its function as a painting, just as a chair that is never sat on is still a chair.

The crucial part of the mayor analogy is this: that becoming mayor is a status that some pre-existing object (Jones) acquires at a particular time. It is a status that could be given up. The change wrought on the world is a change of status not the introduction of anything new into the world. Jones-as-mayor is identical to Jones; there is just one object here and Jones himself, *as a man*, stays the same before, during, and after his elevation. It would be absurd to suggest that when Jones becomes mayor a new object has appeared in the world. Is this true of works? Is it the case that to bring a work into existence is merely to change the status of something that already exists? Is a work identical to its constituting material? The view I shall defend is that this is not a good analogy and that to bring a work into existence is indeed to bring something new into the world.

The problems I have with the mayor analogy will best emerge through consideration of the third suggestion, which centres on the idea that creating a work essentially involves bringing something new into the world.

2.7. Third Suggestion

On the face of it the idea that something new comes into existence when a work is completed is hardly surprising or new. However, characterizing exactly what happens is not so straightforward. Roman

---

[15] Goodman, 'When is Art?', footnote 10, p. 19.   [16] Ibid., p. 18.

Ingarden has raised the issue in the mode in which I want to pursue it: 'whether a work of art is a physical object having a specific form or whether it is rather something that is constructed on the basis of a physical object as an entirely new creation brought into being by the creative activity of the artist.'[17]

The core of the argument that a work (e.g. a sculpture) is not identical to its constituting material (e.g. clay or marble or bronze) appeals to applications of Leibniz's Law or the Indiscernibility of Identicals. This law states that if an entity *a* is identical with entity *b* then, for any property, if *a* has that property then *b* has that property or, put another way, there can be no property possessed by *a* that is not also possessed by *b*. Should there be such a property then *a* cannot be identical with *b*. Philosophers have found the principle readily applicable to works of art. Thus, Joseph Margolis writes: 'artworks possess, where "mere real things" do not, Intentional properties: all representational, semiotic, symbolic, expressive, stylistic, historical, significative properties. If that is granted, then of course artworks cannot be numerically identical with "mere real things" '.[18] A similar conclusion, drawn at a linguistic rather than metaphysical level, is reached by Kit Fine who observes that a range of descriptive predicates—e.g. *defective, substandard, well* or *badly made, valuable, ugly, Romanesque, exchanged, insured*, or *admired*—might be truly applied to the statue but not to the piece of bronze.[19] The argument is not restricted to physical objects. Jerrold Levinson, who defends the thesis that 'Musical works must be such that they do *not* exist prior to the composer's compositional activity, but are *brought into* existence *by* that activity' (italics in original),[20] argues, by appeal to Leibniz's Law, that two musical works constituted by the same sound-structure-type would nevertheless not be identical because, being 'indicated' in different contexts, they would have different aesthetic and artistic properties.[21]

But the argument about different properties possessed by a work and by its constituting material needs to be handled with care. After

---

[17] Roman Ingarden, 'Artistic and Aesthetic Values', *British Journal of Aesthetics*, vol. 4, no. 3, 1964, p. 198.
[18] Joseph Margolis, *What, After All, Is a Work of Art?* University Park, PA: Pennsylvania State University Press, 1999, pp. 34–35.
[19] Kit Fine, 'The Non-Identity of a Material Thing and Its Matter', *Mind* 112, 2003, p. 206.
[20] Levinson, *Music, Art & Metaphysics*, p. 68.   [21] Ibid., p. 69.

all, might not Margolis's argument find an analogy with the Jones-as-mayor case? If, as Margolis argues, artworks possess Intentional properties, but 'mere real things' do not, then can we not say that Jones-as-mayor possesses Intentional properties, such as constitutional powers and obligations, that the man himself does not possess? Jones-the-man does not possess the power to legislate; that is only a power he acquires during his term of office and when acting in that role. Yet, as we have seen, it would be odd to conclude that Jones-the-mayor is not identical with Jones. If that is right then perhaps we should hesitate to conclude, with Margolis, that artworks are not numerically identical with 'mere real things'.

In this context it is tempting for the identity theorist to deploy the idiom of *qua*-objects, in spite of the controversial nature of that notion.[22] When we reflect on Jones-*qua*-mayor we confine our reflections to certain aspects of his actions and interests. We might be ignorant of his other characteristics. Similarly it could be argued that it is only *qua*-statue that the piece of bronze possesses, say, aesthetic properties; *qua*-piece-of-bronze it does not possess such properties. After melting down, the bronze survives *qua*-piece-of-bronze, but not *qua*-statue. Being a work or being a painting or, more specifically, being a painting of Diana and Actaeon might, returning to our earlier hypothesis, be an aspect that a physical canvas possesses at some but not necessarily all times of its existence. Perceiving or thinking about the canvas-*qua*-work or the canvas-*qua*-representation-of-Diana-and-Actaeon might bring into salience a range of art-related properties, including aesthetic properties. On this account it is simply question-begging to say that objects, unlike works, cannot have such properties.

But the appeal to Leibniz's Law and differences in properties has not been defeated. The idea that something can have properties *qua*-this but not *qua*-that is pretty obscure. However, it becomes worse than obscure, in fact incoherent, when *essential* properties are at issue. If we think of essential properties as *de re* necessities, which hold of objects

---

[22] Criticisms of *qua*-objects appear in, e.g., Harry Deutsch, 'The Creation Problem', *Topoi* 10, 1991, pp. 212–213; Mark Johnston, 'Constitution is Not Identity', *Mind* 101, 1992, p. 91; and Stefano Predelli, 'Musical Ontology and the Argument from Creation', *British Journal of Aesthetics* 41, 2001, pp. 288–289. For a more positive account, see Kit Fine, 'The Problem of Non-Existents I. Internalism', *Topoi* 1, 1982, pp. 97–140.

under any description, then there could be no essential properties of object O *qua-φ* but not of O *qua-ψ*. Yet in the art case there do seem to be properties essential to works but not essential to the material that constitutes the works. Eddy Zemach gives an example:

Fountain and the urinal are distinct things, since they have different essences. Being a part of a certain artworld is essential to *Fountain*; out of that context *Fountain* cannot exist, for it would lack its essential aesthetic property, its contrast to traditional artworks, which makes it the artwork it is. Its significance is due to its appearance as an artwork at a specific historical and art-historical period. For the urinal, on the other hand, its relation to that artworld is inessential; it can survive without it.[23]

It is not just essential properties of this kind that might differ between a work and its constituting material but also perhaps *causal* properties, where a similar problem arises for *qua*-objects. Here is Lynne Rudder Baker:

When a large stone is placed in certain circumstances, it acquires new properties, and a new thing—a monument to those who died in battle—comes into being. And the constituted thing (the stone monument) has effects in virtue of having properties that the constituting thing (the stone) would not have had if it had not constituted a monument. The monument attracts speakers and small crowds on patriotic holidays; it brings tears to people's eyes; it arouses protests. Had it not constituted a monument, the large stone would have had none of these effects. When stones first came to constitute monuments, a new kind of thing with new properties—properties that are causally efficacious—came into being.[24]

How could O-*qua-φ* have causal properties not possessed by O-*qua-ψ*? Baker's explanation is that the monument is 'a new kind of thing

---

[23] Zemach, *Real Beauty*, University Park, PA: Penn State University Press, 1997, p. 160.
[24] Lynne Rudder Baker, *Persons and Bodies: A Constitution View,* Cambridge: Cambridge University Press, 2000, pp. 32–33. Baker has developed the theory primarily in relation to persons but sees it as applying also to: 'the relation that obtains between an octagonal piece of metal and a Stop sign, between strands of DNA molecules and genes, between pieces of paper and dollar bills, between stones and monument; between lumps of clay and statues—the list is endless' (p. 27). For discussion, notably on the constitution issue, see D. Pereboom, 'On Baker's *Persons and Bodies*', *Philosophy and Phenomenological Research*, 2002, 64 (3), pp. 615–622; M. Rea, 'Lynne Baker on Material Constitution', *Philosophy and Phenomenological Research*, 2002, 64 (3), pp. 607–614; G. Wedeking, 'Critical Notice: Lynne Rudder Baker, *Persons and Bodies*', *Canadian Journal of Philosophy*, 2002, 32 (2), pp. 267–290.

with new properties'. If it is right that bringing a work into existence cannot just be changing the properties of something that already exists then indeed it follows that it must involve bringing into existence something that did not exist before.

2.8. A Negative and Positive Thesis

It is helpful to distinguish a negative from a positive thesis in this discussion. The negative thesis, which is widely held, is that a work is not identical to its constituting material. The positive thesis, which can take many forms, states what kind of entity a work is. Agreement on the negative thesis does not ensure agreement on the positive.

Many philosophers have advanced the negative thesis but it is striking how diverse are the views that emerge from a rejection of identity. Kit Fine, for example, like Baker, defends the negative thesis. He gives prime attention to the statue and the alloy from which it is made, yet views that example as paradigmatic of a wider relation between a material thing and its matter.[25] What is important for our purposes are not the detailed arguments for and against constitutionalism in Fine's treatment[26] but the metaphysical conclusion—intuitively disturbing—that two material things might occupy the same space at the same time yet not be identical. A statue is a material entity but not *the very same* material entity as the piece of marble that constitutes it. One reason why this result is not repugnant to commonsense lies in a crucial feature, namely that the coincident objects are not of the *same kind*. The metaphysical principle that commonsense, as well as logic, should preserve is that *no two objects of the same kind can occupy the same space at the same time*.[27] Acceptable versions of the negative

---

[25] Fine, 'The Non-Identity of a Material Thing and Its Matter'.

[26] Kit Fine's argument in 'The Non-Identity of a Material Thing and Its Matter' is primarily linguistic, showing that those defenders of the identity thesis who marshal arguments from 'opacity' to combat putative exceptions to Leibniz's Law are themselves led to 'intolerable consequences'. Baker's argument, in contrast, is not primarily linguistic but metaphysical in showing that properties like *being a statue* are not only relational properties but are also essential in some cases.

[27] See David Wiggins, *Sameness and Substance*, Cambridge, MA: Harvard University Press, 1980, p. 16.

thesis maintain that works and 'mere' physical things are *not* of the same kind, even in the cases where the works are physical things.[28]

Let us look at three rather different versions of the negative thesis to see if there is any common ground to be found for constructing a positive thesis. Roman Ingarden, in defending the negative thesis, insists that 'in its structure and properties a work of art always extends beyond its material substrate, the real "thing" which ontologically supports it, although the properties of the substrate are not irrelevant to the properties of the work of art which depends upon it'.[29] From this starting point he develops a view of the work as a collaborative effort between artist and observer centred on the notion of 'concretion':

> The *concretion* of the work is not only the reconstruction thanks to the activity of an observer of what was effectively present in the work, but also a completion of the work and the actualisation of its moments of potentiality. It is thus in a way the common product of artist and observer.[30]

As the 'material substrate' itself is clearly not the common product of artist and observer the negative thesis is reinforced, although the latter on its own does not entail the positive thesis on offer. There is a role for observers (or interpreters) in the identity conditions of works but a somewhat different idiom, as we shall see, captures this better than Ingarden's.

A second, more radical, version of the negative thesis distances works altogether from their physical substrates. On the idealist theory the work—even of ostensibly a physical kind—does not occupy space at all. Here is R. G. Collingwood:

> A work of art in the proper sense of that phrase is not an artifact, not a bodily or perceptible thing fabricated by the artist, but something solely in the artist's head, a creature of his imagination; and not only a visual or auditory imagination, but a total imaginative experience. It follows that the painted picture is not the work of art in the proper sense of that phrase.[31]

However, Collingwood does not suppose that the act of putting paint on canvas is entirely fortuitous to the work itself for the act

---

[28] The point is also emphasized by Robert Stecker in *Interpretation and Construction: Art, Speech, and the Law*, Oxford: Blackwell, 2003, pp. 91–92.
[29] Ingarden, 'Artistic and Aesthetic Values', p. 198.   [30] Ibid., p. 199.
[31] R. G. Collingwood, *The Principles of Art*, Oxford: Clarendon Press, 1938, p. 305.

of painting is incorporated into the very experience that the painter expresses:

> There is no question of 'externalizing' an inward experience that is complete in itself and by itself. There are two experiences, an inward and imaginative one called seeing and an outward or bodily one called painting, which in the painter's life are inseparable, and form one single indivisible experience, an experience which may be described as painting imaginatively.[32]

Later he writes that 'the painter "records" in his picture the experience which he had in painting it' and 'the picture . . . produces in [the audience] sensuous-emotional or psychical experiences which, when raised from impressions to ideas by the activity of the spectator's consciousness, are transmuted into a total imaginative experience identical with that of the painter'.[33] So the material object, the painted picture, is both part of the artist's act of expression and causally connected to an audience's appreciative response but nevertheless is not identical with the work itself, which exists entirely in the mental realm.

A third, equally radical, defence of the negative thesis, by Jean-Paul Sartre, seems to hold that works (of art) per se do not even exist, strictly speaking, but are projections of the imagination. They are not objects of perception but objects of the imagination and only objects of perception are *real*. 'The Seventh Symphony', Sartre writes, 'is in no way *in time*. It is therefore in no way real. It occurs *by itself*, but as absent, as being out of reach. . . . It is not only outside of time and space—as are essences, for instance—it is outside of the real, outside of existence.'[34] Something similar is true of pictures too. Sartre thinks that paintings—that is, representational paintings—act much like images; to reveal their content, and thus their identity as pictures, requires an act of imaginative consciousness, a 'radical change' and 'negation' that shifts consciousness from perception to imagination. All that we can *perceive* is the paint and canvas; only when we attain an imaginative consciousness can we bring to mind what he calls the 'ethetic object', in effect the work itself.

---

[32] R. G. Collingwood, *The Principles of Art*, pp. 304–305. [33] Ibid., p. 308.
[34] Jean-Paul Sartre, *The Psychology of Imagination*, New York: Carol Publishing Group, 1991, p. 280.

Here then are three distinct views of the work consequent on accepting the negative thesis that the work and its constituting material are not identical: the work is a product of artist/audience collaboration; the work exists entirely in the mind of the artist; the work is a projection of the audience's imagination onto a material analogue. These views and others like them emerge under pressure of an assumption that a work is a different kind of entity from the materials underlying it. Works are not simply changes in pre-existing objects or rearranged items in the world. That at least is a view I believe ought to be endorsed. Nor are these the only candidates for a theory of the work. Works have been characterized, among other things, as action-types, performance-tokens, indicated structures, and culturally emergent entities.[35]

2.9. Steps Towards a Positive Thesis

Once we have embraced the negative thesis that a work is not simply a change of state in existing materials and once we have acknowledged the cultural embeddedness of works, there are few options in seeking a general characterization of the kind of entity that comes into existence when a work is completed. In short, a work must broadly be a 'cultural' or 'institutional' entity of some sort.

We already have the ingredients at hand to offer an answer of a *general* kind to our enquiry, about how the world changes when a work comes into existence. The important considerations are these: works are the product of human agency and intention; they emerge when work on them has been completed; work is completed, as opposed to abandoned, under a conception of the finished product; the work a maker undertakes in producing a completed work involves the manipulation of a 'vehicular' medium constrained by

---

[35] By, respectively, Gregory Currie, *An Ontology of Art*, Basingstoke: Macmillan, 1989; David Davies, *Art as Performance*; Jerrold Levinson, 'What a Musical Work Is', in *Music, Art & Metaphysics*; Joseph Margolis, 'Works of Art as Physically Embodied and Culturally Emergent Entities', *British Journal of Aesthetics*, vol. 14, 1974.

an 'artistic' medium; completed works possess intentional properties of an aesthetic, artistic, or representational kind; the possession of those properties is made possible only in the appropriate cultural context.

Herein lies what truth there is in institutional accounts of art. There have to be established 'practices'—perhaps something like an 'artworld', though that idea is notoriously problematic—to make possible the existence of works (paintings, sculptures, symphonies, etc.). This is where the analogy with becoming a mayor is at its most plausible. Mayors only exist where the appropriate constitutional and legal systems are in place. But, as we saw, being elected mayor gives Jones a new status but does not introduce a new object. Becoming a work, in contrast, does introduce a new—'institutional'—object. Works are like schools, churches, and laws. A new school is a genuinely new (institutional) object in a community not identical with the buildings that comprise it. The buildings might or might not be new themselves. A church ceases to be a church when it is sold, deconsecrated, and turned into a coffee house. Something is lost, but not the building. To use a final hoary analogy, if I am missing a chesspiece I might mould a bit of plasticine into a convincing shape and thereby *make* a rook. A new chesspiece has come into the world but not a new bit of plasticine.

The institutional requirement for work-existence casts doubt on the strongly mentalistic accounts offered by Collingwood and Sartre. Works cannot exist just in the mind or in the imagination. They need the cultural setting as outlined. But mentalistic elements are present. There have to be appropriate beliefs, attitudes, modes of appreciation, and expectations for works to come into, and be sustained in, existence; these are constrained by the conventions of established practices in the arts. Works cannot survive as works if these practices are lost. If no-one is any longer in a position to judge that something is a work of a particular kind then works of that kind no longer exist.[36] This is partly the truth behind Ingarden's observation that works are the 'common product of artist and observer'. It is only through a kind of social compact between people with like-minded interests that the recognition of a work as a work is possible.

[36] See Ch. 3 'Work and Object'.

We should conclude, then, that to bring a work into existence is indeed to bring a new entity into the world, not just to reorder what is there already. The conclusion is important, if hard won, because it means that whenever a work is completed there has been genuine creation. All too often in the ontology of art that simple conclusion has been denied.

3
Work and Object

There is more to a musical work than just a sequence of sounds, more to a literary work than just a sequence of words, more to a pictorial work than just a configuration of line and colour, more to a sculpture than just a shaped block of marble. But what more? The point is not merely, as is obvious, that not all sound-sequences are music or word-sequences literature or line-configurations pictures or shaped blocks of marble sculptures but, more substantially, that no instances of the former are ipso facto instances of the latter. In virtue of what, then, is something a *work*? The answer I shall propose is that works are a species of cultural objects whose very existence rests on essential possession of fairly complex intentional and relational properties. The proposal is not in itself unusual but the nature of the thesis and some of its consequences have not always been adequately acknowledged.

Although the discussion applies to works of art it is not restricted to art in any narrow sense but encompasses a wider class of works that includes the simplest of tunes or popular music, folktales, children's stories, genre fiction, amateur drama, as well as run-of-the-mill paintings, sketches, and sculptures, few of which would normally merit the label 'art'. There is no absolutely clear boundary for what is admissible into this wider class, any more than there would be for the more restricted class. But, even though evaluative matters will turn out to be crucial in the delineation of identity conditions for works, it is important not to focus exclusively on the most revered and well-known works of art, for this can lead, as we shall see, to theoretical distortions. The enquiry is one of ontology, in particular the issues: what makes something a work and what are its identity and survival conditions as a work? I shall not offer a definition of art, although among the implications of the thesis will be considerations favourable to certain aspects of institutionalist definitions.

3.1. Particulars and Types

Our talk about works is riddled with ambiguities of tokens and types. Already in mentioning sound-sequences and word-sequences I could be referring to some actual token sequences on an occasion, the sounds I am hearing now, the text I have before me, or to sequence-types of which these sounds and that text are instances. Of course both usages are acceptable. In practice strategies of disambiguation are usually at hand. Of token sound-sequences we ask what works they are *performances* of. Of token texts we ask what works they are *copies* of. It is a further question what relation there is between work and performance or work and copy. To have heard a performance of the 'Moonlight' Sonata is to have heard the 'Moonlight' Sonata, just as to have read a copy of *Pride and Prejudice* is to have read *Pride and Prejudice*. Yet neither *that* performance nor *that* copy is identical with the works in question for the latter could exist without the former. Musical performances can vary to a considerable degree yet still count as performances of one and the same work. This flexibility is important for performers, allowing scope for inventiveness on their part, but is troubling for the ontologist and calls for explanation. The existence of arrangements, versions, adaptations, variations and transpositions only emphasizes a further looseness of fit between performance and work. A similar looseness pertains between literary works and copies or dramas and dramatic performance. To have read a translation of *War and Peace* usually counts as having read *War and Peace* and to watch a slightly shortened version of *Hamlet* usually counts as having watched *Hamlet*.

Type–token ambiguities occur too in our talk about pictures and sculptures. The expression 'same picture' is ambiguous between type and particular, whatever global view we take of the ontology of pictures. It could be said truthfully that you and I have the *same picture* on our walls in virtue of owning reproductions or even copies of the work done by the same artist. Yet your picture is not numerically the same object as mine. Whether it is the same *work* depends on whether we use the type or token construal of 'work-identity' and ordinary language is tolerant of both. Picture and sculpture identity, like musical or literary work-identity, allows for indeterminacies of other kinds. The same work can survive quite severe forms of physical deterioration or quite radical acts of restoration.

Much recent discussion of the ontology of art has focused on the question whether or not works of art divide into two categories: on the one hand, types or abstract entities of some kind and, on the other, particulars or physical entities of some kind. There are those who seek a uniform account in this regard, placing all works into one category or the other, most commonly into the category of types.[1] Others have sought to maintain the divide, placing, for example, paintings and sculptures into the category of physical particulars and placing musical and literary works into the category of types, allowing multiple instantiations.[2] In the present context I can largely bypass this debate, but I offer the following comments that bear on the matters at hand.

First of all, we should resist pressure to find common ground in *all* respects between the inevitably heterogeneous collection of entities we classify as works of art (or works *tout court*). As it happens, we shall find substantial commonalities among works, as cultural objects with a peculiar kind of intentionality, but in the particular/type or singular/multiple dimension we need not press for uniformity, and should be suspicious of those who claim to find it.

More controversially, as a second point, even if we do retain this categorial divide, I see no reason why it should fall uniformly between art forms. While it might seem natural enough to suppose that paintings

---

[1] Joseph Margolis sees all works of art as particulars (e.g. *Art and Philosophy: Conceptual Issues in Aesthetics*, Atlantic Highlands, NJ: Humanities Press, 1980, p. 22), as does Eddy M. Zemach (*Real Beauty*, University Park, PA: Pennsylvania State University Press, 1997), although Zemach argues that particulars themselves are types (op. cit., p. 144). Gregory Currie holds that all works of art are types and that no work of art is a physical object, i.e. particular: Currie, *An Ontology of Art*, Basingstoke: Macmillan, 1989, p. 7.

[2] The most prominent advocate of this view is Richard Wollheim (*Art and Its Objects*, Cambridge: Cambridge University Press, 2nd edition, 1980); another version is developed by Jerrold Levinson ('The Work of Visual Art', in *The Pleasures of Aesthetics: Philosophical Essays*, Ithaca, NY: Cornell University Press, 1996). A related but not identical distinction is that between the autographic and the allographic, as drawn by Nelson Goodman in *Languages of Art*, Brighton: Harvester, 2nd edition, 1981.

and (carved) sculptures are physical objects and musical or literary works are abstract objects (types or kinds), further reflection suggests that this division is not hard and fast.[3] All works are reproducible, through copies, replicas, photographic reproductions, and in other ways, and the question of work-identity rests to a considerable degree on the status and value given to these reproductions. With many paintings seeing even a good reproduction seems (and is) something less than seeing the original of which it is a copy. In contrast, hearing a good performance of a musical work is not just *as good as* hearing the work itself but *counts as* hearing the work. To the extent that some pictures seem to be essentially unique physical objects this is partially because to *see* the work requires seeing that particular object. You haven't *seen* the *Mona Lisa* if you haven't been to the Louvre (assuming the work hasn't been moved), however many excellent reproductions or replicas you might have seen. (Incidentally, you might reasonably claim to be knowledgeable about the painting and even have an appreciation of its beauty and power through studying reproductions alone.) Not all pictures, though, meet this condition. Some pictures are made to be reproduced and in such cases seeing the reproduction can indeed count as seeing the work. You can rightly claim to have seen the latest Gary Larson cartoon if you have seen it in a newspaper or book, without having seen his original drawing. Cartoons, illustrations for stamps or brochures, sketches in court, even the kind of mass-produced paintings that turn up in hotel lobbies, owe their identity more to a specific configuration of line and colour, as a type with multiple instances, than to a unique physical object. The original drawings might be valued in the manner of an original score or manuscript but the works' survival, arguably, does not depend on the survival of any such artefact. This simple test for what counts as *seeing the work* offers a way of dividing pictures into particulars and types. But it still calls for an explanation. The answer must lie, so I shall argue, in the kinds of experiences demanded of a work.

[3] Frank Sibley has powerfully advanced the case that our practices concerning paintings show us systematically ambivalent between treating paintings as physical objects and as types. He suggests there might even be two distinct *concepts* of the visual arts underlying this ambivalence. See Sibley, 'Why the *Mona Lisa* May Not be a Painting', in Frank Sibley, *Approaches to Aesthetics: Collected Papers on Philosophical Aesthetics*, J. Benson, B. Redfern, and J. Roxbee Cox, eds., Oxford: Oxford University Press, 2001.

What about musical and literary works? Do they all fall on the type side of the divide? No, not necessarily. Normally, of course, we do not identify such works with any individual object or event, a score or manuscript or performance. However, some musical works are (arguably) identical with a unique particular performance. This might be true, for example, of certain improvisations or works performed for a specific occasion. To have heard the work you would have had to have been present at the performance. Even were the performance to be recorded, the recording would have the same status as a reproduction of the *Mona Lisa*. It would give you some access to the work and some chance of appreciating it but it would not present you with the work itself. I imagine that similar examples could be found among literary works, notably those performed, like poetry or drama. It seems clear, on the other hand, that works like the 'Moonlight' Sonata or *Pride and Prejudice* are not tied to particular performances, are not individual entities of this kind, and can appear in different instantiations, even those, as we have seen, showing considerable variation one from another. The lesson I draw from all this is that the classification of works as particulars or types is not given a priori as determined by generic classes but is *derived,* case by case, from other features taken to be important or valuable in a work, which in turn dictate how the work is to be correctly regarded.

3.2. Desiderata for an Ontology of Works

In attempting to characterize the identity and survival conditions of works, I am constrained by a number of desiderata that strike me as commonsensical and desirable, fit to be preserved. Although I shall not offer proofs that each is true I at least hope that my own conclusions do not conflict with them, indeed that they offer further support for them. Remarkably, each desideratum has been denied in the aesthetics literature. Works (of art) are *real,* not ideal, entities (they do not exist only in the minds of those who contemplate them); they are *public* and *perceivable* (they can be seen, heard, touched, as appropriate, and by different perceivers); they possess their properties *objectively*, some essential, some inessential; they are *cultural objects,* dependent for their inception and survival on cultural conditions; more specifically, they are entities essentially tied to *human acts* and *attitudes*; they are *created*, for example, by artists; they can *come into* and *go out of existence* (they are not eternal, even those that are types); and their identity conditions, being value-laden, are distinct from those of functionally-defined artefacts and physical objects in the natural world.

3.3. Works and Mere Real Things

Let us return to the assertions with which I began, that in each of the cases considered there is more to a work than just, as it were, the stuff that constitutes it. Applications of Leibniz's Law, the principle that if two things are identical then they must share the same properties, are often invoked to show that a work cannot be identical with, in Arthur Danto's provocative phrase, a 'mere real thing'.[4] Thus, a statue is not identical with a piece of bronze *simpliciter*, so it is argued, because, for example, (i) the very same piece of bronze could exist *before* the statue is cast, so bronze and statue can exist at different times, or (ii) if the bronze were melted down, it would still be the same piece of bronze but the statue would have ceased to exist,[5] or (iii) an artist created the statue but the artist did not create the piece of bronze,[6] or (iv) a part of the statue—a hand, say—might break off and be replaced by a new part but while this does not affect the identity of the statue, which stays the same, it does affect the identity of the piece of bronze, which is now different,[7] or (v) the statue has aesthetic, expressive, and representational properties that the piece of bronze per se does not possess.[8]

---

[4] Arthur Danto, 'Works of Art and Mere Real Things', in *The Transfiguration of the Commonplace*, Cambridge, MA: Harvard University Press, 1981.

[5] A version of these arguments is given in Allan Gibbard, 'Contingent Identity', *Journal of Philosophical Logic* IV, 1975, p. 190.

[6] I take it this is a version of an argument by Joseph Margolis: 'Duchamp made something when he created *Bottlerack* but he did not make a bottlerack . . . If the bottlerack were said to be identical with Duchamp's *Bottlerack* . . . , we should be contradicting ourselves': Margolis, *Art and Philosophy: Conceptual Issues in Aesthetics*, Atlantic Highlands, NJ: Humanities Press, 1980, pp. 20–21.

[7] A similar argument appears in Judith Jarvis Thompson, 'The Statue and the Clay', *Nous* 32, 1998, p. 152.

[8] Margolis writes: 'artworks possess, where "mere real things" do not, Intentional properties: all representational, semiotic, symbolic, expressive, stylistic, historical, significative

It is striking how different are the kinds of properties cited in these arguments: temporal properties, relational properties, properties of material constitution, intentional properties. But is the possession or non-possession of all such properties sufficient to establish the non-identity conclusion? Compare the hoary case of Superman and Clark Kent. Ordinary usage suggests that there is a property possessed by Superman, *being admired by Lois Lane*, not possessed by Clark Kent, and a property of Clark Kent, *being an object of Lois Lane's contempt*, not possessed by Superman. Could we not also say that Superman existed before Clark Kent, that Superman could exist without Clark Kent existing, and that Clark Kent might disappear without Superman disappearing (or vice versa)? Yet none of this apparently impugns the identity of Superman and Clark Kent. One way to accommodate such intuitions is to introduce *qua*-locutions. Superman is admirable *qua*-Superman but contemptible *qua*-Clark Kent (just as Bill Clinton might be admirable *qua*-President, contemptible *qua*-husband). On this account it might be inferred that Lois Lane *does* admire Clark Kent (unknown to herself) but only in the guise of Superman, or *qua*-Superman. It is worth noting another feature of this explanation, namely that when Lois Lane perceives Superman-*qua*-Clark-Kent, and feels contempt, her perception is not unduly subjective or idiosyncratic or peculiar to her own situation. Other people have the same perception and share the same attitude. Superman's Clark Kent persona is not like a temporary illusion, existing only in the mind, but is objective, persists over time, can be characterized in detail, and is open for all to observe. What about the apparent temporal divergences between Superman and Clark Kent, the fact that Superman and Clark Kent are not temporally co-extensive? One explanation would be to treat *being Clark Kent* as a phase-property of Superman. Superman becomes Clark Kent when he wants to disguise his true powers. He could be rid of the Clark Kent guise whenever he desires. But, again, that does not make Clark Kent *distinct* from Superman.

These simple observations have a bearing on the identity of works. They should make us wary of over-hasty appeal to Leibniz's Law to

---

properties. If that is granted, then of course artworks cannot be numerically identical with "mere real things" ': Margolis, *What, After All, Is a Work of Art?*, University Park, PA: The Pennsylvania State University Press, 1999, pp. 34–35.

reject the identity of work and 'mere real thing' and they hint at other possible relations between the two. Might not the piece of bronze *become* the statue in virtue of certain other facts about the bronze, including its form and relations it enters into? Might not *being a statue* or *being-the-statue-David* be a property that a piece of matter possesses at a time, without changing the essential identity of the piece of matter?[9] The appeal to *qua*-objects might also carry over to works, in spite of the much-remarked obscurity of that notion.[10] On this idiom it is only *qua*-statue that the piece of bronze possesses, say, aesthetic properties; *qua*-piece-of-bronze it does not possess such properties. Or after the melting of the bronze, the bronze survives *qua*-piece-of-bronze, but not *qua*-statue. Of course that does not yet settle the identity question, whether the statue *is* the piece of bronze. That depends on the status of *qua*-objects. Whatever we say about *qua*-objects, we cannot do without some appeal to *aspects* when characterizing works. To view an object (or a sound- or word-sequence-type) as a work is to view it aspectivally, in the sense of attending in perception to selected (art-related) aspects of the object (or type). More on that will emerge in due course.

Where does this leave works and 'mere real things'? It might be that the strategy of appealing to *qua*-objects or aspects of objects or objects 'under a description' is just another way of putting the claim that works are not 'mere' objects, for is not a 'mere' object one to which work-descriptions are withheld? But there remains a difficult, and crucial, ontological choice. Are we to say, on the one hand, that *one and the same object* is now a 'mere real thing', now a work of art? Or are we to say, on the other, that a *new* object, even a new *kind* of object, a work of art, has come into existence, either co-existing with, or superseding, another object, the mere real thing.[11] To accept the former is to accept a kind of identity theory and to encourage the parallel with Superman and Clark Kent. It implies that statues are 'basically' pieces of matter that acquire (for whatever reason and in whatever manner)

---

[9] This is a hypothesis entertained, but ultimately rejected, by Thompson in 'The Statue and the Clay', pp. 149–152. It is also debated in section 2.6 of Chapter 2 above.

[10] For further discussion, see section 2.7 in Chapter 2 'On Bringing a Work into Existence'.

[11] Eddy M. Zemach raises the issue in his *Real Beauty,* University Park, PA: The Pennsylvania State University Press, 1997, p. 147.

additional, mostly relational and intentional, properties for at least part of their existence. Correspondingly, for type-based arts, musical and literary works are 'basically' sound- or word-sequence-types that acquire art-related properties at and for a time. To accept the other alternative might at first not seem all that different. For it implies too that statues are material objects, for example, made of bronze, and musical and literary works are sound- or word-sequence-types, and it too attributes to these entities probably the same range of art-related properties, including intentional and relational properties. The difference, though, is this: on the former account the presence of a work of art is explained in terms of a change occurring in a pre-existing thing in the world, a thing that remains essentially the same, albeit with evolving properties, while on the latter a *new* thing is introduced into the world when a work of art is made. This new thing is still a physical object or a sound- or word-sequence-type but it is not the *same* physical object or type as existed earlier.

How do we make this choice? The former choice has simplicity and seemingly ontological parsimony on its side and, if the Superman parallel can be sustained, it meets several of our theoretical desiderata (see above). In the end, though, two arguments seem persuasive in favour of the latter choice. The first concerns creation. One of the desiderata was that works are created (by artists). The idea that an artist brings something new into the world, i.e. a work of art, which did not exist prior to the artist's efforts, is a powerful intuition not to be abandoned lightly.[12] Yet merely altering the properties of something, without bringing anything new into the world, as on the first proposal, seems a pale shadow of creativity. It does not explain the activities of the great artists, nor do justice to the status of the works they create. A potential problem crops up, however, for the second proposal, at the other end of the scale, with minimalist or found-art, which seems to require very little creativity. Can an artist bring a new object into existence just by his say-so, as when Duchamp exhibited a bottlerack and titled it *Bottlerack*?[13] The best response in such cases is to stress other, non-material

---

[12] For a well-known and eloquent defence of this intuition, see Jerrold Levinson, 'What a Musical Work Is', in *Music, Art & Metaphysics*, Ithaca, NY: Cornell University Press, 1990, pp. 66–67.

[13] This problem worries Eric T. Olson in 'Material Coincidence and the Indiscernibility Problem', *Philosophical Quarterly* 51, 2001, p. 347.

(e.g. cultural or intentional) properties of the new object. A far deeper, more intractable, problem concerns type-based arts, notably music, where the nature of creativity is hotly disputed.[14] If types are eternal and musical works are sound-structure-types of some kind then it is hard to see how they can be brought into existence by the activities of a composer. What needs to be shown is that among the *essential* properties of a sound-structure-type that serves to identify a musical work are time-anchored (or historically-anchored) properties.[15]

The second argument in favour of the new-object view draws on just such essential properties. Even though we might make sense of the idea that Superman and Clark Kent are one and the same being yet differ, perhaps as *qua*-objects, in certain intentional properties, we could not suppose they are identical yet differ in *essential* properties. While we might be tempted by the thought that Superman-*qua*-Superman is essentially all-powerful and Superman-*qua*-Clark-Kent is essentially a weakling, these could at best be *de dicto* necessities applying to different aspects of the same being, not *de re* necessities of any kind, for *de re* necessities apply to objects under any description. Likewise, we could not allow, following the first proposal, that the statue is just the piece of bronze in one of its temporal stages and at the same time suppose there to be essential properties of the statue that are not essential properties of the piece of bronze. Yet there do seem to be such essential properties, so the first proposal must be abandoned. What are essential properties of works? This takes us to the next stage of the argument, to follow, but one *prima facie* candidate, in the case of any given statue, is *being a statue*.[16] The statue *David*, arguably, is *essentially* a statue, such that if it ceased to be a statue it would cease to exist. In contrast, if the material from which *David* is made ceased to be a statue it would not cease to exist. Exactly that material could exist without *David* existing, indeed without any statue existing, so *being a statue* is not an essential property of the constituting material. But

---

[14] For clear statements of opposing views, see Levinson, 'What a Musical Work Is' and Julian Dodd, *Works of Music: An Essay in Ontology*.

[15] I cannot here defend the view that musical works are created but were I to do so it would be roughly along the lines of Levinson's 'initiated types', as in Levinson, 'What a Musical Work Is'. For a further defence, see Robert Howell, 'Types, Indicated and Initiated', *British Journal of Aesthetics* 42, 2002.

[16] Lynne Rudder Baker makes this case in 'Why Constitution is Not Identity', *Journal of Philosophy* XCIV, 1997, pp. 599–621; see in particular pp. 601–602 and p. 620.

then it follows that *David* could not be identical with its constituting material and that of course is the conclusion of what I have called the new-object—i.e. the non-identity—view.

3.4. Preliminary Conclusions

Works, then, are objects (or types) brought into existence by the activities of artists (or humans generally). They are constituted by material substances or types (usually word-or-sound-sequence-types) yet are not identical with those constituting materials.[17] These constituting materials, as I call them, might pre-exist the works they come to constitute and indeed they might continue to exist after the works have vanished. What interests me are the conditions that must obtain for a work to come into existence and the conditions under which it is sustained in existence. The enquiry does not centre on the activities of artists (or others) in making works for these are largely contingent matters and there are unlikely to be substantial generalizations about common features in the workshops of painters, sculptors, poets, dramatists, and composers. But the need for human activities is not quite the anodyne premise it might seem. It rules out, for example, a certain kind of speculation about the origin of works. Had an object, indistinguishable in material composition, configuration, and appearance from Michelangelo's *David,* broken off from a cliff face in the Palaeozoic era it would not *be David*, nor an instance of *David*, nor even a statue. Likewise, more controversially, if the sound-structure-type associated with the 'Moonlight' Sonata had existed in the Palaeozoic era—as would follow if the type were eternal—or indeed had actual tokens of that type been miraculously conjured by wind blowing in the rocks in that same era, again it would not *be* the 'Moonlight' Sonata, nor an instance of the work. What is missing,

---

[17] I have helped myself, without argument, to the idea of 'constitution', as defended, for example, by Baker (op. cit.) and Johnston (op. cit.) and many others, but I am aware of criticisms, e.g. by Olson (op. cit.), Michael B. Burke ('Copper Statues and Pieces of Copper: A Challenge to the Standard Account', *Analysis* 52, 1992, pp. 12–17), and D. Zimmerman ('Theories of Masses and Problems of Constitution', *Philosophical Review* 104, 1995, pp. 53–110). Very little in my discussion hangs on the details of 'constitutionalism', except for the non-identity view just defended.

minimally, is the presence of a creative activity, not to say *the* creative activity of Michelangelo and Beethoven. The important conclusion, now familiar from discussion of indiscernibles cases,[18] is that works are underdetermined by their physical or structural properties, or, more strongly, that there are possible worlds where, for any given work in this world, a structurally isomorphic object (or type) exists that is not a work at all or not that work. We will look at further consequences of this point in a moment.

Before then, another feature of the act of creating works must be noted. When artists (or others) create works they do so with at least some conception, however vague, of what they seek to achieve in the work, as well as what effects they desire, what responses would be appropriate, what relation the work has to other works or to a tradition, and so forth. That creativity is connected with *some* conception of what is created follows from the fact that creation is an intentional act. Creating works also takes place at a time, in a context, and this context will help condition both the artist's conception (including what is *possible*) and the very resources for realizing that conception. Undoubtedly the character of a work, its salient features, its value, broadly conceived, indeed its very identity as a work, will be bound up, to a greater or lesser degree, with the historical and cultural context of its creation. Many of its essential properties, as we shall see, are grounded in this context.[19]

3.5. Generic Embeddedness Conditions

Essential properties of a work occur at different levels of generality: those essential to its being a *work* and those essential to its being the

---

[18] See, e.g., Danto, *Transfiguration of the Commonplace*, Chapter I, Kendall L Walton, 'Categories of Art', *Philosophical Review*, 79, 1970, pp. 334–367, and G. Currie, *An Ontology of Art*, Basingstoke: Macmillan, 1989, Chapter 2. For my own comments, see Lamarque, 'Aesthetic Value, Experience, and Indiscernibles', *Nordisk estetisk tidskrift* 17, 1998, pp. 61–78, and other chapters in this volume.

[19] David Wiggins puts it like this: 'The work has necessarily—is such as to be *de re* inconceivable or unenvisageable as definitely lacking—any sufficiently rich complex of features that has essential occurrence in the artist's own implicit or explicit account (placed as it is in whatever context of cultural understanding and artistic theory) of this very piece of work' (*Sameness and Substance,* Oxford: Blackwell, 1980, p. 126).

particular work that it is. At each level we can distinguish conditions of *production*, that is, necessary conditions pertaining to a work's origins, and conditions of *reception*, which, as I will show, yield necessary conditions for a work's survival.

3.5.1. Conditions of Production

Let us look, first, at conditions of production at the generic level. Works are essentially embedded in the human world of action and attitude. Not only is it essential to works that they be the product of intentional human activity but that activity must, in a broad sense, be social. Works—pictures, sculptures, music, dance, poetry, drama—are made in a social context, for an immense variety of ends certainly, but always constrained, even if loosely, by practices, conventions, expectations, and interactions. In this, as alluded to earlier, lies the important core of truth in institutionalist definitions of art. Nothing can be a work (of art) if it does not play a role, or be fit to play a role, in a human practice where a sufficient number of informed practitioners recognize its status and respond appropriately. Furthermore, the human world without which there would be no works, presupposes human traits much as they are, for all their diversity. If human beings had radically different psychological or social dispositions, having no concern for beauty, being robot-like in their response to the world, not inclined to value things beyond the utilitarian, being unexpressive, unemotional, and unconcerned with the pursuit of pleasure, then there would be no art (or works as described). Art and the urge for art, although recognized to be universal features of human life, might not have been so; they are universal but not essential to human existence. Perhaps humans will evolve to a state where art is redundant.

3.5.2. Conditions of Reception

Generic conditions of reception also stress the embeddedness of works in the human world and human practices. But here the emphasis is on 'uptake' and matters become somewhat more contentious. Appropriate social conditions must obtain not only for a work to come into existence but for its continuing to exist. The distinction between work and object again applies, for the persistence conditions of objects ('mere real things') and of works do not coincide. Take the case of literary works. Suppose the language in which a work is written has been entirely lost but suppose also that a *text* of the work—as a string of sentences—remains. It seems fairly clear that while the text survives, the *work* has not survived.[20] Text-survival is not sufficient for work-survival. Literary works depend for their survival on competent readers with sufficient background to grasp the basic meanings of the work. Musical works too only survive in a context in which they can be played and appreciated. The existence of a score does not guarantee the survival of a work unless there exist people in principle competent to read the score.

The point can be generalized. The continued existence of any work depends on the continued possibility of the work's being *responded to* in appropriate ways.[21] A work is sustained in existence partly in virtue of the attitudes, beliefs, and desires of those who recognize its role as a work and as the work it is. But I say 'possibility' because it is not an essential condition for the continued existence of a work that it be constantly an object of attention or interest in some individual mind. It is not an 'ideal' entity, existing only in some mind (that was one of our desiderata), but it is an *intentional* entity, depending essentially on facts about how it is *taken to be* by qualified observers.[22] We need a notion of what is 'culturally possible' to explain how reception conditions for works can obtain or be lost.[23] There is no sharp line between a time when the required responses are possible

---

[20] The point is argued in Amie L. Thomasson, *Fiction and Metaphysics,* Cambridge: Cambridge University Press, 1999, p. 11. See also 'Aesthetic Essentialism' in this volume.

[21] In this, works share common features with other institutional objects or facts. John Searle writes:

The secret of understanding the continued existence of institutional facts is simply that the individuals directly involved and a sufficient number of members of the relevant community must continue to recognize and accept the existence of such facts. Because the status is constituted by its collective acceptance, and because the function, in order to be performed, requires the status, it is essential to the functioning that there be continued acceptance of the status. The moment, for example, that all or most of the members of a society refuse to acknowledge property rights, as in a revolution or other upheaval, property rights cease to exist in that society. (Searle, *The Construction of Social Reality,* London: Allen Lane, 1995, p. 117).

[22] Searle's notion of 'collective intentionality' might be useful for explaining the status of works: *The Construction of Social Reality,* pp. 23–26.

[23] I say more about the idea in Ch. 5 'Aesthetic Essentialism', p. 117.

and when they are not. In consequence we find that works can fade into oblivion rather than being lost at an instant. They fade as cultural conditions change and cultural memories are lost, rather as a language can slowly die as fewer people use it and less of it is known.

It is not only the literary or musical arts that can be lost when reception conditions cease to obtain. It is true for the singular arts as well, although it is less easy to think of examples where the physical artefact remains but not the work. Prehistoric cave paintings, however, might be one such example. The line and colour configurations are still there to see but, arguably, the *works* are lost. Because we know nothing of the conditions under which they were produced or appreciated, and these facts are unrecoverable, the original *works*—assuming they were works arising within a practice—have not survived for we have no conception of what could count as a correct response to them. Perhaps different works have arisen in their place. The physical configurations have been appropriated and disseminated as works of representational art, discussed in the context of later traditions of representation. It would be a mistake, however, to assume that the appropriated works, with which we are familiar, are identical to the original works.[24]

Another striking consequence of making reception conditions essential to work-identity is what might be called the doomsday scenario. What becomes of works when all human beings are finally extinct? The answer is: the works too vanish. What makes the claim striking is that we can imagine a scenario where there are no more humans but the old museums and their (physical) contents remain, even records and videotapes and CDs playing endlessly on abandoned machines. So isn't that the *Mona Lisa* still there in the Louvre or the 'Moonlight' Sonata still playing on the CD? The answer is no: the works have gone but the material objects and the sounds remain. There are a number of reasons why we intuitively resist this conclusion. The first is the Berkeleyan reason that in imagining the scenario we putatively imagine ourselves observing it, but of course were

---

[24] I discuss the case of prehistoric art in this context in: Lamarque, 'The Aesthetic and the Universal', *Journal of Aesthetic Education* 33, 1999, pp. 1–17, and in 'Palaeolithic Cave Painting: A Test Case for Trans-Cultural Aesthetics', in Thomas Heyd and John Clegg, eds., *Aesthetics and Rock Art*, Aldershot: Ashgate, 2005, pp. 21–35.

we to observe it the works would indeed remain. Yet the scenario requires no human presence and no possibility of such. A second reason is that we have no ready means of referring to the objects or the sounds per se without referring to the works. We can't help but *say* that the *Mona Lisa* is present because that is how we refer to the object we know in the Louvre. A third reason is a false analogy with other kinds of artefacts. Artefacts like screwdrivers, CD players, or wheelbarrows can survive the doomsday scenario. A screwdriver is still a screwdriver even if there are no people to use it (although there must have been people who *made* it). Its identity is bound up with its function and it possesses its function as a disposition, which can obtain without ever meeting its conditions of use.[25] Work-identity, however, is more stringent than artefact identity in the matter of 'uptake'.[26] The intentionality of works connects them far more directly with what is *thought* or *perceived* (and what *can* be thought and perceived) than is the case with screwdrivers. A better analogy would be with Searle's institutional facts.[27] The sign says 'Keep Off the Grass' but in the doomsday scenario the sign survives but not the prohibition. There are no laws or institutions or rights—or *works*—in a world where humans have disappeared forever.

3.6. Work-specific Identity Conditions

Some of these points should become clearer as we turn to the conditions for a work's being the particular work it is.

3.6.1. *Conditions of Production*

Again, first of all, there are conditions of production. Much of the debate has focused on questions about the necessity of origins for

---

[25] Nick Zangwill has offered a defence of aesthetic functionalism, one implication of which is that a work of art could retain its function, therefore its identity, even though no-one is in a position to appreciate it: Zangwill, 'Aesthetic Functionalism', in Brady and Levinson, eds., *Aesthetic Concepts: Essays After Sibley*.

[26] Andrew Brennan impressed on me the implication of my account that the identity conditions of works and (non-art) artefacts must diverge in this regard; his book *Conditions of Identity* (Oxford: Clarendon Press, 1988) has helped me see the importance of survival conditions as well as, or even in place of, identity conditions.

[27] See note 21 above.

works.²⁸ Could anyone other than Beethoven have composed the *Eroica*? Could *Don Quixote* have been written by a twentieth-century symbolist poet? My own view is that we cannot generalize across cases. Judgements about the identity of specific works are inextricably tied to judgements of value.²⁹ A property is essential to a work only if its presence makes a relevant difference to the experience of the work (when correctly experienced) and bears on the work's value as a work.³⁰ More precisely, *if the presence or absence of a feature f in work w makes no difference to the quality of the experience of w (in a suitably informed perceiver) then f cannot be essential to the identity of w*. Features of works here can include both intentional and relational properties, many of which have been counted among essential properties. Where does that leave the essentiality of origins? Is *being by Beethoven* an essential property of the *Eroica*? Perhaps it is, and if so that is because in order to experience the work correctly, to understand it, and appreciate it for what it is, we *must* locate it in that composer's oeuvre, we *must* identify the specific context of its composition and the influences on it. But with other works—less complex, less iconic, less indispensable to the canon, less paradigmatically influential—it seems increasingly implausible that the composer or author should be essential to a work's identity. What about advertising jingles, football chants, minor pop songs, children's nursery rhymes, or indeed the wealth of anonymous poems or songs or ballads? Have we failed to grasp the identity of these works by not knowing who composed them? Or have we failed to experience them adequately? Perhaps we need to know roughly the period in which they were written to identify some of their essential properties, their genre, their style, whether they are pastiche

---

²⁸ Prominent contributions have been Levinson, 'What a Musical Work Is', and other essays in *Music, Art & Metaphysics,* and Currie, *An Ontology of Art.* For Levinson's criticisms of Currie, see Levinson, 'Art as Action', in *The Pleasures of Aesthetics,* Ithaca, NY: Cornell University Press, 1996.

²⁹ Here I am much influenced by Zemach, *Real Beauty.* He writes: 'identity conditions are not value-free . . . What is valuable in an artwork . . . is what is essential to it,' p. 149. See also Zemach, 'No Identification Without Evaluation', *British Journal of Aesthetics* 26, 1986.

³⁰ I have not defended the connection between artistic value and experience, though I broadly follow Malcolm Budd's thesis that the value of a work of art as a work of art is 'the intrinsic value of the experience the work offers': see Budd, *Values of Art: Pictures, Poetry and Music,* London: Allen Lane, The Penguin Press, 1995.

or serious, and so forth. But for many works little more is needed. Why? *Because these works neither demand nor reward more detailed attention.* The mode of appreciation appropriate to simple or ephemeral works is not so multi-layered that it needs to be informed by comprehensive knowledge of their conditions of production.

3.6.2. *Conditions of Survival*

In the discussion of generic embeddedness conditions, we saw that conditions of reception were inextricably bound up with conditions of survival.[31] What about survival conditions for specific works? There are obvious cases of works being lost or destroyed. Typically, these are cases where a physical object—a canvas, a mural, a sculpture—has been irreparably destroyed. Not every such case is clear-cut. Conditions for work-survival are more flexible, more work-specific, and more value-laden, than is often supposed. Clearly, if an essential property is lost then the work is lost. The principle enunciated earlier for essential properties of works thus has a direct bearing on work-survival. We must focus, as the principle requires, on the experience a work affords and on its value. How important is the physical constitution of a work? Perhaps surprisingly, it is not essential to a painting that it be made of precisely *those* physical materials. Surely Leonardo might have used paint from a fractionally different part of his palette to achieve exactly the same effect?[32] The result would still have been the *Mona Lisa*. Likewise, take the case of a painting that has been extensively, although gradually, restored over the years so that little of the original paint remains but the discernible configuration of line and colour is largely as it was. Arguably, the work survives, even if it belongs in the category of works 'fading' from existence. Hasn't something comparable happened with Leonardo's *Last Supper*? Enough of the work remains for it to have retained its essential aesthetic character and value. The artist's original conception is still in evidence and able to inform our experience of the work. Yet we

---

[31] For a brave, but in the end, I think, unsuccessful, defence of the thesis that '[a]rt has nothing essential to do with an audience', see Nick Zangwill, 'Art and Audience', *Journal of Aesthetics and Art Criticism* 57, 1999, pp. 315–332.

[32] Arguments of this kind are used in John Dilworth, 'A Representational Theory of Artefacts and Artworks', *British Journal of Aesthetics* 41, 2001.

would not be so sanguine about a work's survival if all the original paint were to be removed at one time and a reproduction painted in its place. Wholesale repainting and reconstruction, as at the Palace at Knossos in Crete, makes work-survival doubtful. Something *like* the work survives but not the work itself.

Inaccurate performance of music is comparable in some respects to physical degeneration in paintings. Again there is marked flexibility in assessment of work-survival in performance. *Pace* Goodman, a few wrong notes in a performance do not in themselves compromise work-identity, assuming that the admired qualities of the work are retained; yet sticking slavishly to a sequence of notes is not sufficient, for playing the correct sequence, even in accurate relative time-duration, at a tempo that makes the work unrecognizable, would destroy its distinctive aesthetic character and the work would be lost in performance.

We could run through any number of potential candidates for essential properties, the loss of which would entail the loss of the work. For any work w and any feature f, we can ask: would w be *same work* if it lacked (or lost) f? If so, then f cannot be essential to w. Thus, for example, being owned by X, being heavier than Y, being framed in a particular way, are revealed to be inessential properties of a painting. The aesthetic value of a painting per se is not affected by these external relations, nor do they bear on the experience the painting itself demands of a qualified viewer.[33] What about other features? Take colour, which might seem essential to a painting's identity. But colours fade over time. The colours now in Titian's *Diana and Actaeon* are not what they were in the mid-sixteenth century. Is what we see in the National Gallery in Edinburgh the same work as Titian painted? Most would agree, yes. A sufficient number of the salient features remain for us to value the painting as it has always been valued and there is continuity of the appropriate kind with the original.[34] What about a work's very ontological category, as discussed

---

[33] An ugly frame might of course detract from the experience of a painting but that is a contingent matter, comparable to a crowded gallery, not relevant to an assessment of the painting itself.
[34] Anthony Savile has argued, persuasively, that certain properties of works—including colours—are 'fixed' in relation to an artist's original conception, such that even though the properties are no longer perceivable (as when colours fade) they are still possessed by the

earlier: a unique particular or a multiply instantiable type? The reason that the most revered works of pictorial or sculptural art are particulars (not types)[35] is that there is a unique experience (and value) attached to seeing the original object, a live causal connection with genius.[36] With less iconic works and works made to be reproduced the required experience is satisfied by the reproducible appearance alone.

3.7. Works and Norms

I have spoken of the experiences 'demanded' by a work, with the implication of a strong normativity in responses to works. It is surely the case that there are better or worse, even in many cases right and wrong, ways of responding to a work. For example, in order to appreciate a work *as the work it is* we need to place the work in its proper category, for to fail to do so would be to fail to identify (and thus to perceive) its aesthetic properties.[37] The response a work demands is a function of several factors, including the artist's own aims and conception, the conventions of a genre or category, the norms established by the critical tradition. However, it would be wrong to

work and form a standard for the work's understanding and evaluation. If we accept this thesis, we might need to refine what counts as an adequate experience of a work. Perhaps knowledge of the true colours of the Titian should somehow inform the experience of its current, faded, colours. Non-perceptual properties, like semantic properties in the case of literature, are easier to accommodate, for the 'experience' of the work already incorporates thoughts about its original nature. See Savile, 'The Rationale of Restoration', *Journal of Aesthetics and Art Criticism* 51, 1993, pp. 463–474.

[35] Here I disagree with Zemach, for whom: 'The identity conditions of paintings are such that paintings may exist at more than one place at the same time' ('No Identification Without Evaluation', p. 244).

[36] Leonard Meyer puts it well: 'The original is . . . more valuable and more exciting aesthetically [than the "finest reproduction"] because our feeling of intimate contact with the magic power of the creative artist heightens awareness, sensitivity, . . . and the disposition to respond' (Leonard B. Meyer, 'Forgery and the Anthropology of Art', in Denis Dutton, ed., *The Forger's Art*, University of California Press, 1983, pp. 86–87). Levinson produces powerful arguments for the uniqueness of paintings, based on the practices of art lovers and curators: Jerrold Levinson, 'Zemach on Pictures', *British Journal of Aesthetics* 27, 1987, pp. 280–282.

[37] The point is familiar and well established by Walton in 'Categories of Art'. There are dissenting voices, though: cf. Nick Zangwill, 'In Defence of Moderate Aesthetic Formalism', *Philosophical Quarterly* 50, 2000.

pretend to a degree of definiteness which is unrealistic. Of course responses to art, the experiences (even of fully informed perceivers) elicited by particular works, and the values placed on different aspects of a work admit of considerable variability. The priority given to features of a work will always be, to an extent, interest-relative, albeit constrained by norms of critical practice. It is for this reason that judgements about work-identity and work-survival have an inevitable degree of indeterminacy. Among art critics who, relative to institutionally accepted norms, value highly the actual materials used by an artist, some kinds of restoration count as a serious threat to a work's survival. In another example, those philologically inclined critics, for whom the precise phrasing and linguistic nuances of a literary work have the highest priority, will diminish the value of translations.

That work-identity and work-survival should be relative to judgements of value should not impugn the objectivity of the properties of works. This objectivity, though, takes an unusual form given the unusual nature of art-objects. As cultural objects, essentially dependent on cultural conditions and human responses, art-objects have intentional and relational properties essentially, as part of their natures. This can seem strange, metaphysically. *Being a statue* is both an objective property of *David,* a property it possesses *in itself* and essentially, but also a property necessarily bound up with factors *external* to the work. An intentional property is a property something possesses in virtue of how it is *taken*, or *thought to be*, or *perceived*. A work is a peculiar kind of object, necessarily connected to human interests (this is not true of any natural object). But this need not imply subjectivity, for art-related properties do not reside in the mind of the observing subject. They are public and perceivable (further conforming to our desiderata), even if for complex works a considerable amount of background knowledge is required to perceive them correctly.

But what is it to perceive a work *as a work*? It is a kind of aspect-perception. To hear music is not just to hear sounds but to hear a distinctive organization of tones, in Scruton's words, 'an order that contains no information about the physical world, which stands apart from the ordinary workings of cause and effect, and which is irreducible to any physical organisation'.[38] To hear music, rather

[38] Roger Scruton, *The Aesthetics of Music,* Oxford: Oxford University Press, 1997, p. 39.

WORK AND OBJECT 77

than just sounds, is something only humans can achieve, but it is an experience of a real phenomenon, not just a phenomenologically real experience.[39] Musical aspects of sounds are objective and shareable. In a different, but parallel, manner, to attend to a literary work as a literary work is also aspectival, also an experience of a distinct kind, imbued with an expectation of value.[40] It calls for an unusual kind of attention—recognizing fictionality, looking for character and thematic development, noticing structural connectedness, irony, symbolism, and so forth—an attention which would not be appropriate for reading different kinds of text, scientific or philosophical. Finally, the perception of paintings is itself a perception not just of lines and colours but of representations or expressions. We perceive the representational aspects *directly*; they are not inferred from more basic perceptions.[41] Both the practices and the experiences of art perception confirm the thesis that work and object are distinct. They also go a long way to support the robustly realist desiderata for a theory of works that I have outlined.

[39] Levinson criticizes the idealist tendency in Scruton, in his review of *The Aesthetics of Music*, *Philosophical Review*, October, 2000.
[40] For an account of literary reading as *sui generis*, see Peter Lamarque and Stein Haugom Olsen, *Truth, Fiction, and Literature*, Oxford: Clarendon Press, 1994, esp. Chapter 10.
[41] Joseph Margolis has long defended the view that art objects are real objects of perception and has criticized Arthur Danto for allegedly holding that only 'mere real things' are perceived: Margolis, 'Farewell to Danto and Goodman', *British Journal of Aesthetics*, 38, 1998, pp. 353–374.

4
Distinctness and Indiscernibility in the Allographic Arts

4.1. Types and Particulars

Not all musical works or literary works are types. Some are particulars. That possibility at least should not be ruled out a priori.[1] It is in principle possible that a musical work be identical with a unique performance. A work performed for a specific occasion might be of this kind, as might be certain improvisations. Only someone present at the performance could be said to have heard the work. If a recording of the performance were made, it would have the same status as a reproduction of a painting. It would provide some access to the work and some chance of appreciating it but it would not present the work itself. Similar examples could be found among literary works, where facts about the presentation of the work are also deemed essential to its identity. Certain public performances of poetry or drama might fall into this category.

However, even with musical and literary works that are particulars there will always be an associated type: a sound-structure-type in the case of music, a word- or sentence-structure-type in the case of literature. Not any tokens of these types—like recordings of occasion-specific performances—will count as proper tokens of the works, but that is because the works being particulars do not have tokens. Only one individual token, that produced on the relevant and unique occasion, counts as the work. There is a parallel with

---

[1] See section 3.1, ch. 3 'Work and Object'.

paintings. Paintings are normally classed as particulars but associated with each painting is a colour-line-configuration-type that can have separate tokens and indeed is instantiated every time the painting is reproduced or copied. If paintings are classed as particulars then only one token of the configuration-type—that produced by the artist on an occasion—counts as the work.

There is a view, however, that holds that paintings are multiply instantiable types and that any proper token, accurately reproduced, can count as the work.[2] If that is right—and it might seem to be true at best of only *some* paintings—then paintings are not particulars and their identity conditions do not reside in the identity of any single physical object.

A further complication is that even among types there is thought to be a distinction between types per se and 'indicated' types. Indicated types are provenance-specific. They are still types, not particulars, but facts about their provenance—who created them, when, and where—are thought to be essential to the identity of the types.[3] This makes the identity of tokens—actual sound-sequences or actual sentence-sequences—problematic. Two type-identical sound-structures or sentence-structures might be tokens of distinct indicated types. So how is it determined what indicated type is this particular token a token of? In the case of sound-structures is this a performance of musical work *a* or musical work *b*? In the case of sentence-structures, which literary work is this a copy of? (Note that if paintings are indicated types then the same question arises: is this configuration in front of me painting *a* or painting *b*?) The criteria of identity for tokens of indicated types are not clearly defined. This is a problem not sufficiently addressed, I maintain, by those who hold that distinct musical and literary works can be constituted by identical sound- or word-structures.

---

[2] See P. F. Strawson, 'Aesthetic Appraisal and Works of Art', in *Freedom and Resentment*, London: Methuen, 1974. Also Frank Sibley, 'Why the *Mona Lisa* May Not be a Painting', in F. Sibley, *Approaches to Aesthetics: Collected Papers on Philosophical Aesthetics*, J. Benson, B. Redfern, and J. Roxbee Cox, eds., Oxford: Oxford University Press, 2001. Gregory Currie holds that all works of art are action-types: Currie, *An Ontology of Art*, Basingstoke: Macmillan, 1989, Chapter 3.

[3] Jerrold Levinson, 'What a Musical Work Is', in *Music, Art & Metaphysics*, Ithaca, NY: Cornell University Press, 1990.

4.2. Autographic and Allographic

Musical and literary works that are particulars (neither types nor indicated types) are 'autographic' in Nelson Goodman's terminology and thus can, unproblematically, be subject to forgery. An item purporting to be such a work and experientially similar to it could be presented with a false history of production.

However, not all musical and literary works are particulars. Most, it would seem, are multiply instantiable types (indicated or otherwise). One and the same literary work, characteristically, can be instantiated in printed copies, readings, even memory states, just as one and the same musical work can be instantiated in distinct performances at different times, even performances with different experiential properties.

It is a matter of some controversy whether musical and literary works that are types can be forged and are 'allographic' in Goodman's sense. No-one disputes that manuscripts and autographed scores can be forged or even that musical performances can be, in a slightly extended sense (purporting to be Klemperer with the Berlin Symphony Orchestra but in fact no such thing). Furthermore, we should distinguish between cases of forgery where an exact copy is made of an *existing* work, as in Goodman's Rembrandt example,[4] and cases, such as van Meegeren's 'Vermeers', where what is copied is a *style* rather than a particular work. Jerrold Levinson calls the former 'referential' forgery, the latter 'inventive' forgery.[5] Inventive forgery does seem relatively unproblematic for music and literature. A simple model might be Kant's 'rogue of a youth' mimicking a nightingale.[6] Although it might be somewhat arch to describe the youth's offering as a forgery he is nevertheless falsely trying to pass off his own sounds as something that they are not ('made by a nightingale').

---

[4] See Nelson Goodman, *Languages of Art,* Indianapolis: Hackett, 1968, Chapter 3 (reprinted as 'Reality Remade: A Denotation Theory of Representation', in Philip Alperson, ed., *The Philosophy of the Visual Arts,* New York: Oxford University Press, 1993).

[5] Levinson, 'Autographic and Allographic Art Revisited', in *Music, Art & Metaphysics,* Ithaca, NY: Cornell University Press, 1990, p. 103.

[6] Kant, *Critique of Judgment,* Part I, Book II, §42. This is discussed in Chapter 6 'Aesthetic Empiricism'.

However, is referential forgery possible for music and literature? Levinson thinks it is, although deems it a 'relatively harmless possibility'.[7] In this he disagrees with Goodman, for whom such arts are allographic and not forgeable (in this sense). Goodman defines forgery in the relevant sense as an object's 'falsely purporting to have the history of production requisite of the (or an) original of the work',[8] and yet holds that for allographic arts history of production is not necessary for work-identity. All that is required for something's being a genuine instance of a musical or literary work is that it complies with the relevant notation (or 'spelling'): 'all that matters for genuine instances of a poem is what may be called *sameness of spelling*' and 'the constitutive properties of a performance of the symphony are those prescribed in the score'.[9] It follows that any notationally correct instance counts as an instance of the work so no referential forgery is possible just by producing a notationally identical facsimile. Peter Kivy concurs with Goodman: 'when versions of a work are note for note identical, they are the same version of the same work, hence cannot bear the relation of forgery to original.'[10]

Levinson disagrees with Goodman and Kivy about identity conditions of musical and literary works. He holds that identical sound-structure-types might constitute different works with different aesthetic and artistic properties. The pattern of argument is familiar from indiscernibles cases, as in Kendall Walton, Arthur Danto, and Gregory Currie, all of whom aim at finding an indispensable role for facts about a work's history of production in identification and individuation conditions for the work. Here is Levinson:

A work identical in sound-structure with Schoenberg's *Pierrot Lunaire* (1912), but composed by Richard Strauss in 1897 would be aesthetically different from Schoenberg's work. Call it '*Pierrot Lunaire**'. As a Straussian work, *Pierrot Lunaire** would follow hard upon Brahms's *German Requiem*, would be contemporaneous with Debussy's *Nocturnes*, and would be taken as the next step in Strauss's development after *Also Sprach Zarathustra*. As such, it would be more *bizarre*, more *upsetting*, more *anguished*, more *eerie* even than Schoenberg's work, since perceived against a musical tradition,

---

[7] Levinson, 'Autographic and Allographic Art Revisited', p. 103.
[8] Goodman, *Languages of Art*, p. 122.　　　　　　　　　　[9] Ibid., pp. 115, 117.
[10] Peter Kivy, 'How To Forge a Musical Work', in *New Essays on Musical Understanding*, Oxford: Clarendon Press, 2001.

a field of current styles, and an *oeuvre* with respect to which the musical characteristics of the sound structure involved in *Pierrot Lunaire* appear doubly extreme.[11]

Levinson produces several such cases in seeking to establish that 'there is always some aesthetic or artistic difference between structurally identical compositions in the offing in virtue of differing musico-historical contexts'.[12]

We should agree with Levinson about the identity conditions of musical and literary works, at least in his insistence that notational identity or 'sameness of spelling' alone is not sufficient for work-identity and reference must be made to provenance-related factors. Indeed the point is of considerable importance in understanding what a work (of any kind) is. We must, though, be careful to limit its scope and consequences. There is no simple formula in determining exactly what provenance-related factors bear on the individuation of works and this can vary to a considerable degree from case to case, depending on the nature of the work and the kind of appreciation it demands.[13] What is accepted is only that some such factors are involved in every case. Levinson asserts that there are 'no existing art forms in which historical factors are wholly irrelevant to the question of the genuineness of works or instances'.[14]

However, consequences concerning the possibility of forgery for musical and literary works and relatedly the identity of individual tokens of such works do not follow quite as inevitably as Levinson supposes. For Levinson, only provenance-related facts about a performance of a musical work or a copy of a literary work will determine what work each is an instance of, so the possibility of misrepresenting that provenance in a forgery is real. To make sense of this, we need a two-step process: first, establish that two notationally (or structurally) identical items could be distinct works, then, suppose that one of these works is misrepresented as being the other. While we might grant the

---

[11] Levinson, 'What a Musical Work Is', p. 80. In fact, in a later paper, Levinson invites us to substitute for Schoenberg's *Pierrot Lunaire* his work *Five Pieces for Orchestra*, op. 16, 1909, because of problems with the former example due to its literary component. But nothing for our purposes hangs on this. See J. Levinson, 'What a Musical Work Is, Again', in *Music, Art & Metaphysics*, p. 225, fn. 22.

[12] Levinson, 'What a Musical Work Is', p. 81.   [13] See Chapter 3 'Work and Object'.

[14] Levinson, 'Autographic and Allographic Art Revisited', p. 101.

first step, the second, arguably, is problematic. Let us look a bit more closely.

4.3. Literary and Musical Forgeries

Levinson offers a literary and a musical case. In the literary case we are to suppose that White and Black, by eerie coincidence, but independently, pen poems that consist of the very same word-sequence. Because of the different acts of 'indication' and the resulting difference in aesthetic and artistic properties the poems are distinct works, calling, no doubt, for distinct interpretations and modes of appreciation. In exactly parallel fashion, in the musical case, a waltz written by Z is identical in structure and notation to a waltz written by Y, although again, because of a difference in provenance and consequently in aesthetic and artistic properties, they are distinct as works.

Let us grant this scenario, although we shall return to it. Now here is Levinson's forgery claim: 'If I knowingly present a copy of White's poem as if it were a copy of Black's (identically worded) poem, forgery has occurred. If I knowingly give a performance of Z's waltz (from Z's score and with Z in mind) while presenting it as a performance of Y's (identically scored) waltz, this too is forgery'.[15]

But Levinson immediately identifies a problem:

If what makes a performance a performance of Z's waltz is that the performer intentionally relates the performance to Z and Z's creative activity, then how can this performance serve as a forgery of Y's waltz? Wouldn't that require the performer to think of the performance *as being of* Y's waltz as well, and if so, *wouldn't* it be of Y's waltz, and hence not a forgery? The way out of this puzzle is to recognize that forgery can occur in virtue of the difference between the *generation* of a performance as an instance of a particular work and the *presentation* (or *labeling*) of the performance as an instance of a particular (possibly different) work. To forge Y's waltz the performer must deceitfully *put forward* the performance as being of Y's waltz; but the performer need not and must not *think* of it as deriving from and relating to Y's creative activity.[16]

---

[15] Ibid., p. 102.   [16] Ibid., p. 102, fn. 27.

But how can this work? Let us elaborate the story, following Levinson's suggestion that Z is a 'Dadaistic composer', and suppose that the difference between Z's waltz and Y's is that the former, unlike the latter, is *ironic, pokes fun at the traditional waltz form, alludes to Duchamp, is a wry comment on the sterility of modern composition*. It would be possible to imagine a performance of Z's waltz that subtly brought out these features, albeit within the constraints of the score and its instructions (identical to Y's score). Someone listening to Z's waltz under these conditions indeed would (and *should*) discern (and attend to) the ironic and allusive elements. Levinson's scenario, though, requires that a performer (the alleged forger) *pretend* that none of those features are present, indeed strives in the performance to remove any hint of their presence and plays the waltz exactly as Y intended it. The performer's intention is to invest the performance with all the expressive properties associated with Y's work—and none of the properties of Z's. So what do the audience hear? Surely they hear a performance of Y's work, not Z's? The fact that at the back of the performer's mind is the thought that what is *really* being played is Z's work seems insufficient to make that the case. The problem is that the association with Z is too tenuous. Nothing of Z's conception is informing the performance—the Dadaistic spirit that makes the work what it is has been deliberately effaced, to the extent, one might suppose, that to hear that spirit in the performance is somehow to *mishear* it. In the Rembrandt/copy example the fact that there is no direct causal input from Rembrandt into the copy bears crucially on the experience of the copy. But Levinson admits that no causal connection is required from a performance to the composer; what is needed is 'intentional relatedness'.[17] But the intention that a performance be heard *as if* it were of Y's work and the performance's being *of* Y's work are not sufficiently distinct to allow the deception in the performance to gain any purchase.[18]

This discussion has cast some doubt on the possibility of referential forgery in the case of music, as conceived by Levinson, but it has

---

[17] Levinson, 'Autographic and Allographic Art Revisited', p. 105.
[18] I have been influenced in this paragraph by an illuminating discussion of the issue by Christopher Janaway in 'What a Musical Forgery Isn't', *British Journal of Aesthetics*, 39, 1999, pp. 62–71. Janaway holds that a referential forgery of a musical *work* is incoherent but allows that a performance might be a referential forgery.

not cast doubt on the possibility of two notationally identical items constituting different musical works. What it does highlight, though, is the difference between attending to a token of a musical or literary work and attending to a painting. In the latter case the provenance of the object in front of me is crucial in determining what work I am giving my attention. But in music and literature provenance plays a much more complicated role. In music it is not the causal provenance of a score[19] nor the hidden thoughts of a performer that determines what work is performed so much as appropriate modes of interpretation (or appreciation) encouraged and taken up. Likewise, in literature the provenance of the copy in front of me is far less important than how it is apprehended.

Take White's poem and Black's (identically worded) poem and consider the following scenario. The poems are to be published in separate volumes but by the same publisher. At the printing stage 500 copies of the identical text of the two poems are produced without thought to which is which. Late in the process the binder decides, arbitrarily, that the first 250 off the press will go into White's volume, the second 250 into Black's. At that point, but not before, the texts become texts of the different works. A proof-reader picks up the sheets from White's volume and reads the poem. Being of literary inclination he, the proof-reader, not only dwells on the typography of the text but finds time for appreciative reflection on this delightful new addition to White's distinctive oeuvre. An hour later an emergency call goes up that only 200 copies of White's book are needed but 300 of Black's. The sheet that the proof-reader so diligently attended to is transferred to Black's pile. Not recognizing the sheet (would it matter if he had?) the proof-reader turns his attention to Black's volumes and reading from the very same, transferred, sheet revels in the dark, and distinctive, humour of Black's poem. By a cruel twist of fate, a further decision is made that indeed only 200 copies are needed of Black's volume as well. The unwanted sheet now twice proof-read is put in the waste bin. Days later a cleaner, indifferent to the merits of either White or Black, picks out the sheet, takes it home and frames it (as a valuable memento of the last print run of a famous, but now

---

[19] Levinson concedes this point in footnote 23, 'Autographic and Allographic Art Revisited', pp. 99–100.

defunct, press). Is it White's or Black's poem on the cleaner's wall? Strictly of course only the text appears on the wall. But whose poem is it the text of? There is no determinate answer. The provenance of the sheet provides no discriminating criterion. The text itself could be read as either White's or Black's poem. The determining factor rests not on the history of the sheet but on a decision by whoever turns their attention to it.[20]

What the example highlights is the possibility of complete arbitrariness in whether a token of a text is one work or another (in the case where the works are textually—or notationally—identical). What determines the matter in the example is a simple, unconstrained, decision made by the person reading the text—and different decisions could be made by people viewing the text on the cleaner's wall on different occasions. The underlying truth remains that it is always a matter of decision (by the reader) how a text is read. Of course in normal cases the context in which the text is presented encourages a decision one way or another. When the text of the poem is read in a volume with White's name on the cover then there is a presumption in favour of reading it as one of White's poems. But it is not obligatory. If a devotee of Black is keen to engage with Black's poem but has no copy of it to hand, only a copy of White's volume, then he might well—in the full knowledge that the works are distinct if textually identical—read the text in White's volume *as* the text of Black's poem. A conscious decision of this kind could not be counted as a *mistake* or a *misreading*. Nor would it in any way detract from a full appreciation of the work. Of course that is not to say that a mistake could not be made. A reader who intended to read the text as a poem by White and believed that this was White's poem but who identified in it aesthetic and artistic properties associated with Black's poem has misread the poem, in effect by responding to it inappropriately.

It is interesting, again, to contrast the literary indiscernibles case with the pictorial one. No *decision* on the part of the viewer can make

---

[20] The scenario outlined here goes much further in showing the indeterminacy of token identity than that offered by Levinson to show that intentional considerations often override causal ones in determining token identity: see footnote 23, 'Autographic and Allographic Art Revisited', p. 99.

appreciation of the replica Rembrandt equivalent to appreciation of the real thing. The provenance of *this object* is all important in constituting the full aesthetic appreciation. Treating an object *as if* it were by the hand of Rembrandt will always fall short of viewing an object that *is* by his hand. The provenance of this instantiated text-token or this copy of a literary work is never a determining factor in how it should be read. Reading a text as if it were by White—regardless of the history of the text-token in front of the reader—yields the appropriate response to White's poem. That is not to say that there is anything arbitrary about the distinction between *a-correct-response-to-White's-poem* and *a-correct-response-to-Black's-poem*.

4.4. Pierre Menard

This discussion provides an important perspective on Jorge Luis Borges's short story 'Pierre Menard, Author of the *Quixote*'[21] which has come to epitomize, for philosophers, thought-experiments about indiscernibles. Borges's story is frequently held to offer further support for the distinction between text and work. Danto himself appropriated the story in support of his thesis that 'works are in part constituted by their location in the history of literature as well as by their relationships to their authors'.[22] In the story, Menard, a (fictional) early twentieth-century Symbolist poet, has the ambition to write *Don Quixote*, not by merely copying the original, but by a fully inspired act of literary creation. Here is a key, and often quoted, passage from the story:

It is a revelation to compare Menard's *Don Quixote* with Cervantes's. The latter, for example, wrote (part one, chapter nine):

. . . truth, whose mother is history, rival of time, depository of deeds, witness of the past, exemplar and adviser to the present, and the future's counsellor.

---

[21] Jorge Luis Borges, 'Pierre Menard, Author of the *Quixote*', in *Labyrinths*, Harmondsworth: Penguin, 1971, pp. 62–71.

[22] Danto, 'Content and Causation', in *Transfiguration of the Commonplace*, pp. 35–36. Danto states that 'Borges's contribution to the ontology of art is stupendous', op. cit., p. 36.

88 WORK AND OBJECT

Written in the seventeenth century, written by the 'lay genius' Cervantes, this enumeration is a mere rhetorical praise of history. Menard, on the other hand, writes:

... truth, whose mother is history, rival of time, depository of deeds, witness of the past, exemplar and adviser to the present, and the future's counsellor.

History, the *mother* of truth: the idea is astounding. Menard, a contemporary of William James, does not define history as an inquiry into reality but as its origin. Historical truth, for him, is not what has happened: it is what we judge to have happened. The final phrases—*exemplar and adviser to the present, and the future's counsellor*—are brazenly pragmatic.

The contrast in style is also vivid. The archaic style of Menard—quite foreign after all—suffers from a certain affectation. Not so that of his forerunner, who handles with ease the current Spanish of his time.[23]

For philosophers, the passage once again presents a familiar feature in discussions of work ontology: indiscernibility at the surface but different meaning and artistic properties further down. It might be thought that the lesson from Borges's tale is all too familiar and unexciting, at least from the point of view of philosophy of language: the same sentence-type can bear different meanings and what speakers mean by any token of a sentence-type might differ from occasion to occasion. The sentence-type quoted from *Don Quixote* could be *used* on different occasions to mean (and connote) different things. But what Danto and others draw from the story is deeper than this, a further illustration of the thesis that text identity does not imply work-identity: what makes something the work it is rests not on its textual properties alone but on facts about its origin, including the intentions of its creator.

The trouble is it is far from clear that the story does support this thesis. There is some doubt, even internal to the story, that the process by which Menard arrives at his *Quixote* is even intelligible. A striking fact, for example, is the tone of the narrative voice. Isn't there a hint of scepticism in the narrator, who describes Menard's task as 'impossible', 'from the very beginning, futile'? The narrator identifies a character trait of Menard's: 'his resigned or ironical habit of propagating ideas which were the strict reverse of those he preferred'.[24] Isn't there a suggestion that both Menard and the

[23] Borges, 'Pierre Menard, Author of the *Quixote*', p. 69.   [24] Ibid., p. 69.

narrator know that the task is absurd? That both are revelling in a lost cause? Couldn't we—shouldn't we?—perhaps read the story as a witty *reductio ad absurdum*, a description of a magnificent, pathological, hopelessly flawed enterprise, rather than solemnly taking it as literally credible?

Furthermore, it is not even clear that the story, taken literally, implies any thesis about distinct but indiscernible works. We are explicitly told that Menard's ambition is not to create a different work but 'to compose *the Quixote*' ('he did not want to compose another *Quixote*—which is easy—but *the Quixote* itself'). The truth is that Borges is not working with any theoretically informed notion of a *work*, in contrast to a *text*, and we should not lose sight of the fact that he has written a playful fiction, not an essay in ontology.

A view of Borges's story quite different from Danto's is taken by Nelson Goodman and Catherine Elgin, these latter insisting that Menard has not produced a new work, merely 'another inscription of the text'.[25] They elaborate as follows:

> Menard may in some way have proposed or inspired a new interpretation of the text. But no more than any other admissible interpretation offered before or since or by others, does the Menard reading count as *the* work *Don Quixote*, or even as *a* work *Don Quixote*. All are merely interpretations of the work. Moreover, all and only right interpretations of Cervantes' text are right inscriptions of Menard's. If it is incorrect for a contemporary reader to interpret Cervantes' text as archaic, it is equally incorrect to so interpret Menard's. For the 'two' texts are one.[26]

For Goodman and Elgin, a work is a text. Any tokening of a type-identical text ('same spelling') is a tokening of the work. This is at the heart of Goodman's notion of the allographic and a reason, for him, why allographic, notationally-based arts do not admit of referential forgery. At most Menard can be credited with 'having produced a replica of the text without copying it; and having formulated

---

[25] Nelson Goodman and Catherine Elgin, 'Interpretation and Identity: Can the Work Survive the World?' in Eileen John and Dominic Lopes, eds. *Philosophy of Literature: Contemporary and Classic Readings: An Anthology*, Oxford: Blackwell, 2004, p. 96. (Originally published in *Critical Inquiry* 12, 1986, pp. 567–574.) For powerful arguments against Goodman and Elgin, see Gregory Currie, 'Work and Text', *Mind*, 100, 1991, pp. 325–340; rept. in John and Lopes, eds., *Philosophy of Literature*.

[26] Goodman and Elgin, 'Interpretation and Identity', p. 96.

or inspired a new interpretation of the work—a way of reading it as a contemporary story in an archaic style'.[27] This account is certainly compatible with the story itself. Indeed at the end of the story Borges suggests that the lesson we should draw is not Danto's but rather a lesson about the possibilities of *reading*, applying a technique of 'deliberate anachronism and . . . erroneous attribution' and encouraging us, for example, 'to go through the *Odyssey* as if it were posterior to the *Aeneid*'. There is nothing to suggest that the text of the *Odyssey* might support distinct works (pre- and post-*Aeneid*) and the proposal for new ways of reading sounds very like what Goodman and Elgin call interpretation.

It is important, though, to draw the right lesson from all this. We should keep distinct the issue of whether works are identical to texts and the issue of whether the provenance of a text-token is decisive in determining what work it is a text of. Take the second issue first. We have reason to believe, from looking at Levinson's Black/White example, that the provenance of any given text-token is not decisive for work-identity. Similarly, what is crucial about the two quoted type-identical snippets from *Don Quixote* in the above passage is not some facts about the history of the printed word-tokens but the instruction to read one as by Cervantes and the other as by Menard. At this stage of the argument there is nothing to distinguish between Goodman's and Elgin's hypothesis that we are simply being offered different ways of interpreting the single work *Don Quixote* and the suggestion that there are different works with different interpretative implications. Significantly we do not begin by observing the different stylistic and connotative properties of the two quotations and infer their different provenances; rather, if we want to follow the second suggestion, we start by assuming they have different provenances (and are tokens of different indicated types), then we notice their different properties. What the Borges story shows—and the ending makes all but explicit—is that any text-token can be treated *as if* it were a token of different indicated types (i.e. different works). That holds true whether or not there actually exist, in particular cases, different works or indicated types. The latter will depend on quite specific and extremely rare circumstances of creation.

[27] Goodman and Elgin, 'Interpretation and Identity', p. 96.

That brings us back to the first of the two issues that need to be separated, namely, whether two identical texts *can* be instances of distinct works. Goodman and Elgin believe not, but application of Leibniz's Law, or the 'indiscernibility of identicals', suggests otherwise, i.e. the principle that if a is identical with b then a and b share all the same properties.[28] If we can find instances of identical text-tokens that possess different work-related properties then that implies that texts cannot be identical with works. Levinson suggests what sort of properties these might be—'aesthetic and artistic'—and Borges suggests stylistic and interpretative ones. Yet we have just seen that looking for properties such as these is not something we do first, then infer work differences. Instead we look at provenance-related facts to see if there are genuinely distinct historical conditions of creation that could underpin a difference of properties. If we can show this then the Goodman/Elgin hypothesis looks increasingly implausible and unmotivated, with its insistence that entirely anachronistic interpretations (like those associated with Menard's text) are legitimately applied to a single work.[29] But these provenance-related facts bear on the type itself—as an indicated type—and only obliquely on the particular tokens under investigation.

In this regard it is helpful to distinguish two kinds of tokens, which I will call *type-creating* tokens and *type-instantiating* tokens. Type-creating tokens are, as implied, those tokens the production of which brings into existence a new (indicated) type. When Cervantes wrote *Don Quixote* his text was a type-creating token. The type he created is the work. My copy of *Don Quixote* is merely a type-instantiating token of that original type. While provenance is important for type-creating tokens it is not so for type-instantiating ones. The question often asked of Borges's story is whether it offers a plausible scenario for the creation, by Menard, of a distinct type-creating token. Perhaps it does not—the case is debatable—but that does not impugn the fact that there could be two works with type-identical tokens.

Any given token of the *Don-Quixote*-text-type, *even the type-creating token produced by Menard*, can count as a type-instantiating token of

---

[28] For a discussion of the applicability of Leibniz's Law in this context, see 'Work and Object'.
[29] This is Currie's objection in 'Work and Text'.

either Cervantes's or Menard's work. Again the Black/White example suggests that while the history of some actual type-instantiating token might be an *indicator* of the relevant type it is rarely decisive in determining what type is instantiated in cases of distinct type-identical works. We are led, then, to the surprising conclusion that the provenance of a token can be irrelevant to the identity of that token even though provenance determines the (indicated) type of which it is a token.

What makes the Borges story problematic for appropriation into the ontology of a work is not the idea that two texts might sustain different works but, as it were, the more local difficulty of making coherent the process by which Menard arrives at his own text. While we might grant that he did not *copy* it in any straightforward sense,[30] or transcribe it from memory—and he dismissed trying to *become* Cervantes as 'too easy'!—nevertheless his achievement is not sufficiently independent of the original work to determine decisively the distinctness of the works: in other words, the production of a genuine type-creating token. To grant the theoretical possibility of textually identical but distinct works it is important to suppose that the creative acts giving rise to the works are independent of one another. So in spite of the fact that the text-token produced by Menard does not have the standard provenance of being a copy or reproduction of Cervantes's text we cannot conclude from that fact alone that it is the text of a distinct work. And of any given type-instantiating token presented to us it is a matter of decision whether to read it *as if* it were by Menard or by Cervantes.

4.5. Concluding Remarks

So we can return, finally and briefly, to the allographic/autographic distinction and the question of whether referential forgery is possible

[30] Michael Wreen, in 'Once is Not Enough?', *British Journal of Aesthetics*, 30, 1990, pp. 149–158, argues that to all intents and purposes it is a copy of Cervantes's work and thus is not distinct. Christopher Janaway, in 'Borges and Danto: A Reply to Michael Wreen', *British Journal of Aesthetics*, 32, 1992, pp. 72–76, rejects this on the grounds that some crucial conditions for copying are missing in the Menard case.

for the allographic arts. The central argument of this chapter is that we should keep separate the issue of how far 'autographic' (i.e. historical or provenance-related) factors bear on work-identity and the question of whether literary and musical works can admit of referential forgery, which I have interpreted as an issue about the status and identity of individual tokens. I am inclined to side with Levinson against Goodman on the former and Goodman against Levinson on the latter. There is an important difference between producing a replica of a painting or carved sculpture and passing it off as the original and producing a 'replica' token of a poem or performance-token of a musical work and trying to pass it off as the original. Levinson himself admits there is a difference but sees it as one of degree.[31] I maintain that the difference is deeper because it rests on quite fundamental relations that writers and readers have to copies of poems or performers and listeners to performances of music.

I agree with Levinson (and Currie and Danto)—against Goodman and Elgin—that there is a distinction between work and text. A poem is a text-structure suitably contextualized. Two distinct works can (albeit in highly exceptional circumstances) share identical text-structures. What then is a copy of a poem? It is a token of a text-structure-type. Identical text-structure-types share identical tokens. But White's poem and Black's poem might be distinct, not in virtue of being distinct text-structure-types but in virtue of different creative acts. A copy of White's poem is indistinguishable from a copy of Black's poem. The difference between the two poems comes out not at the level of the copies themselves—the text-tokens—but in what is *done* with the copies, how they are read, appreciated, interpreted, and indeed how they are presented. A copy of a poem can be thought of as a route to the work. By attending to the copy, supplemented with an instruction, implicit or explicit, to read it *as a copy of a particular work*, a reader comes to appreciate the work. Crucially, there can be no difference between presenting a copy of White's poem and presenting a copy of the shared White/Black text with the instruction to read it

---

[31] Levinson, 'Autographic and Allographic Art Revisited', pp. 104–106.

as White's poem.[32] That is why referential forgery is not possible in such cases. For the forger, attempting to forge White's poem, must present a copy of a text as if it were White's poem (and urging that it be taken that way) while somehow holding in mind the thought that it is in fact a copy of Black's poem. But 'presenting a copy of a text as if it were White's poem', i.e. with the instruction to read it as White's poem, just is presenting White's poem. No provenance-related facts about the copy—the text-token itself—will make a difference. What matters is the way the copy is offered and taken. Similar remarks, *mutatis mutandis*, apply to the performance of a score as if it were a performance of Y's waltz.

Once again, the disanalogy with the painting case is striking. There is an obvious difference between presenting Rembrandt's sketch and presenting an indiscernible replica *as if* it were Rembrandt's sketch. I take it that the intuition underlying this disanalogy was a prime motivation behind Goodman's original allographic/autographic distinction in terms of forgeability. It is an intuition that should not be lost.

[32] This of course is on the assumption that White's poem does exist—i.e. has been produced by a distinct act of creation or 'indication'. If there has been no such creative act and White's poem does not, in that sense, exist then clearly presenting a text as if it were by White cannot be equivalent to presenting White's poem. This recapitulates the point made earlier which kept separate the possibility of reading *Don Quixote* as if it were by Pierre Menard (which Borges establishes) and the actual existence of an independent Menard-created *Don Quixote* (which even in the story is doubtful).

5
Aesthetic Essentialism

5.1. The Thesis

My central claim in this chapter is simple. When we attribute aesthetic properties to works of art or, expressed more cautiously, when we apply aesthetic predicates to subject terms designating works of art, our purpose is not always to offer a factual description but at least in some cases to state a necessary truth. The aim of such judgements is to characterize a work, in the sense of saying not just what kind of work it is but what partly constitutes it as the work it is. The judgements serve, in part, to identify and define the work itself. If we construe aesthetic terms, as I am inclined to, in a realist manner, as standing for properties, then my claim implies the more controversial thesis:

(T) Some aesthetic properties are possessed essentially by some works of art

In fact it is precisely T that I do want to defend. Some works of art, maybe even all works of art, have necessarily and essentially a certain aesthetic nature or character and some, though not all, aesthetic descriptions of works of art are necessary truths identifying that aesthetic character.

5.2. Neighbouring, but Distinct, Essentialist Theses

Thesis T as stated speaks only of what is true of 'some works of art'. I am inclined to think that we can be more precise about which works of art, namely all those that possess aesthetic properties, although if that proves indefensible I am happy to revert to T in its basic formulation above. The stronger version might be expressed as follows:

(T*) All works of art that possess aesthetic properties possess at least some of them essentially

I will call T and T* 'individual essentialism' (or I-essentialism) for they allude to essential properties in individual works (allowing for there to be different essential properties in different works).

There are other essentialist theses in aesthetics and it is important not to run them together or confuse them with the thesis I am defending here. The most familiar kind arises from attempts to offer definitions of art in terms of properties that works of art must possess to be works of art. Often defended are instantiations of (1):

(1) There is at least one property that all works of art possess necessarily[1]

Let us call (1) an example of 'class-essentialism' (or C-essentialism) in that it asserts the possession, essentially, of some specific property by all members of a class (as a condition of class-membership). I believe that (1) is most likely true, though I doubt that the property or properties are aesthetic in nature or even intrinsic to the objects that possess them. The most promising candidates are some species of relational, historical, or institutional properties. I will not be defending, or discussing, (1). It is of course distinct from:

(2) There is at least one aesthetic property that all works of art possess necessarily

This is almost certainly false and is not equivalent to or implied by T (or T*), which I am defending. Yet another thesis is different again:

(3) All works of art are such that necessarily they possess at least one aesthetic property

---

[1] Perhaps the location of the necessity within the quantifier, suggesting necessity *de re*, rather than locating it outside, implying merely necessity *de dicto* ('Necessarily, some property is possessed by all works of art') makes this version tendentious. But I want a version which implies essentialism (which the *de re* version does) even though it is not uncommon to speak of essentialism in both contexts.

When P. F. Strawson argues that it is self-contradictory to speak of judging something as a work of art but not from the aesthetic point of view, he perhaps rests his claim on something like (3) as a premise.[2] If (3) is true it is not uncontroversially so. Maybe some works of art (conceptual art, 'transfigured' urinals or snow shovels) have no aesthetic properties. Because of the controversial nature of (3) I am not inclined to defend a version of I-essentialism, that is stronger than T*, relying on the truth of (3), namely:

(4) All works of art are such that there are at least some aesthetic properties that they possess necessarily.

5.3. The Prima Facie Counterintuitiveness of Aesthetic I-Essentialism

On the face of it I-essentialism, in the aesthetic application of T or T*, seems counterintuitive, even contrary to good sense. Given the hard-fought battle to make aesthetic realism palatable it might seem a step too far to press for aesthetic I-essentialism. Essentialism of any kind is still only marginally acceptable in philosophy but essentialism in aesthetics (that is, I-essentialism not C-essentialism) seems to contradict the very nature of the aesthetic realm. It should be said, however, that it is not entirely undefended: both Eddy Zemach and Nicholas Wolterstorff, for example, have presented theories with I-essentialist implications, though both are tied to somewhat unusual ontologies,[3] and Jerrold Levinson, among others, is an essentialist about artistic origins.[4]

There are many prima facie problems and objections. If aesthetic properties are, as seems plausible, at root relational properties, that is, involving relations between objects and human responses, then

---

[2] P. F. Strawson, 'Aesthetic Appraisal and Works of Art', in *Freedom and Resentment and Other Essays*, London: Methuen, 1974. Originally in *Oxford Review* 3, 1966.

[3] Eddy Zemach, *Real Beauty*, University Park: Pennsylvania State University Press, 1996; Nicholas Wolterstorff, *Works and Worlds of Art*, Oxford: Clarendon Press, 1980, Part II, Chapter IV.

[4] Jerrold Levinson, 'What a Musical Work Is', in *Music, Art & Metaphysics*, Ithaca, N.Y.: Cornell University Press, 1990.

how could such properties essentially inhere in those objects? Isn't it obvious that there will be worlds where an object has different aesthetic qualities from those it has in this world? The essentialist thesis requires that in all possible worlds where a work exists it retains at least some of its aesthetic properties (its essential ones). But suppose these worlds contain radically different kinds of art institutions and art appreciators. If aesthetic properties depend on observers and contextual features as well as intrinsic physical properties then there is no reason to think they will (even can) remain invariant across worlds. Cannot objects even change their aesthetic qualities across time in this world without threatening their identity? There are problems, too, about irresolvable disagreements in aesthetics, which seem to strengthen the hand of the anti-realists. If there are such disagreements then they make I-essentialism epistemologically as well as metaphysically suspect. Why should there be a determinate answer to the question which properties a work possesses if even the most qualified appreciators cannot agree? Finally, what are we to make of the alleged quasi-evaluative nature of so many aesthetic characterizations? Could *evaluative* properties be essential? The problems mount up alarmingly.

5.4. Aesthetic/Non-Aesthetic and Supervenience

Before addressing these problems a bit more ground-clearing is needed. The thesis makes reference to aesthetic properties. What are they exactly? Sibley, who initiated the modern discussion, lists the following as examples of 'aesthetic concepts': *unified, balanced, integrated, lifeless, serene, sombre, dynamic, powerful, vivid, delicate, moving, trite, sentimental, tragic*.[5] I shall take these concepts to designate the corresponding class of aesthetic properties, though without commitment to a view as to what the properties have in common. Sibley contrasts such concepts (he later calls them 'qualities'[6]) with non-aesthetic qualities of a more straightforwardly perceptual, physical, or formal kind

---

[5] Frank Sibley, 'Aesthetic Concepts', *Philosophical Review*, 68, 1959, p. 421.
[6] Frank Sibley, 'Aesthetic and Nonaesthetic', *Philosophical Review*, 74, 1965, p. 135.

(being red, having five acts, having the structure of a fugue). He has two central theses concerning aesthetic qualities: the first, that they are perceivable only through an exercise of aesthetic sensitivity or 'taste', the second, that they are 'emergent' from and dependent on non-aesthetic properties, even if not inferable from them.

There are epistemic as well as metaphysical consequences of Sibley's theses. For simplicity's sake, let us call aesthetic properties A-properties and non-aesthetic properties B-properties. Then Sibley's theses imply that (i) it is possible to be fully apprised of a work's B-properties but remain in ignorance of its A-properties (failing the requisite *gestalt* or aesthetic receptivity) and (ii) any change in A-properties must result from a change in B-properties.

Much of the subsequent debate about aesthetic properties has focused on the precise relation between A- and B-type properties. A familiar claim, deriving from Sibley, is that A-properties supervene on B-properties, though this is open to different interpretations. It could mean, as Sibley has it, that there could be no difference in A-properties without a difference in B-properties. Or it could mean, more demandingly, that if something has an A-property then it has B-properties such that if anything, in any world, has just those B-properties then it has that A-property.[7] (In the literature these two interpretations are generally labelled 'weak supervenience' and 'strong supervenience'.) The interest of aesthetic supervenience lies in the nature of the base (or B-)properties. If the base properties are restricted to intrinsic (physical or structural) properties of objects, which is probably what Sibley believed, then the thesis would have philosophical bite, particularly in its strong form (for one thing it would suggest close parallels between aesthetic properties and secondary qualities). However, that thesis is almost certainly false. Arthur Danto's work on indiscernibles and Kendall Walton's on 'categories of art' show beyond reasonable doubt, albeit in different ways, that objects identical in physical composition and appearance could have different aesthetic properties, when for example the objects

---

[7] I owe this formulation to Nick Zangwill, who in turn draws on Jaegwon Kim's 'Concepts of Supervenience' in his *Supervenience and Mind*, Cambridge: Cambridge University Press, 1993. See also Gregory Currie's 'Supervenience, Essentialism and Aesthetic Properties', *Philosophical Studies*, 58, 1990: pp. 243–257; and Jerrold Levinson, 'Aesthetic Supervenience', in *Music, Art & Metaphysics*.

are located in different art-historical contexts or rightly perceived as belonging to different categories.[8]

If there is aesthetic supervenience, the supervenience base has to include relational properties, of a historical, cultural, dispositional, or provenance-sensitive kind (the latter involving, for example, an artist's intentions). But now the supervenience claim looks in danger not of falsity but of triviality. If we allow so broad a range of base properties, including facts about the dispositions of appreciators, then it is totally unsurprising that there could be no changes among aesthetic properties (involving responses among appreciators) without a change somewhere in the supervenient base. Worse still, it would seem that the combination of relational and intrinsic properties in the base would encompass all the identity conditions for an individual work. It then looks as if any objects possessing identical B-properties, in this broad conception, might of necessity be (numerically) identical works, and it is of no interest that one and the same work possesses the same A-properties as itself.[9] I shall return to supervenience later.

The importance of the Sibley tradition lies not just in the supervenience thesis but also in the notion of a special epistemic access to aesthetic properties, ascribing them an epistemic character different in kind from non-aesthetic properties. Accommodating that to the essentialist thesis will prove more difficult but also more decisive in the defence of essentialism.

5.5. Motivating Aesthetic Essentialism

What are the intuitions that might motivate I-essentialism of the kind expressed in T or T*? What sorts of examples might make it plausible? The thesis is not that all aesthetic attributions make a claim to necessity, only a subclass, which can be thought of as having a distinctive illocutionary character, that of a constitutive judgement,

---

[8] A. C. Danto, *The Transfiguration of the Commonplace*, Cambridge, MA.: Harvard University Press, 1981; and Kendall L.Walton, 'Categories of Art', *Philosophical Review*, 79, 1970, pp. 334–367.

[9] Currie advances a version of this argument in 'Supervenience, Essentialism and Aesthetic Properties', pp. 248–249.

an identification, or a (partial) statement of identity conditions. Thus, the assertion, for example, that the final scene of *King Lear* is tragic can be construed not just as stating a matter of opinion, or even a matter of fact, but of saying something that *must* be true, that could not possibly be false.[10] The assertion is related, obviously, to the more explicit classificatory judgement that the play as a whole is a tragedy, that it belongs in the category of tragedies. But the asserted content that interests me says more than that for the classificatory judgement is not yet an aesthetic judgement. I am interested in the aesthetic judgement that certain scenes in the play have the aesthetic character of being tragic, and have that character essentially. Against this, a strong prima facie objection is that the ending of *Lear* is only tragic to certain viewers, albeit ideal or appropriately positioned viewers. Given radically different viewers, or different kinds of viewers, so the objection goes, the ending simply might not be tragic at all. I shall be returning in detail to that objection for it could be raised about all cases.

Meanwhile, what are other examples? I think they are numerous, though my case does not hinge on the plausibility of particular examples. Here are some more or less at random. Fra Angelico's fresco *Lamentation over the Dead Christ* (in the San Marco convent in Florence) has essentially a sorrowful intensity to it, just as Piero della Francesca's *Baptism of Christ* has a mood of tranquillity and serenity; the second movement of Brahms's Violin Concerto in D Major, op. 77 is essentially calm and peaceful, while Dvořák's Piano Quintet in A Major; op. 81 ranges from melancholy introspection to sudden joy. Yeats's 'Sailing to Byzantium' shows essentially a tension between the sensual and the spiritual, as well as a yearning for lost youth; Thomas Hardy's 'The Darkling Thrush' expresses a glimmer of hope amid a pervading gloom.[11] So I could go on. As I say, I hope

---

[10] Note that more than just an epistemic reading of these claims is required. It is not simply that I *couldn't* be wrong about *Lear* on this matter—something that non-essentialists could concede—but that the statement itself is necessarily true.

[11] Following Walton in 'Categories of Art', I am including representational properties among aesthetic properties. Not all meaning properties, however, are representational properties in this sense. Semantic facts (for example, that 'thrush' means thrush) are not representational and do not require any *gestalt* for their recognition. Broadly speaking, properties that involve interpretation or are symbolic or thematic are included among 'aesthetic' representational properties.

without incurring too much suspicion, I am not resting the thesis on these examples. I might be wrong about individual cases—perhaps the properties I have identified are not essential to the works mentioned. That might be revealed by deeper analysis. My claim does not entail infallibility. It is not an epistemological claim and it is not about certainty so much as about necessity. It is a claim about the very identity of individual works of art.

In general, I believe that expressive and representational qualities are prominent in the class of essential properties. Works of art can be essentially sad or triumphant, essentially representations of a certain kind. One reason why these qualities are prominent is that they have the strongest claim to objectivity within the appropriate parameters of the aesthetic. Among all aesthetic qualities these are most naturally thought of as 'objectively possessed' by the works concerned, and thus the least dependent on subjective idiosyncrasies of appreciators. Purely evaluative properties or properties with a strong evaluative vector are probably not to be found among essential properties. It is not a necessary truth that a work is a masterpiece or mediocre. Without impugning the objectivity, to a suitable degree, of aesthetic evaluations, it seems clear nonetheless that evaluative criteria can be subject to historical or cultural variability. Tolstoy's eccentric judgements about Shakespeare, Beethoven, even his own novels, are weird but not self-contradictory. We could conceive a society that adopts his criteria. Nor is any work essentially beautiful, again not because of doubts about a Kantian 'subjective universality' of beauty but principally because there is an implicit *comparison* in judgements of beauty. There is no such thing as absolute beauty indifferent to humanly based 'standards of taste'.

It is not entirely fortuitous that composers use terms of expression as well as tempo (in fact the two sometimes merge[12]) in their instructions to performers. 'Allegro' means cheerful as well as lively and fast, and other musical terms are purely aesthetic: *appassionato* (passionately), *lacrimoso* (sadly), *scherzando* (playful). At the beginning of *La Bohème*, Puccini marks all the parts *ruvidamente* meaning roughly or harshly. Arguably these aesthetic prescriptions are as essential to the passages

---

[12] It is worth noting that this puts pressure on the aesthetic/non-aesthetic distinction; if that distinction is not tightly drawn then the supervenience thesis is again weakened.

so marked as any other notation in the score and while, of course, performances may fail to realize the aesthetic qualities—performances may fail to adhere to any notation—an adequate rendering will *demand* characterization in these terms.[13]

Part of what is involved in the necessity of aesthetic descriptions is the normativity of a class of judgements. These judgements, although in the form 'work w possesses property P', convey the sense 'no complete characterization of w, as it stands, as we have it in actuality, would be *correct* without reference to P'. The norms can also be norms of response arising from dispositional properties of works, according to which those who fail to respond in a particular way to a work have failed to understand the work. This is a point now familiar in relation to literary works, especially as regards emotional response.[14] What is interesting about the normativity of response is that it introduces a cognitive element into appreciation, in this case linking appropriate affective response to the conditions of correct understanding. Although none of this implies essentialism, essentialism can nevertheless draw

---

[13] It might be objected that the same kind of problem arises here as plagued Nelson Goodman's theory (in *Languages of Art*, Indianapolis: Hackett, 1968) of the identity of allographic works. It was an implication of Goodman's theory, which grounded the identity of allographic works in their notation, that any performance of a musical work w which deviated by even one note from the prescribed score of w could not count as a performance of w (see Stefano Predelli, 'Goodman and the Wrong Note Paradox', *British Journal of Aesthetics*, 39, 1999, pp. 364–375, for a discussion of the issues). Similarly, if a musical work is essentially passionate, say, then it would seem to be an implication of aesthetic essentialism that any non-passionate performance could not be a performance of that work. For some this might seem just as counterintuitive as Goodman's position (or more so). I offer two responses. First, if a musical work is essentially passionate then this expressive quality is likely to be deeply embedded in the notation itself, making it difficult for that quality not to manifest itself to some degree or other, even in otherwise poor performances. Of course, if the notation itself is altered or the basic tempo, cadences, or phrasing, then there would be a stronger case for saying that the work strictly speaking has not been performed. The second response is that the criteria for what counts as a performance of a work are notoriously unclear. In common speech we have the notion of a version of a work which allows considerable latitude. A drastically compressed twenty-minute performance of *Hamlet* might still count as a 'version' of the play even though it leaves out the bulk of the lines and several characters and treats the play as slapstick comedy. The essentialist thesis is about work-identity rather than performance-identity and has implications only for a performance ideal. The possibility of inaccurate versions does not falsify the thesis.

[14] As argued by writers like Jenefer Robinson, Susan Feagin, and Martha Nussbaum: J. Robinson, *Deeper than Reason: Emotion and Its Role in Literature, Music, and Art*, Oxford: Oxford University Press, 2005; S. L. Feagin, *Reading With Feeling*, Ithaca, N.Y.: Cornell University Press, 1996; M. Nussbaum, *Love's Knowledge: Essays on Philosophy and Literature*, Oxford: Oxford University Press, 1990.

on it. If aesthetic properties have a relational aspect, including the eliciting of normative responses, then it is not such a major step to the view that a work essentially possesses an aesthetic character, which demands a certain kind of receptivity.

5.6. A Distinction at the Core of the Argument

The argument for aesthetic I-essentialism, in this version, requires as a crucial first premise the distinction, once again, between a *work of art* and the *object* that embodies it. Arthur Danto's well-known 'gallery of indiscernibles' helps to focus the distinction we need in this context. Recall his example, from *The Transfiguration of the Commonplace*, of nine visually indistinguishable rectangular canvases all painted unbroken red. Each, Danto proposes, embodies a different work of art: one is about the Red Sea after the Israelites had crossed and the Egyptians drowned, another is a 'minimalist exemplar of geometrical art' entitled 'Red Square', the next a still-life executed by an embittered disciple of Matisse, called 'Red Table Cloth', and so on, and so on.[15] Danto is having fun. The theoretical point, though, is serious. The works of art are underdetermined by the surface physical properties of the canvases. As physical objects, the canvases are qualitatively identical (in colour, structure, texture, etc.) yet the works of art they embody are distinguishable in terms of their art-related properties. The latter are not only representational properties, concerning what the paintings are about but include also stylistic properties, one being in the style of Matisse, another in the style of geometrical art, and so forth. Assuming we enter into the spirit of the thought-experiment, we could no doubt identify other aesthetic properties that differ in the different works, to do with mood, serenity, power, or emotional resonance.

We do not have to agree either with Danto's own characterization of the thought-experiment or with his conclusions to draw important lessons from it.[16] It might seem tendentious, for example, for Danto

---

[15] Danto, *The Transfiguration of the Commonplace*, p. 1f.
[16] Powerful reservations about the nature of the thought-experiment have been expressed by Richard Wollheim in 'Danto's Gallery of Indiscernibles', in Mark Rollins, ed., *Danto and*

to describe the case in terms of what is 'indiscernible at least with respect to anything the eye . . . can determine'. It is arguable that a viewer *informed with the appropriate knowledge of title, provenance, and art-historical context* might undergo different experiences (and visual experiences at that) when viewing the different works.[17] The red canvas in the style of Matisse might genuinely *look* different from the red canvas depicting the Red Sea. If this seems fanciful then consider an example where there are not two objects but one and the same object viewed at different times: e.g. Van Meegeren's *Christ and His Disciples at Emmaus* viewed before and after its exposure as a forgery of Vermeer. It does not seem implausible to suppose that the painting came to *look* different when seen as a forgery, even though ex hypothesi there is no physical difference in the object at the two viewings.[18]

The general point, though, derivable from Danto, is well established: works of art are identifiable not only by their material properties—paint and canvas or their equivalent in the case of visual art, sound-sequences in the case of music, verbal, or textual properties for the literary arts—but by complex relational properties which embed the works in a cultural, art-historical, and broadly institutional, context. Without appropriate cultural and institutional background conditions there would be no works of art even if there were by chance objects physically indistinguishable from those we call works of art. Works of art are not natural kinds, nor physical objects *tout court*. Using a different terminology they are, as Joseph Margolis says, culturally emergent. Margolis argues that even if we do (as he commends) link works of art necessarily to physical objects they are not reducible to physical objects. He writes:

> to be aware of . . . [an artwork] . . . is to construe physical objects or marks as supporting a certain culturally emergent object. So, works of art are said to be the particular objects they are, in *intensional* contexts, although they may be identified, by the linkage of embodiment, through the identity of what may be reliably specified in *extensional* contexts. Works of art are

---

His Critics, Oxford: Blackwell, 1993. Other criticisms appear in Joseph Margolis, 'Farewell to Danto and Goodman', *British Journal of Aesthetics*, 38, 1998.

[17] This idea is developed in Ch. 6 'Aesthetic Empiricism'.
[18] The case is considered further in Ch. 7 'Imitating Style'.

identified extensionally in the sense that their identity (whatever their nature) is controlled by the identity of what they are embodied in; but to identify them *as* what they are is accomplished only intensionally (by reference to the very cultural tradition in which they may actually be discriminated).[19]

There are familiar non-artistic parallels with cultural or institutional objects of other kinds (coins, chesspieces, etc.). We can even generate essentialist claims (of both C- and I- varieties) for these other non-artistic examples. Are not the following necessary truths: that a ten pence coin is a unit of currency (indeed with the value of ten pence); that the bishop in chess can move only diagonally on its own colour; that the British monarch is head of state; that the Faust-character makes a pact with the devil? Note that in each case the essentialist claim rests on an implicit *qua*-operator qualifying the subject-term. It is only *qua* monarch that the British monarch is head of state. Of any particular monarch, *qua* person, it might have been the case that that person were not head of state. It is only a contingent fact that, say, George of Hanover became King George I of England. The distinction between person and role offers at least a prima facie parallel with the distinction between object and work of art.[20]

How do these philosophical commonplaces help to establish aesthetic I-essentialism? They show that we need a threefold distinction between object, work of art, and aesthetic properties. Many aestheticians attempt to make do with just a twofold distinction between objects, characterized by Sibleyan non-aesthetic properties, and aesthetic properties taken to be emergent from them. Essentialism could never be defended on this basis, as a relation between an object per se and an aesthetic property. The essentialism I am defending is a relation between a *work of art* and an *aesthetic property*. It is always only a contingent fact that an object O possesses aesthetic property P. It is also a contingent fact that a work of art w emerges from O. My claim is only that a property P can in certain cases be an essential property of w.

Now we can see why the debate about supervenience in aesthetics, whether A-properties supervene on B-properties, is largely a red

---

[19] J. Margolis, *Art and Philosophy: Conceptual Issues in Aesthetics*, Atlantic Highlands, N.J.: Humanities Press, 1980, p. 41.

[20] For qualifications, see Ch. 2 'On Bringing a Work into Existence'.

herring. Once we have abandoned the thought that A-properties supervene on intrinsic, non-relational properties, and once we have embraced the thought that essentialism holds between a work of art and (some of) its A-properties, then any insights supposedly derivable from supervenience vanish. It would be futile to look for a relation of supervenience between the A-properties of a work of art and its other (art-related) properties for there will be no principled way of dividing the two sets. Being culturally emergent, institutionally-grounded, intentional objects, works of art will not yield any non-arbitrarily demarcated supervenience base on which to explain aesthetic properties. The salient properties of works of art are already an inextricable mix of the physical, the functional, and the meaning-based.

I suggested in the *King Lear* example that being tragic is an essential property of the ending of the play. Other independent considerations might point in the same direction. *Lear* could be taken as a paradigm case of the tragic, helping define the meaning of the term 'tragic' (if Lear's fate is not tragic, then nothing is). Or *Lear* might epitomize a Waltonian 'category' (*Lear* belongs, and cannot but belong, in the artistic category of tragedies). Or it could be argued that *Lear*'s being tragic is demanded by what Umberto Eco has called the *intentio operis*, the intention of the work, based on the most coherent possible reading.[21] The essentialist claim I am advancing, however, goes beyond these considerations. It is stronger, more metaphysical, a claim about the very nature of the work. It says that *Lear* could not possibly be other than tragic; that the play is necessarily so; that it is tragic in every possible world in which it exists.

5.7. The Relational Aspect of Aesthetic Properties

To establish this stronger claim—and comparable ones in other cases—we need to examine a feature of aesthetic properties, their

---

[21] Umberto Eco, *Interpretation and Overinterpretation*, Cambridge: Cambridge University Press, 1992, p. 25.

supposed relational nature, which might be thought to present an insuperable obstacle to essentialism. There seems to be wide agreement among contemporary aestheticians—it is already evident in Sibley's earliest work—that aesthetic properties admit of a relational analysis: that is, they are grounded in a relation between a work's lower-level perceptual properties and the responses of a class of ideal or appropriate perceivers. As John Bender puts it: 'a work's having an aesthetic property, F, such as grace, power, or starkness, is for it to have some set of (other) features and relations which makes the work evoke in some relevant class of perceivers or critics certain responses and judgments, including the judgment that it is appropriate to call the work F.'[22] Versions of this relational analysis are widespread.[23]

Linking aesthetic properties to the responses of qualified perceivers makes the metaphysical nature of the essentialist thesis problematic for, as earlier intimated, it seems easy enough to conceive of variations among responses without corresponding variations in the object. At first, the problem seems only to be compounded when we re-introduce the earlier, Sibleyan, factor of the special epistemic access required for aesthetic properties: the idea that knowledge of non-aesthetic properties is not sufficient for recognition of aesthetic properties. In fact I hope to show how a proper understanding of this latter desideratum goes some way towards mitigating the problem posed by the relational analysis.

Connected to this relational analysis is another widely held view: that aesthetic characterizations are essentially perceptual or experiential. Philip Pettit puts it like this:

the putatively cognitive state one is in when, perceiving a work of art, one sincerely assents to a given aesthetic characterisation, is not a state to which one can have non-perceptual access. What I seem to know when, having seen a painting, I describe it as graceful or awkward, tightly or loosely organised,

---

[22] John W. Bender, 'Realism, Supervenience, and Irresolvable Aesthetic Disputes', *Journal of Aesthetics and Art Criticism*, 54, 1996, p. 371.

[23] A relational analysis appears in all the following: Alan Goldman, 'Realism About Aesthetic Properties', *Journal of Aesthetics and Art Criticism*, 51, 1993, pp. 31–37; Jerrold Levinson, 'Being Realistic About Aesthetic Properties', *Journal of Aesthetics and Art Criticism*, 52, 1994, pp. 351–354; Gregory Currie, 'Supervenience, Essentialism and Aesthetic Properties'.

dreamy or erotic, inviting or distancing, is not something which you can know in the same sense, just through relying on my testimony.[24]

The point nicely pulls together the relational thesis (of aesthetic properties) and the Sibleyan epistemic thesis (of aesthetic judgements). Roger Scruton uses such a point to argue for an anti-realist construal of aesthetic descriptions:

> the acceptance condition of an aesthetic description may not be a belief but may rather be some other mental state which more effectively explains the point of aesthetic description. To agree to an aesthetic description is to 'see its point', and this 'seeing the point' is to be elucidated in terms of some response or experience. . . . Hence aesthetic descriptions need not have truth conditions in the strong sense, and to justify them may be to justify an experience and not a belief.[25]

Setting aside the anti-realist strand in Scruton's argument (nothing in the passage amounts to an outright rejection of aesthetic properties), it is possible to see here further evidence of the different functions of aesthetic descriptions. Scruton is right in suggesting that to endorse such a description is at least sometimes to respond directly to a work of art rather than merely assenting to a proposition. The underlying thought, so I shall argue, in Bender's, Pettit's, and Scruton's formulations—the connection of aesthetic description to experiential response—far from being an impediment to essentialism can in fact be utilized in its defence.

It should be noted first of all that no insuperable difficulty, with regard to the relational analysis, arises from the essentialist claim that some aesthetic descriptions are necessary truths. The question might be raised how grasp of necessary truths could ever rely essentially on perception. Are not necessities graspable a priori? Two points can be made here, the first a mere preliminary, the second taking us to the heart of the issue. The first is that not all necessary truths are definitional, analytic, or tautological. To assert that the end of *King Lear* is necessarily tragic is not to say something trivial or something

---

[24] Philip Pettit, 'The Possibility of Aesthetic Realism', in Eva Schaper, ed., *Pleasure, Preference, and Value: Studies in Philosophical Aesthetics*, Cambridge: Cambridge University Press, 1983, p. 25.
[25] Roger Scruton, *Art and Imagination*, London: Methuen, 1974, p. 55. The passage is quoted in and discussed by Pettit, op. cit.

that can be looked up in a dictionary. It arises ultimately from a response to the play, a response, if the thesis is right, that is demanded by the play, a normative response, a necessary condition not only for a correct understanding of the play but for the recognition of the play as the play it is.

The second, deeper point is that the perceptual or experiential underpinning of aesthetic characterization can be carried over to the identification of works of art. In other words, the thought that there can be no non-perceptual access to the appropriate cognitive state for assenting to an aesthetic description (as Pettit puts it) holds true also, at least in many cases, for the state required for the identification of a work of art as the work it is. To recognize a work for what it is—the Fra Angelico as sorrowful, but also a depiction of the dead Christ, a painting in the devotional tradition, and so forth—is to be in a cognitive state internally related to the experience the work affords. No external judgement, based on testimony, physical description, or even a priori deliberation, can properly ground recognition of this kind.[26]

Here we must move carefully. 'Recognizing a work for what it is' admits of two interpretations, or perhaps two stages: recognition that it is a work of art and recognition of what work of art it is. Both stages involve what Scruton calls 'seeing the point', which, I suggest, is something akin to the *gestalt* of Sibley's theory. It would be possible to be fully apprised of all an object's non-aesthetic properties but still fail to recognize that it is a work of art (thus a fortiori what work it is). The obvious examples would be 'found art' or ready-mades (driftwood, snow shovels, etc.) that do not in any sense 'look like' art. But strictly no works of art, as culturally emergent entities, bear

---

[26] Note that the emphasis here is on the grounds for aesthetic description or art-recognition, claiming that appropriate experience must ultimately underpin such judgements. Scepticism about the need for direct acquaintance has been voiced in Malcolm Budd, 'The Acquaintance Principle', *British Journal of Aesthetics*, 43, 2003 and Paisley Livingston, 'On an Apparent Truism in Aesthetics', *British Journal of Aesthetics*, 43, 2003. Derek Matravers and Aaron Ridley have also made important contributions to this issue. In 'Aesthetic Concepts and Aesthetic Experiences', *British Journal of Aesthetics*, 36, 1996, pp. 265–277, Matravers offers a thoughtful account of how aesthetic beliefs are grounded in aesthetic experiences. Ridley, in 'The Philosophy of Medium-Grade Art', *British Journal of Aesthetics*, 36, 1996, pp. 413–423, argues that sometimes, in the case of 'medium-grade' art, aesthetic judgements can be warranted on the strength of testimony alone. A seminal paper on this topic, of older vintage, is Alan Tormey, 'Critical Judgments', *Theoria* 39, 1973, pp. 35–49.

their art status, as it were, 'on their sleeves'. Being a work of art is not a directly perceivable property, like being red or square, but rather is an intentional property, involving the thought of an object *under-a-description*. Once an object is recognized as a work of art—albeit with the help of background knowledge—that will affect the way the object is perceived or experienced.[27] A *gestalt* switch, or 'seeing as', is needed from experiencing the driftwood, for example, as a mere piece of driftwood, to seeing it as an artwork. Knowledge or third-person testimony alone will not guarantee the shift. To *recognize* an object *as* a work of art requires just the kind of special epistemic access that Sibley postulated for aesthetic properties.

Such recognition, however, is still not sufficient for the second-stage recognition of what the work is. Works can be misidentified and that can radically affect the way in which they are experienced. I suggested earlier that Van Meegeren's forgeries look different when viewed as genuine Vermeers or as forgeries. Other cases can be multiplied. In Walton's well-known example, *Guernica* evokes a different experience when categorized not as a painting but as a *guernica*.[28] Misinterpretation, misattribution, failure to recognize irony, parody, or figuration can all affect responses to a work. So much is obvious. What is less obvious, but crucially important for the argument, is that it is not only aesthetic properties that are related essentially to the responses of perceivers but works of art themselves. To identify a work for what it is is at least partly to respond to it (experience it) in a certain way. More than that, the very identity of the work is bound up with the responses it elicits.

5.8. Work and Response

This takes us back once again to the prima facie objection I mentioned when I first began to characterize the essentialist thesis. The objection, put simply, envisages audiences who react to works of art quite

---

[27] There is no commitment here to any particular theory of artistic perception, nor need the argument take sides in this well-worn controversy: whether there is such a thing as aesthetic perception, whether the correct attitude is disinterestedness, psychic distance, or the rest. Minimally some form of directed attention is presupposed in perceiving an object *as a work of art*.

[28] Walton, 'Categories of Art', p. 347.

differently from us, but nevertheless regularly and predictably. They see nothing tragic in the ending of *Lear*, nor anything sorrowful in the *Lamentation*, but they do perhaps have other aesthetic responses. The point is not that such audiences merely differ in their evaluations, finding these works dull or uninspiring while we think of them as masterpieces, but that they must be conceived as differing in their considered aesthetic descriptions. In any case, I have set aside evaluative properties in my defence of essentialism.[29]

The obvious point to make about audiences that fail to assent to what we take to be normative[30] aesthetic descriptions—a point that might be sufficient in a defence of aesthetic realism—is that the audiences are not, in Levinson's terms, 'appropriately backgrounded'; they are not the ideal perceivers envisaged in the relational analysis. Of course there is a danger in this move of begging the question, of eliminating the very possibility of deep aesthetic disagreement by imposing tight constraints on whose judgements can count as appropriate. But the essentialist is at least in no worse position on potential disagreement than the realist. Necessary truths are no more immune from disagreement than contingent truths, nor is necessity equivalent to certainty.

The more pressing question for the essentialist is what to say about those worlds in which audiences or perceivers are fundamentally different from humans in this world. Perhaps they respond differently because they have quite different psychological constitutions. If aesthetic properties rest partially on the responses of suitably qualified audiences what becomes of a work in a world where no audience can so qualify? My brief answer is this: *in such a world either what we call works of art would not be works of art at all or they would be different works.* In a world where audiences are constitutionally unable to perceive *Lear* as tragic the work *King Lear* simply does not exist.

---

[29] Of course it is not entirely uncontroversial to postulate a sharp distinction between the descriptive and the evaluative. Alan Goldman, for example, in 'Realism About Aesthetic Properties', bases his version of anti-realism on the idea that attitudes and evaluations inform virtually all aesthetic characterizations. However, I am sufficiently persuaded by Levinson's argument, in 'Being Realistic About Aesthetic Properties', that even for terms that bear an evaluative force there is a non-evaluative experiential content that is isolatable.

[30] Note that 'normative' here does not mean 'evaluative'. These are descriptions that are *required*, according to appropriate norms of response, but need not be, or imply, value judgements.

AESTHETIC ESSENTIALISM 113

Surely, it will be objected, this, if anything, is begging the question. I think not. But it takes us deeply into what we understand by art. First of all, we need to recall the distinction between an object and a work of art. In the world described there might well be a text word-for-word identical to the text of *Lear* (or films of the play or recordings of performances) but, as we have seen, the existence of an object (or objects) of this kind does not imply that the *work* exists in that world. Text and work have different identity conditions.

But, second, the institution of art itself is founded on certain human responses to the world, to people, to suffering and joy, arising out of deeply rooted human values, needs, and aspirations. In a world without those responses or those needs and values there would be no works of art. This is why the idea of art already has an evaluative element within it. Works of art not only elicit, as they are intended to elicit, certain kinds of responses (including aesthetic pleasure and more cognitive attitudes) but they also (standardly) reward a distinctive appreciative attention. Where there is no *possibility* of such response or attention there is no art. The very same (or similar) conditions that determine the ideal perceptual or experiential responses to a work of art can also serve to characterize what makes it art in the first place.[31] Although a perceiver can recognize the properties of a mere *object* without any evaluative or appreciative attitude to the object, the properties of works of art, *qua* art, are inevitably connected to responses of just such a kind.

Stanley Cavell asks: 'Could we imagine that there is a culture for which *Othello*, say, reads like science fiction—a group who just have no first-hand knowledge of the need for trust or of the pain of betrayal?' He replies: 'It would not be a group of humans.'[32] In contrast, I would say: it would not be a culture that possesses the work *Othello*.

Clearly more needs to be said about the conception of work-identity behind this claim. Why, it might be asked, can we not, for example, index a work to the world in which it was created and

---

[31] Something like this is the deep truth in Eddy Zemach's aphorism: 'No identification without evaluation'. See Eddy Zemach, 'No Identification Without Evaluation', *British Journal of Aesthetics*, 26, 1986, pp. 239–251.
[32] Stanley Cavell, *The Claim of Reason*, Oxford: Oxford University Press, 1979, p. 458.

then conceive of that same work transposed into radically different worlds? We might even employ a rich 'historicist' criterion of work-identity and still pursue our counterfactual speculations; that is, we might retain the necessity of origins and provenance, including broad cultural embeddedness. *Lear*, then, becomes that work entitled 'King Lear' written by Shakespeare between 1604 and 1605 in England, performed at court in 1606, first printed in quarto in 1608, and so forth;[33] the *Lamentation* is that work, depicting the lamentation over the dead Christ, on a wall in the San Marco convent in Florence painted in the 1440s by Fra Angelico (no doubt with the help of others). These are identifying descriptions. Suppose we use them to fix the reference, in Kripke's terms, of two works of art such that the names *King Lear* and *Lamentation over the dead Christ* rigidly designate those works in all worlds where they exist. Going along with this scenario, what then becomes of the aesthetic properties of these works in worlds where all perceivers are profoundly and constitutionally different from normal humans beings (not just Europeans from the past 500 years but, let's say, any human beings who have ever existed)? One could imagine speculation going in two directions. Either, it might be claimed, the works come to acquire different aesthetic properties (if any) in accordance with the (normative) responses of the observers in their new context; or, in less relativistic mode, it might be said that the aesthetic properties are just what they were in the world of origin (on the grounds that, like the works, they too are indexed to a world and to 'ideal' perceivers in that world), with the consequence that the 'alien' observers must be deemed radically mistaken in their aesthetic characterizations. A parallel question might be what becomes of a coloured object in a world without light. Those impressed by the former position might reason that the object loses its colour in such a world, those impressed by the latter might be persuaded that the object retains its 'real' colour even though conditions make it impossible to observe that colour.

---

[33] For the purposes of this argument we can ignore the complication that a different form of the play was printed in the First Folio, 1623, and that scholars debate the relation between the quarto and Folio texts. If anything it simply reinforces the inherent indeterminacy of work-identity.

Although the second alternative might seem congenial to the aesthetic realist and the aesthetic essentialist, it remains highly counter-intuitive. It is not a route I recommend. Instead I suggest that the whole scenario of rigidly designating works across worlds is misconceived (or at the least should be handled with great care). Work-identity, like the identity of all intentional objects, is 'soft' identity. It is dependent on what is 'thought' as well as what merely is. It rests, as argued earlier, not just on cultural factors but on values, perceptions, meanings, 'seeing as'. A work of art is not just a thing with intrinsic properties contingently related to its environment that can be transported 'objectively' from world to world. As already observed, there would be no art without a determinate human and institutional setting.

Of course historical conditions change, as do tastes, judgements, expectations, background beliefs. Works can be resilient to such changes but it should not be presumed that they always are. Take a case where it would seem uncontroversial that a work is lost. Suppose a text is found of a linguistic work once deemed of high artistic import in its originating culture but in a language that is completely lost. If the meaning is unrecoverable then the work is lost, even though the text remains and even though it is known, from contextual sources, that this was a work of importance. Nor does the case hinge on peculiarities of the linguistic arts for it seems to me that pictorial works can be lost as well even though the physical objects in which (to use Margolis's terms) they are embodied survive. Plausible candidates might be the Palaeolithic cave paintings, about which virtually nothing is known. If the purposes that give sense to the works and the normative responses to them are lost, then the very conditions that made the works possible no longer obtain and the works too, arguably, are lost.

Anthony Savile has proposed a criterion by which a work of art survives the test of time: 'if over a sufficiently long period it survives in our attention under an appropriate interpretation in a sufficiently embedded way'. He goes on: 'This condition will only be satisfied if the attention that the work is given is of a kind that generates experience relevant to its critical appreciation and attracts the attention that is given to it in its own right.'[34] If my own argument

---

[34] Anthony Savile, *The Test of Time: An Essay in Philosophical Aesthetics*, Oxford: Clarendon Press, 1982, pp. 11–12.

is right then some such criterion applies not just to surviving the test of time but surviving as a work *tout court*.[35] Another way of putting the point is to say that a condition of work-survival is a kind of *uptake*. Works survive only when they are apprehended as works and as the works they are.

I have discussed the extreme case where we consider worlds with people constituted in a radically different way from ourselves. But what of worlds in which people differ only somewhat from ourselves? They value works differently, they tend to find dull and monotonous what we find exciting, they are uplifted by what we find banal, in general they are affected in different ways. Must we say that our works do not exist in such a world? That not only seems implausible but seems like a desperate measure to preserve essentialism.

We do not, I think, need to take this line. What should be emphasized is that only certain aesthetic properties are rightly thought of as essential to works of art, as partially constitutive of the works, and these, I have suggested, will usually be drawn from the class of expressive or representational properties. They will tend not to include purely affective properties such as being moving, disturbing, exciting, evocative, erotic, invigorating, challenging, and so forth. The point about affective properties is not that they rest on a direct causal relation between work and audience, for a work could be invigorating without as a matter of fact making any given spectator feel invigorated, but that they are directly dependent on the psychological dispositions of perceivers. A work is only exciting because it will tend, other things being equal, to cause a suitably backgrounded perceiver to feel excited. Audiences with different psychological dispositions will not respond in this way and it is thus just a contingent fact that a work will have such an affective quality: it is contingent on the existence of appropriate dispositions in perceivers. But the lack of those dispositions, or the relative strength or weakness of them, should not affect the identity of the works perceived.

The same, I have argued, is not true of expressive or representational properties that depend in a less direct manner on the dispositions

---

[35] I am not committed to all the elements of Savile's thesis, particularly the existence of a single right interpretation for each work, but his remarks about the attention given to a work being 'of a kind that generates experience relevant to its critical appreciation' seem to capture well the ideas I have been developing about work-identity.

of observers and look more like objective properties of works themselves. Unlike affective properties, they do not demand an emotional response. Works can remain expressive even though an audience remains (literally) unaffected. In this I reject simple arousal theories of expressive properties. A work is sad not because it causes sadness in an audience, or even because it is disposed to do so, but rather because of how it is correctly perceived, for example on analogy with a sad person. I should emphasize that in making these comparisons I am not rejecting the basic relational analysis of aesthetic properties. Expressive and representational properties do rest ultimately on modes of response from suitably qualified observers but the route is more indirect than with affective properties. My claim is that there is nothing more relational about certain aesthetic properties than about works of art themselves, as intentional objects. Indeed it is precisely for this reason that the thesis of aesthetic essentialism is made possible. Works of art have some aesthetic properties essentially only *qua* works of art, fully embedded in human cultural practices.

However, the problem of audiences that differ only in certain respects from us—at a deep cultural, not a deeply human, level—but enough, seemingly, to threaten a work's core aesthetic properties is not one that I dismiss lightly. In trying to get clearer on the subject, one idea that might be worth pursuing is that of what is 'culturally possible' (for a people, at a time). We need to ask whether it is *culturally possible* for an audience to identify and respond to (what I take to be) a work's essential aesthetic properties. This is determined by background knowledge, psychological disposition, historical context, social conditioning, and no doubt other factors as well. What is culturally possible, at a point in history for a community, relies not on the idiosyncrasies of individuals but on the limits of what can be grasped (perceptually, imaginatively, intellectually) by an appropriately informed and receptive audience. Thus, I contend, it is not culturally possible for us, in our present circumstances, to get an appreciative grasp of *Guernica* under the category of a *guernica* (as in Walton's example above). It is not that we cannot make sense of Walton's thought-experiment (intellectually) but we cannot adequately grasp what it would be to operate such a category, how it might affect other perceptions, how it might have come into being. Likewise, it would not have been culturally possible for a fourteenth-century

Siennese artist to appreciate *Les Demoiselles d'Avignon* (as a work of art). In contrast, looking backwards in art history, it *is* culturally possible for a twentieth-century (Western) audience to perceive the expressive properties in *The Lamentation of Christ* or to comprehend what is represented in the *Divine Comedy*, even though in such cases we are often stretched to the limit in trying to do so, and our own (modern) sensibility is exposed as remote from that of the original intended audience. The point is not that we respond in the same way as that audience but that we know enough—just—to recreate what is demanded of a qualified perceiver and to locate the required conditions of appreciation in an appropriate cultural context. This is something, as I argued earlier, that we cannot do with the prehistoric cave paintings. Where it becomes no longer culturally possible to identify a work's core (essential) aesthetic properties, then, I maintain, the work does not survive. To the extent that the conditions of work-identity are bound up with the conditions of cultural possibility it seems inevitable that work-survival will be at least partially a matter of degree. Works can fade into oblivion as cultural conditions change and as cultural memories are lost. An analogy might be the gradual disappearance of a language. A language dies as fewer and fewer people are able to interpret its symbols (sounds and/or marks) and as fewer and fewer symbols remain interpretable. A language is lost where there is no-one left with the requisite knowledge, and the knowledge is unrecoverable.

Before addressing the question of what hangs on the essentialist thesis, let me offer a further remark about its scope. Aesthetic essentialism, as I defend it, applies only to works of art and not to natural objects. It is never essential to an object *qua* object that it possesses an aesthetic property. A birdsong might be melancholy, a range of mountains awe-inspiring, a person elegant and poised but these are never necessary or defining features. The kind of necessity I have identified arises in connection not just with a certain kind of artefact but with intentional or cultural objects whose very nature is already grounded in a web of human relations, responses, and practices. Does this mean that the attribution of expressive properties to natural objects has different truth conditions from their attribution to works of art and thus perhaps that the correlative aesthetic terms have different meanings in these applications? No, there is no such implication, any more than there is in saying that a square has four equal sides—stating a necessary truth—and Malevich's painting has four equal sides, stating a contingent truth.

5.9. Why does it Matter?

Aesthetic essentialism might well look like just another arcane philosophical theory. If my arguments have seemed plausible then the thesis might be grudgingly accepted by like-minded philosophers but nonetheless elicit a world-weary 'so what?'. In fact I think there are several reasons why the truth of the thesis makes a difference.

First of all, there are a couple of philosophical reasons. The thesis gives some insight into what might be called the metaphysics of cultural objects, going beyond the confines of aesthetics. The language of 'essences' has traditionally been applied to natural objects, although 'nominal essences' have been attributed to human artefacts. The thought that there could be *de re* necessities pertaining to cultural, as well as natural, objects forces one to reflect on the kinds of 'things' they are, what constitutes them, what their identity conditions are, and what kinds of properties they possess. In looking at works of art, the unusual case of aesthetic properties, and the relations that these can bear to each other, I hope to have illuminated an otherwise murky ontological topic. Furthermore, by offering a benign version of essentialism in this context I might have helped to open the way to a more favourable view of essentialism elsewhere and to a new approach to the ontology of cultural objects.

But the thesis has more direct implications for the philosophy of art. It suggests, for example, interesting consequences for the survival of works. Where a work possesses essential aesthetic properties, the survival of physical or non-aesthetic properties will not be sufficient for survival of that work. Works could fail to survive even though all their non-aesthetic properties (or at least all their non-relational non-aesthetic properties) do survive.

This in turn has consequences for the practice of restoration (for autographic arts) or for performance (for the performing allographic arts). Restorers would have to ensure that they preserve the essential *aesthetic* character of a work, not just its material composition, in order to preserve the work itself. In a slightly different manner, performers would have to be constrained by the aesthetic qualities, as well as the purely notational, in their rendering of a work, to determine that it is *that work* which they are presenting.

There are implications, too, for the relation between a work and an interpretation (in both the performing and the semantic sense, though here I am concerned with the latter[36]). To the extent that the interpretation of art involves the identification of aesthetic properties (as it does in some but not all cases) then some interpretations will turn out not just true but necessarily so. In many ways, this is a remarkable conclusion, not least in the light of pressures towards relativism. Note that the interpretative statements that are necessary truths (those that identify essential aesthetic properties) are by no means trivial truths. In featuring aesthetic properties they will *ipso facto* demand that species of discernment, that distinctive epistemic access, which holds for all aesthetic properties. Although necessary, they will not be certain, nor accessible through mechanical, non-reflective means.

Finally, the insistence on a distinction between work and object, on which the thesis rests, has important consequences across the arts, not least for literary criticism. It is a further reminder of the need to distinguish work and text for, if the thesis is right, works are underdetermined by texts. There is more to a (literary) work than a set of sentences in a language. Literary criticism cannot be textual criticism *tout court*. 'Explication de texte' is never a sufficient enquiry for determining the properties of a literary work. The competent literary critic cannot ignore the facts (a) that literary works are cultural objects whose very existence rests on their embeddedness in a literary tradition, and (b) that such works demand an aesthetic, as well as purely linguistic, understanding.[37]

5.10. Back to Sibley

Where does all this leave Sibley's claims about aesthetic properties? There is little doubt that Sibley was edging towards a kind of aesthetic

---

[36] The distinction between 'performative' and 'semantic' interpreting comes from Jerrold Levinson.
[37] This idea is fully worked out in my *Philosophy of Literature*, Oxford: Blackwell, 2009.

realism, although in stressing that aesthetic properties are emergent he emphasized their distinctness from other, as it were, 'natural' properties, including secondary qualities, like colour, with which they share so many features. In defending aesthetic *essentialism*, even if only in a limited range, I have gone significantly beyond aesthetic realism. But unlike Sibley my focus has been on the relation between aesthetic properties and works of art rather than between such properties and objects per se. This does not entail, however, discarding the intuition behind Sibley's claim about the special epistemic status of aesthetic appreciation and I have acknowledged something comparable in the identification of works of art themselves. Only someone suitably trained or experienced can offer informed aesthetic characterizations of works of art or can say what makes them the works they are. Finally, like Sibley I have been concerned with the underlying logic of a certain kind of aesthetic judgement. What Sibley recognized is that the form of aesthetic judgements is something that needs further analysis. Not all descriptions are performing the same simple predicative function and surface form is no sure guide to deeper truth conditions. I have suggested that there is a class of aesthetic descriptions that turn out on analysis to be rather different from standard descriptions and are much more like partial definitions or identifications. This has led me to a defence of aesthetic essentialism, and the perhaps surprising claim that some works of art necessarily possess a distinct aesthetic character. Sibley would no doubt be heartily sceptical of the conclusions I have reached, but I hope he would recognize the spirit of the enquiry I have engaged—for it was he, as much as anyone, who initiated enquiries of this kind.

6
Aesthetic Empiricism

The expression 'aesthetic empiricism', probably coined by Gregory Currie,[1] seems to be used more often than not to designate a position that the user seeks to reject.[2] The received wisdom is that aesthetic empiricism is false and furthermore that this can be demonstrated conclusively by appeal to cases of indiscernibles.[3] But I think it merits a closer look. There are certainly some close relatives of the theory that should not be abandoned and are not refuted by indiscernibles.

6.1. Characterizing Aesthetic Empiricism

Currie's initial formulation of aesthetic empiricism is this: 'What is aesthetically valuable in a painting can be detected merely by looking at it. Features that cannot be so detected are not properly aesthetic ones.'[4] This is extended to other arts by including other sense modalities, e.g. hearing for music. Currie incorporates literature by adding 'verbal understanding' to sensory perception: 'the boundaries of the aesthetic are set by the boundaries of vision, hearing or verbal understanding,

---

[1] Gregory Currie, *An Ontology of Art*, Chapter 2. The term 'empiricism' is also used in this context by Joseph Margolis, in 'Art Forgery, and Authenticity', in Denis Dutton, ed., *The Forger's Art*, Berkeley: University of California Press, 1983, pp. 153–154.

[2] An exception is Gordon Graham, who offers a nuanced defence of aesthetic empiricism in 'Aesthetic Empiricism and the Challenge of Fakes and Ready-Mades', in Matthew Kieran, ed., *Contemporary Debates in Aesthetics and the Philosophy of Art*, Oxford: Blackwell, 2006.

[3] David Davies has launched a sustained attack on aesthetic empiricism, e.g. in 'Aesthetic Empiricism and the Philosophy of Art', *Synthesis Philosophica*, 15, 2000, pp. 49–64; *Art as Performance*, Oxford: Blackwell, 2004, Chapter 2; and 'Against Enlightened Empiricism', in Matthew Kieran, ed., *Contemporary Debates in Aesthetics and the Philosophy of Art*.

[4] Currie, *An Ontology of Art*, p. 17.

depending on which art form is in question.'⁵ Currie is a prime example of someone who thinks that this view in its various formulations is demonstrably false, notably as shown by indiscernibles cases.

David Davies, another opponent, characterizes aesthetic empiricism as 'the thesis that the focus of appreciation is what we may term the "manifest work"—an entity that comprises only properties available to a receiver in an immediate perceptual encounter with an object or event that realises the work'.⁶ He elaborates by asserting that to 'oppose aesthetic empiricism . . . is to argue that at least some features not determinable from inspection of the manifest work bear crucially upon artistic appreciation' (p. 27). It is just such features that he seeks to describe. Davies identifies a more refined version of aesthetic empiricism, dubbed 'enlightened empiricism', that acknowledges the relevance of contextual factors in art appreciation but still holds that 'all artistic value must ultimately reside in characteristics of the experiences elicited in receivers *in a suitably informed engagement* with an instance of the work' (italics added).⁷ Davies rejects this version too.

The association of aesthetic empiricism with, on the one hand, certain kinds of *properties*—surface or perceptual properties—of works and, on the other, with the *appearance* of works or how works *look*, while innocent enough in an initial formulation, leads, as we shall see, to complications later on. In fact immediately Currie moves to extend the class of relevant properties to include aesthetic as well as more narrowly conceived perceptual properties. The point is that without such an extension it is hard to see how the aesthetic empiricist is going to get an account of aesthetic value off the ground, given that many judgements of aesthetic value are advanced on the basis of a work's aesthetic properties, such as its being graceful, dynamic, vibrant, and so forth, as well as just its colours or sounds. Currie suggests that the aesthetic empiricist can comfortably accommodate aesthetic properties by appeal to an intimate dependence (supervenience) of aesthetic properties on directly perceptual properties, such that 'if two pictures look exactly alike—if they have the same pictorial properties—they will have the same aesthetic properties'.⁸

---

⁵ Ibid. p. 18. ⁶ David Davies, *Art as Performance*, pp. 26–27.
⁷ David Davies, 'Against Enlightened Empiricism', p. 27.
⁸ Currie, *An Ontology of Art*, p. 20.

So now aesthetic empiricism looks like the view characterized by Kendall Walton at the beginning of 'Categories of Art', a view he also goes on to reject:

> Works of art are simply objects with certain properties, of which we are primarily interested in perceptual ones—visual properties of paintings, audible properties of music, and so forth. A work's perceptual properties include "aesthetic" as well as "non-aesthetic" ones—the sense of mystery and tension of a painting as well as its dark coloring and diagonal composition; the energy, exuberance, and coherence of a sonata, as well as its meters, rhythms, pitches, timbres, and so forth; the balance and serenity of a Gothic cathedral as well as its dimensions, lines, and symmetries. Aesthetic properties are features or characteristics of works of art as much as non-aesthetic ones are. They are *in* the works, to be seen, heard, or otherwise perceived there. Seeing a painting's sense of mystery or hearing a sonata's coherence might require looking or listening longer or harder than does perceiving colours and shapes, rhythms and pitches; it may even require special training or a special kind of sensitivity. But these qualities must be discoverable simply by examining the works themselves if they are discoverable at all. It is never even partly *in virtue of* the circumstances of a work's origin that it has a sense of mystery or is coherent or serene. Such circumstances sometimes provide hints concerning what to look for in a work, what we might reasonably expect to find by examining it. But these hints are always theoretically dispensable; a work's aesthetic properties must "in principle" be ascertainable without their help.... It would not matter in the least to the aesthetic properties of the portrait if the paint had been applied to the canvas not by Rembrandt at all, but by a chimpanzee or a cyclone in a paint shop.[9]

The salient feature of this version of aesthetic empiricism is that the aesthetically relevant properties of a work of art—those properties that form the basis of aesthetic value judgements—are 'discoverable simply by examining the works themselves', that is, examining the perceptual (and aesthetic) properties of a work. Properties relating to the work's origins or provenance are not aesthetically relevant.

---

[9] Kendall L. Walton, 'Categories of Art', *Philosophical Review*, 79, 1970; rept. in Peter Lamarque and Stein Haugom Olsen, eds., *Aesthetics and the Philosophy of Art: The Analytic Tradition: An Anthology*, Oxford: Blackwell, 2003, pp. 142–143 (italics in original, page references to this edition).

A view not unlike this is perhaps behind a well-known passage from Clive Bell:

> To appreciate a work of art we need bring with us nothing but a sense of form and colour and a knowledge of three-dimensional space. . . . [W]e need bring with us nothing from life, no knowledge of its ideas and affairs, no familiarity with its emotions. . . . Great art remains stable and unobscure because the feelings that it awakens are independent of time and place, because its kingdom is not of this world. To those who have and hold a sense of the significance of form what does it matter whether the forms that move them were created in Paris the day before yesterday or in Babylon fifty centuries ago?[10]

Alfred Lessing has proposed a more recent version:

> Aesthetic experience is . . . wholly autonomous. . . . It does not and cannot take account of any entity or fact which is not perceivable in the work of art itself. The historical context in which that work of art stands is just such a fact. It is wholly irrelevant to the pure aesthetic appreciation and judgment of the work of art.[11]

And Jack W. Meiland, defending what he calls 'The Appearance Theory of Aesthetic Value', holds that 'aesthetic value is independent of the non-visual properties of a work of art, such as its historical properties'.[12] There are hints in these formulations of a familiar tradition in aesthetics, going back at least as far as Kant's pure aesthetic judgement, disinterested, non-conceptual and independent of the real existence of the object.

6.2. Positive and Negative Theses

Clearly there are different ideas, and different motivations, underlying these conceptions. I think, though, if we pick our way through the

---

[10] Clive Bell, *Art*, New York: Chatto & Windus, 1949, p. 37.
[11] Alfred Lessing, 'What is Wrong with a Forgery?' in Denis Dutton, ed., *The Forger's Art*, Berkeley: University of California Press, 1983, p. 76.
[12] Jack W. Meiland, 'Originals, Copies and Aesthetic Value', in Dutton, ed., *The Forger's Art*, p. 116. Also in Lamarque and Olsen, *Aesthetics and the Philosophy of Art*, p. 376.

different formulations we can find a core view about aesthetic value or aesthetic qualities or aesthetic appreciation that is recognizably 'empiricist' in the relevant sense but that is not irrevocably committed to formalism or the Kantian pure judgement of taste or indeed to a thesis vulnerable to counterexamples about indiscernibles. This core concerns the ineliminable connection between aesthetic value and perception (or more broadly experience). In many of the formulations we can identify a positive element and a negative element: the positive asserting the connection of the aesthetic with the perceptual, the negative rejecting a connection of the aesthetic with other things. So a positive aesthetic empiricism might say something like this:

> *the aesthetic value of a work of art is essentially related to how the work looks, sounds, . . . or is experienced in an immediate perceptual (or experiential) encounter with the work.*

The negative component glosses this by adding:

> *no factors relating to its history, context, or provenance are relevant to how a work looks, sounds, . . . or is experienced in an immediate perceptual (experiential) encounter so no such factors are relevant to its aesthetic appreciation (or value).*

The negative thesis comes out in Lessing and Bell very clearly. My view is that some suitably refined version of the positive thesis is true but that the negative thesis is not true and is not entailed by the positive one. Note that the emphasis in the positive thesis is not just on 'value' but on 'aesthetic' value. There might be non-aesthetic values of a work that are unconnected to perception or experience.

What needs to be held onto is the importance of perception (experience) in aesthetics. The aesthetic character of a work must reside in, and be accessible to, some appreciative experience or perception of the work. We should endorse what might be called an empiricist constraint, namely: *No aesthetic difference without a perceptual (or experiential) difference.*[13] Works cannot differ in aesthetic character if that difference

---

[13] In effect it is this principle that underlies Nelson Goodman's discussion in Chapter 3 of *Languages of Art*. Robert Hopkins, in exploring Goodman's treatment, identifies two related principles: 'The first ties features of aesthetic significance to experience: (P1) No feature counts as aesthetic unless it makes a difference to our experience of the objects that possess

is not accessible to the senses (or in the case of literature to experience more broadly conceived[14]). It might be supposed—although Currie and Davies do not put it in these terms—that one's attitude to this constraint determines which side of the pro- or anti-aesthetic empiricist divide one occupies. My own support for the constraint suggests I am more in favour than against some version of aesthetic empiricism.

What is an aesthetic difference? Here is an initial simple thought: *X and Y differ aesthetically just in case there is some aesthetic property P such that X possesses P but Y does not possess P*. What is an experiential difference? Again, in an initial formulation: *E is a (qualitatively) different experience from E′ just in case there is some (non-trivial) characterization true of E that is not true of E′*. By 'non-trivial' I mean to rule out the characterization that it is, for example, this rather than that experience, and so forth. The characterization of an experience might encompass its phenomenology (being pleasant, disturbing, vivid) or its intentional content. As we shall see the characterization must be intentional not causal; it is not what the experience is of that matters (in the sense of what causes it) but what it is *thought* to be of.

With these tentative definitions in place I think in fact it can be shown—with some additional premises about aesthetic properties—that the empiricist constraint *must* be true. But the indiscernibles examples also seem to threaten it head-on, as we shall see. A crucial factor in the debate is going to hang on what makes one experience different from another, in particular relating to the kinds of enrichment, as it were, of experience that beliefs about the objects of experience can affect. The reason that the positive and negative aspects of aesthetic empiricism need to be kept apart is that the question of the centrality of perception in aesthetic appreciation is distinct from the question of what kind of background knowledge can

---

it. The second ties what is experienced to discrimination: (P2) A feature—aesthetic or not—figures in experience only if the subject can discriminate cases in which the feature is present from those in which it is not. There is no aesthetic difference without an experiential difference, and no experiential difference without a difference in discriminatory response' ('Aesthetics, Experience, and Discrimination', *Journal of Aesthetics and Art Criticism*, 63, 2005, pp. 119–133, at p.119). Hopkins rejects (P2) but endorses (P1). I agree on both counts, although our reasons differ.

[14] For the relevant notion of 'experience' applied to literature, in the form of 'appreciation', see my *The Philosophy of Literature*, Oxford: Blackwell, 2009, Chapter 4.

inform perception in any context, including that of aesthetics. The negative thesis makes a substantive—as I see it, false—claim about the kind of knowledge required for perception adequate for aesthetic appreciation.

6.3. Putative Counterexamples about Indiscernibles

So let's turn to the alleged counterexamples that are supposed to demonstrate the falsity of aesthetic empiricism *tout court*. There are plenty of indiscernibles examples but we need to be careful to see what each establishes or purports to establish. The obvious place to start is with Arthur Danto's best known example, the series of perceptually indistinguishable canvases painted in monochrome red bearing different titles, *The Israelites Crossing the Red Sea, Kierkegaard's Mood, Red Square*, and so forth. These are, on Danto's story, different works of art, resting on different interpretations; furthermore, some of the red canvases are not even works at all but merely, for example, primed canvases ready for future use.[15] Danto's lesson is that whether an object is a work of art or indeed what work it is if it is a work is not something that merely looking at it can discern. Two perceptually indiscernible objects might be different works or one might be a work and the other not. Being a work and indeed being *that* work rather than some other are underdetermined by the discernible properties of an object. Relational properties, including those bearing on the work's origin, its cultural and historical context, are as essential to its identity as are its intrinsic or structural properties.

Other chapters in this book suggest further reasons for agreeing with Danto, at least on this count: that two objects that are perceptually indistinguishable might be different works. Does that refute aesthetic empiricism? No, because there is no mention of aesthetic, in contrast to artistic, properties. Indeed it is because Danto holds that there is a relation between the aesthetic and the perceptual that

---

[15] Arthur C. Danto, *Transfiguration of the Commonplace*, Cambridge, MA: Harvard University Press, 1981, Chapter 1.

he wants to characterize art without reference to the aesthetic. What makes something art, Danto thinks, is not fundamentally perceptual so it cannot be fundamentally aesthetic. In characterizing aesthetic empiricism it is important to retain a distinction between aesthetic and artistic properties. The following, for example, seems *not* to be true: *If a and b are distinct works of art then there is an aesthetic difference between them*. It seems not to be true because it is at least conceivable that some works of art possess no aesthetic properties (or no aesthetic properties relevant to their identity as works). The relation with experience, though, is fairly complex. Another analogous thesis does strike me as true: *If a and b are distinct works of art then there is an experiential difference between them (when they are experienced correctly)*. It might seem that this follows in a merely trivial way from my earlier account of experiential difference: if E is an experience of *a* and E' an experience of *b* and *a* and *b* are distinct then E and E' are different experiences just in virtue of having different objects. But we must not beg any questions. The thesis seems to conflict in a substantial way with Danto's indiscernibles example because it implies, paradoxically, that two works might be perceptually indistinguishable, like the red squares, yet, as distinct works, afford different experiences. It is that apparent conflict that I want to explore and resolve.

It brings us to another familiar kind of indiscernibles case that does directly bear on aesthetic properties. This is Kendall Walton's famous example from 'Categories of Art':

> Imagine a society which does not have an established medium of painting, but does produce a kind of work called *guernicas*. *Guernicas* are like versions of Picasso's "Guernica" done in various bas-relief dimensions. All of them are surfaces with the colors and shapes of Picasso's "Guernica", but the surfaces are molded to protrude from the wall like relief maps of different kinds of terrain. Some *guernicas* have rolling surfaces, others are sharp and jagged, still others contain several relatively flat planes at various angles to each other, and so forth. Picasso's "Guernica" would be counted as a *guernica* in this society—a perfectly flat one—rather than as a painting. Its flatness is variable and the figures on its surface are standard relative to the category of *guernicas*. Thus the flatness, which is standard for us, would be variable for members of the other society . . . , and the figures on the surface, which are variable for us, would be standard for them. This would make a profound difference between our aesthetic reaction to "Guernica" and theirs. It seems violent,

dynamic, vital, disturbing to us. But I imagine it would strike them as cold, stark, lifeless, or serene and restful, or perhaps bland, dull, boring—but in any case not violent, dynamic, and vital. We do not pay attention to or take note of "Guernica"'s flatness; this is a feature we take for granted in paintings, as it were. But for the other society this is "Guernica"'s most striking and noteworthy characteristic—what is expressive about it. Conversely, "Guernica"'s color patches which we find noteworthy and expressive, are insignificant to them.[16]

For Walton the example shows that what aesthetic properties we perceive in a work depends partially on what *category* we perceive the work to be in: in this case, the category of painting or *guernica*. To establish the *correct* category to perceive it in, we must know something about its origin: 'the correct way to perceive it is determined partly by historical facts about the artist's intention and/or his society' and 'no examination of the work itself, however thorough, will by itself reveal those properties'. He goes on: 'If we are confronted by a work about whose origins we know absolutely nothing . . . we would simply not be in a position to judge it aesthetically.'[17]

Is there an argument here against aesthetic empiricism? On the face of it the example seems to show that we can have one and the same object attributed different and incompatible aesthetic properties when perceived under different categories. Is that not a direct challenge to the empiricist constraint, that there can be no aesthetic difference without a perceptual difference? Care must be taken in answering the question. First, we should note what seems to be a vestigial commitment in Walton to some form of empiricism, in the continuing emphasis on how a work is *perceived*. Walton insists that he is not denying that 'we perceive aesthetic properties in works' and strikingly, at the end of the paper, he writes: 'I do not deny that paintings and sonatas are to be judged solely on what can be seen or heard in them—when they are perceived correctly.' What he does deny is that 'examining a work with the senses can by itself reveal . . . how it is correct to perceive it, [or] how to perceive it that way'.[18] So while finding out the correct category for a work is not a perceptual matter, nevertheless when that knowledge is secured then a *correct perception* is possible. In fact Walton holds that knowledge of the category is not *sufficient* for

[16] Walton, 'Categories of Art', p. 147. [17] Ibid., p. 154. [18] Ibid., p. 156.

AESTHETIC EMPIRICISM   131

correct perception as the latter might require training with objects of a similar kind. The idea of perceptual indiscernibles is problematic in the example. In what sense are Picasso's *Guernica* and the perfectly flat *guernica* indiscernible? Walton envisages Picasso's own painting being appropriated by the *guernica* society and being viewed as a *guernica*. It might be thought that indiscernibility simply follows from the fact that there is only one numerically identical object. But to characterize the indiscernibility as 'perceptual' seems to beg the question for, on Walton's own account, in this new and alien viewing environment the *perceptions* will differ. Walton's account also implies that members of the *guernica* society are perceiving Picasso's work *incorrectly*, in the wrong category, so there is a difference between how it *does* look to them and how it *ought* to look. A variation on the example would conceive of a work physically identical to *Guernica* deliberately made as a *guernica* and thus correctly perceived as a *guernica*. In this case we should say that there are no longer numerically identical *works*. Once again we need to draw on the distinction between physically identical *objects* and distinct *works*. Perception might not tell the former apart but it can register differences in the latter. This makes another remark of Walton's all the more puzzling: 'of two works which differ *only* in respect of their origins—that is, which are *perceptually indistinguishable* [italics added]—one might be coherent or serene and the other not.'[19] But if these two works have different aesthetic properties, and aesthetic properties, as Walton believes, are perceived, then the perceptions of the works—when perceived correctly—must be different. Perceptual indistinguishability is true of the objects only prior to their being identified as works.

Recalling the positive thesis, there seems little doubt that the Picasso and the flat *guernica look* different when viewed under the appropriate category by an informed observer. Do they look different 'in an immediate perceptual encounter', as the thesis demands? Yes, there is nothing indirect or inferential about the experience. The flat *guernica* immediately strikes the *guernican* as cold and lifeless. But isn't this response conditioned by knowledge of the category, experience of other works, etc.? Of course. But that does not make it less immediate

[19] Ibid., p. 154.

or somehow less of a perceptual experience. All perception is informed by background knowledge.

It might be thought, though, that the crux of the matter has not yet been addressed, namely the perceptual indiscernibility of the two works. If the works—the Picasso and the flat *guernica*—were placed side by side no perceptual experience could tell them apart. The *guernican* would react to both as cold and lifeless, you and I to both as violent and dynamic. They could be jumbled about and no-one could tell the difference. But this does not undermine the positive thesis. What it does show is that perception alone is not sufficient to identify the category to which a work belongs. That indeed is Walton's point. We need to know facts about a work's causal history to know what work it is and perception will not reveal those facts—this recalls Danto on the red squares. Yet it is only when such facts are known that we know how to look at a work and when that knowledge is in place our perceptions will differ accordingly. It is one thing to appeal to perception to identify two objects as distinct—*per impossibile* in the indiscernibles cases—another thing to appeal to perceptual differences when objects have already been identified as distinct. It is assumed that aesthetic empiricism falls through failure to establish the former while in fact the core of the doctrine resides in supporting the latter.

In fact the empiricist constraint might even find support from examples of this kind. What Walton's argument establishes so powerfully is that our aesthetic responses are thoroughly determined by our beliefs about what kind of thing we are looking at. We might press a stronger point, in the light of the empiricist constraint, namely that where two works are perceptually indiscernible *as uncategorized objects* there *is* no aesthetic difference between them. Aesthetic differences only arise between works *as categorized objects* at precisely the point where perceptual differences emerge. So the Picasso and the *guernica* side by side have no aesthetic difference between them when perceived as mere objects. Only when perceived as distinct works under different categories do the aesthetic differences materialize. This somewhat speculative characterization concedes a lot to strong aesthetic empiricism. By relativizing aesthetic difference to the categorization of objects it might even be seen as falling in line with Kant's pure judgements of taste, for in such a judgement Kant in effect tells us to set aside all that we know about the object and perceive it purely for its own sake, uncategorized or, in his own terms, not falling under a concept. So, as the empiricist constraint would predict, pure aesthetic judgements about perceptual indiscernibles, *qua* mere objects, must yield the same aesthetic value. But that is compatible with the claim that categorized aesthetic judgements about indiscernibles—judgements about *works* not mere objects—yield different aesthetic values.

When Currie and Davies attack aesthetic empiricism they do so by generating further examples along the lines of Walton's *guernica*. That is, they construct other indiscernibles cases to show that not only facts about a work's *category* but also a whole range of facts about its history of production—provenance-related facts—bear on what aesthetic properties it possesses. The bearing they have is counterfactual such that if the provenance-related facts had been otherwise then the work's aesthetic properties would have been otherwise. And if its aesthetic properties had been different its aesthetic value and thus the potential for aesthetic appreciation would also have been different. So this develops into a powerful seeming *reductio* against aesthetic empiricism.

The argument goes something like this:

(1) Aesthetic value depends only on what can be directly perceived in a work (aesthetic empiricist premise).
(2) What category a work belongs to and other provenance-related facts about it cannot be directly perceived in a work (premise of indiscernibles cases).
(3) So the features mentioned in (2) do not bear on aesthetic value.
(4) But these features do bear on aesthetic value (conclusion from indiscernibles cases).
(5) So aesthetic value does not depend only on what is directly perceived in a work (denial of aesthetic empiricism).

The argument seems to be valid and it is difficult to fault its soundness given that we have already granted both the premise and the conclusion of the indiscernibles cases. To make matters worse I believe that Currie and Davies are right about the importance of provenance-related facts both in the identity conditions of works and in the truth conditions of aesthetic judgements about works. So where does the argument go wrong?

It goes wrong in a number of respects. First, it implies too narrow a concept of direct perception. Second, it under-describes the bearing of provenance-related facts on aesthetic value. And third, as a consequence, it forces too sharp a divide between the aesthetic and the perceptual. The reason that provenance-related facts bear on aesthetic value is (a) that these facts help to determine the identity of a work, (b) the identity of a work helps to determine how the work is perceived by an informed perceiver, and thus (c) this informed perception helps underpin the aesthetic value (and aesthetic character) attributed to the work. This can be seen as generalizing the earlier point about categorization. When perceived *under different categories* two otherwise indiscernible objects can come to look different. Similarly when other facts about provenance are taken into account members of indiscernible pairs might give rise to different experiences. Accordingly aesthetic value *does* depend on what is directly perceived (or experienced) at least when the perception is suitably informed by beliefs about what kind of object is being perceived.

David Davies offers the following objection to this kind of 'enlightened empiricism':

the difference between the value [of an object perceived one way and the same object perceived another way] is surely *not* grounded in the different experiences elicited in us, as receivers, when our perceptual engagements with [the object] are "informed" first by one piece of information about provenance and then by the other. That our experiences differ *reflects* the value we find in the work on each occasion. It isn't the *ground* of that difference in value.[20]

But we must be careful how we interpret the claim that the different experiences do or do not *ground* the difference in value. Davies's point is valid only if we take a causal or temporal view of grounding whereby the experience of the object causes (or temporally precedes) the judgement of value. Having experienced the object a certain way we then infer its aesthetic value (or its aesthetic character); the one, as it were, leads to the other. Davies is right that that ordering does not always occur. But grounding need not take that form and the

[20] Davies, 'Against Enlightened Empiricism', p. 29. (Davies is using the case of van Meegeren's forgeries of Vermeer as his example but I take it the objection can be generalized in the way I have suggested.)

relevant kind of grounding for the enlightened empiricist is not of that form.

The difference in aesthetic value is grounded in the different experiences in the sense that without the difference in experience there could be no difference in aesthetic value. If it means anything to speak of the aesthetic value of a work then that value must be realizable in, appreciable through, an experience. What could it mean to say that a work has aesthetic value if there is no possibility of an experience within which that value is 'grounded'? The aesthetic value could not reside merely in the provenance-related facts that determine the difference in works. Certainly those facts might indicate other kinds of value (one object might be a product of human skill, which we envy or admire, the duplicate a product of nature) but *aesthetic* value does not rest in such facts alone. Differences in aesthetic value must *show* themselves in differences of experience. If there is a causal relation it is between the provenance-related facts and the nature of the experience, not between the nature of the experience and the differential value judgements.

It is perhaps easier to consolidate these points by turning to my third indiscernibles example, which well illustrates the problem with the kind of pure perception that underlies Kant's pure judgement of taste. Ironically, the example comes from Kant himself.

> What do poets set more store on than the nightingale's bewitching and beautiful note, in a lonely thicket on a still summer evening by the soft light of the moon? And yet we have instances of how, where no such songster was to be found, a jovial host has played a trick on the guests with him on a visit to enjoy the country air, and has done so to their huge satisfaction, by hiding in a thicket a rogue of a youth who (with a reed or rush in his mouth) knew how to produce this note so as to hit off nature to perfection. But the instant one realises that it is all a fraud no one will long endure listening to this song that before was regarded as so attractive. (*Critique of Judgment*, Part I, Book II, §42)

Kant offers the example for his own polemical ends. It is part of an argument to show the superiority of natural beauty over art and also to help establish the claim that the interest we have in the beauty of nature is, as he puts it, 'a mark of a good soul'. Yet it runs quite against the tenor of Kantian thinking about beauty. For we might suppose—perhaps in the spirit of strong aesthetic empiricism—that from a purely aesthetic point of view it should make no difference where the sounds emanate from. Recall the negative points from Clive Bell about the irrelevance of provenance in the appreciation of art. It is surprising to find Kant so quick to dismiss as uninteresting and unattractive the very sounds that, when believed to be from the nightingale, were thought so charming. The example is an unexpected concession to the thought that often our aesthetic judgements are far from 'pure' but rest on the very factors that the negative thesis of aesthetic empiricism seeks to play down.

To bring out the challenge of indiscernibles we need to alter the example slightly, along the lines of our modification to Walton's *guernica* case, so that on the one hand we have a genuine nightingale's song and on the other the qualitatively identical song from the rogue of a youth. Now we can ask whether there could be an aesthetic difference between them. Kant himself seems to think there is, while also insisting on their perceptual indiscernibility. The move that needs to be made is analogous to the earlier move, insisting that there is an aesthetic difference but there is also an experiential difference. The experience of the sounds as sung-by-a-nightingale is not the same as the experience of the sounds as sung-by-a-youth. The latter is an experience of a human intentional act; it is assessable in terms of the wit, skill, achievement, or purpose behind the act. The former involves admiration of the wonders of nature. Under these aspects the sounds simply do not sound the same. On the other hand there would be no aesthetic difference if we could attend to the sounds purely for their intrinsic quality—as Kant recommends for the pure aesthetic judgement.

The point about the nightingale example is that it shows it is not merely a peculiarity of art that aesthetic difference can arise in the face of apparent indiscernibility. There is no need to appeal to categories of art to get round the anomaly. It reinforces the idea that all perception is imbued with belief and expectation. What deflates the party-goers in Kant's example is that their assumption that the sounds emanate from a nightingale is undermined. They were never listening to the sounds as pure sounds but already as a nightingale's song—the discovery that they were wrong brought disappointment. The story might have continued with the listeners adjusting their expectations and now enjoying the wit and skill of the youth. The simple point worth emphasizing is the evident *gestalt*-like change in the experience itself.

6.4. Informed Experience

I shall end with some rather speculative remarks about further ways that experiences of indiscernible pairs can differ and the role of provenance-related facts in those experiences. I suggested earlier that two experiences E and E' differ qualitatively just in case there is some (non-trivial) characterization true of E that is not true of E'. But the nightingale example suggests that this cannot be quite right. Suppose a person *a* experiences first the nightingale's song (E) then the youth whistling (E'), can detect no difference between them, and believes they both come from the same source. It seems that for *a* E is qualitatively the same experience as E' yet E is truly characterizable as 'the sound-of-a-nightingale's-song' while E' is truly characterizable as 'not-the sound-of-a-nightingale's-song'. This represents a clear counterexample to the definition in its simple formulation. The characterization of the experience that will differentiate it from another experience must be internalist not externalist. It must be a characterization to which the experiencer assents. Only the person having the experience can give an authoritative characterization both of its phenomenology and its intentional content.

In the case of art the experiences of interest—particularly those that are the basis for value judgements—are normative. They are appropriate, correct, or justified experiences. Along with the idea of normativity comes that of the informed observer, right up to the Humean critic, whose judgements are well-founded and whose experiences set a standard for correctness. Grounded in this context we can ask the following question: *What information about a work to be aesthetically evaluated would an informed observer need in order to experience the work in a manner appropriate to the kind of work it is and sufficient to set a standard for a correct aesthetic response to that work?* It is that question, I believe, that should constrain the search for those provenance-related factors that bear on the aesthetic value of a work. All and only such factors that serve to characterize the intentional content of the experiences of an informed observer are relevant to aesthetic value. Is it enough that the informed observer should use Waltonian categories as part of this characterization? Probably not. The normative experience of Picasso's *Guernica as Guernica* (i.e. as a painting, not as a *guernica*) should make reference not only to the fact that the work is a Cubist painting but also that it is an expression of the horrors of war, a prophetic vision of a collapsing world, symbolic in nearly all its detailed imagery, and also born out of an individual's response to the specific context of the bombing of Guernica, the Spanish Civil War, and so forth. These facts are not merely categorial, nor are they all directly perceivable in the painting itself but they crucially affect the perception of the painting.

The mistake of the naïve aesthetic empiricist is not to base aesthetic value on how a work looks or is experienced but on too narrow a conception of the kinds of experiences relevant to aesthetic appreciation. I spoke earlier of the 'enrichment' of experiences by background beliefs. Now I think we have a clearer idea of how to cash out that metaphor. The enrichment is revealed by the complexity of the characterization of the intentional content of the experience. To experience one of Danto's red squares merely *as-a-red-square*, such that there is no qualitative difference between the experience of this square or that square, is not as 'enriched' an experience as the experience of this red square *as-depicting-the-Israelites-crossing-the-Red-Sea* and that red square *as-depicting-Kierkegaard's-Mood*. These are qualitatively different experiences and differences of this kind, I maintain, are the basis for differential aesthetic judgements (and characterizations). They are the kind of differences that mark off the informed observer of art from the casual or ill-informed observer whose judgements count for less. As I said earlier, though, I do not think it is only the intentional content of an experience that underpins aesthetic appreciation but also the phenomenology of the experience, notably the pleasure, emotional charge, resonance, and so on, that characterizes it. At the heart of aesthetics lies the peculiar interplay between content and phenomenology in our responses to art and nature. My fear is that to abandon aesthetic empiricism altogether is to abandon that insight.

7

Imitating Style

When we say that a work of art is in a particular style, what do we mean? What is it for two works to have the same style? Or different styles? We call certain features or properties of a work stylistic features or properties. But what are these and how are they to be distinguished from other features or properties? It is not at all easy to pin down the defining features of style, even though we would probably have little difficulty recognizing certain well-known styles. Styles are associated with individual artists, regions, periods, and schools; and a simple, albeit not yet substantive, delimitation of stylistic features might be just those characteristics which serve in whatever way to *place* a work in relation to other works. Velasquez's style—say in portraiture—is distinct from van Eyck's; they belong in different stylistic categories; similarly, the style of Mozart's operatic humour is different from that of Monteverdi. Works depicting the same subject matter—the Madonna, the Crucifixion—can do so in different styles. And works from a single artist or school can share a similar style yet depict quite different subjects.

All the arts—painting, music, sculpture, literature, architecture, dance, film—can exhibit styles and stylistic distinctions are often crucial in understanding, appreciating, and comparing works of art. But it is not only works of art that have styles—furniture, pottery, carpets, clothes, and cars exhibit styles and can be classified in terms of style. Nor are styles restricted to artefacts. Actions should be included as well: running, sailing, playing golf, playing chess, dancing, driving, even having a conversation.[1] Perhaps, as is sometimes supposed, how you live your life can have a style, a so-called 'life-style'. Can there

---

[1] For an argument that thinking can have styles, see my 'Style and Thought', *Journal of Literary Semantics*, 21, 1992, pp. 45–54.

be a conception of style that encompasses all these applications and is not vacuous? Does style just mean any distinctive characteristic?

7.1. Two Definitions of Styles

It is helpful to distinguish two putative definitions of style, which I shall call feature-based and act-based definitions. A feature-based definition (of artistic style) defines style simply as those characteristics of a work of art, *qua* work of art, which serve to identify when, where, and by whom, it was produced. This is essentially Nelson Goodman's definition. Style, he argues, 'consists of those features of the symbolic functioning of a work that are characteristic of author, period, place, or school'.[2] Such features might be use of colour, line, compositional techniques, or, in the literary arts, syntactic structure, vocabulary, narrative point of view, or characterization. Note that Goodman identifies style with features of the 'symbolic functioning' of a work. The point is to exclude certain kinds of external or relational properties, like the label on a picture or the chemical properties of pigments, which might contribute to identifying a work. Goodman is happy, though, surely rightly, to include—or at least not rule out—subject matter as a component of style. The characteristic subject matter of Edvard Munch's paintings—isolated or anguished figures in bleak landscapes—can be classified as a stylistic feature, and conforms to Goodman's definition.

One consequence of standard feature-based definitions is that stylistic features are viewed as objective properties of objects, artefacts or performances, such that they can be identified in a more or less formal manner without presupposing further knowledge of the objects or performances themselves. On feature-based definitions, stylistic features are inherent or intrinsic properties. This will contrast with stylistic features conceived under act-based definitions. Under an act-based definition stylistic properties are not inherent properties but emergent properties; they are properties that objects (acts, etc.) have only *under a description*.

---

[2] Nelson Goodman, *Ways of Worldmaking*, Brighton: Harvestor Press, 1978, p. 35.

Although in certain contexts, as we shall see, the identification of objective, inherent features, usually formal features, is sufficient for the classification of styles, there are other more interesting cases of style where the feature-based definition is inadequate. The main reason is that in a large number of cases we cannot even identify a feature as stylistic until we know what it is a feature *of*. A certain kind of movement, for example, might indicate a graceful style of *dancing* but an affected or ungainly style of *running*. We will come to more substantial examples in a moment.

On the alternative act-based definition, style is defined as *a way of doing something*. Not all ways of doing something pertain to style, but style on this view always pertains to ways of doing something.[3] It is a consequence of this definition that a style can only be identified relative to some act being performed. If a style is a way of doing something then what the style is is logically dependent on what is being done. Only when an action is conceived as an action of a certain kind can salient features of the *way* it is performed be identified. The way it is performed emerges only under a description of *what* is being performed. Take the case of colour or line in a painting. These can constitute, or contribute to, stylistic features only relative to the function that the particular line or colour is performing in that work. The point is nicely illustrated by an example from Jenefer Robinson:

> Imagine two painted canvases, perceptually indistinguishable, which consist of a field of red crossed vertically by three thin black or white bands. One of these is a painting by Barnett Newman and has Barnett Newman's style. The other was produced by me and is the unfinished design for my new open-plan living-room, the thin bands marking the positions in the room where I wish to place, respectively, a Japanese screen, a long sofa, and an étagère. Ex hypothesi we cannot tell the two works apart just by looking at them, yet Barnett Newman's painting has Barnett Newman's distinctive style, whereas mine has no style at all. Why is this? The reason is that Newman's work has aesthetic significance whereas mine does not. In Newman's work, the position of the three lines which divide the canvas, the nature of the lines themselves . . . and the exact hue of the four zones of red created by the three lines all have aesthetic significance and all were created with a specific

---

[3] Here I am influenced by Jenefer Robinson, e.g. in 'Style and Personality in the Literary Work', *Philosophical Review*, 94, 1985, p. 228.

aesthetic intention. In my work the positioning of the lines has a practical but no aesthetic significance, while the nature of the lines and the exact hue of the background is a purely accidental feature of the design. My work, I suppose, can be looked at *as if* it were a Barnett Newman, but the fact remains that it was not created with any aesthetic intention and does not have any aesthetic status. It would therefore be absurd to talk of it as a painting with a place in the history of style as the Barnett Newman is.[4]

Style in Robinson's example is just one instance of an aesthetic property and her argument can be assimilated into a general pattern of argument in aesthetics, originating in the work of Frank Sibley, according to which aesthetic properties are 'emergent' or *gestalt* properties. Developing this tradition, Kendall Walton's *guernica* thought-experiment, discussed in the previous chapter, helped to establish the point that we cannot identify aesthetic properties in a work independently of other facts about it, in particular what 'category' it is assigned to. These examples involve comparing objects that are perceptually indistinguishable but which differ, in Robinson's case, with respect to style, in Walton's with respect to a wider class of aesthetic properties, precisely because of external facts about their origin or about their relation to other objects. This framework has interesting bearings on the imitation of style.

7.2. General and Individual Styles

Let me introduce now another distinction, drawn initially by Richard Wollheim, but developed by Jenefer Robinson, between *general* styles and *individual* styles. Broadly speaking general styles are more amenable to feature-based definitions while individual styles seem to require some kind of act-based definition. General styles are taxonomic, i.e. they concern classifications that are imposed by critics, art historians, or artists themselves (acting as theorists). Classification into general styles involves identifying recurrent features which are given salience or significance relative to the classification. Wollheim distinguishes three

---

[4] Jenefer Robinson, 'Style and Significance in Art History', *Journal of Aesthetics and Art Criticism*, 40, 1981, p. 8.

kinds of general style: (1) universal style, e.g. classicism, naturalism, romanticism, the geometric style; (2) period style, e.g. Neoclassicism, Art Nouveau, and Social Realism; and (3) school style, e.g. the style of the school of Giotto (applied to Giotto's followers). General styles can be learned; they can be exhibited in works by different artists. As Wollheim and Robinson put it, they do not have 'psychological reality', they are not expressive of a personality, they are external to an artist, and they are not explicable in terms of some individual artist's psychology or expressive aims.

Individual styles, on the other hand, are expressive of an artist's personality, they have 'psychological reality'.[5] They often manifest themselves in the way that an artist utilizes general style categories. In another essay, Jenefer Robinson has examined the way particular artists work with general styles, bringing out individual expressiveness.[6] For example, the heroic epic style (a 'universal' literary style) is identified by certain modes of composition, diction, repetition, formulaic similes, etc. In the case of Homer, say in the *Iliad*, who uses this general style—the heroic epic—Robinson shows how we can identify beyond this an individual style expressive of certain values, tastes, interests or attitudes stemming from the author himself. In another example, this time of a period style, she looks at the Augustan style of poetry in the eighteenth century with its characteristic features of diction and versification as well as characteristic expressive qualities: civilized, cerebral, elegant, controlled, witty, ironic. However, as she goes on to illustrate, Pope's way of being witty and cerebral is quite different from Swift's.

The important point, in summary, is that individual stylistic features are a manifestation of underlying psychological states or processes and are identifiable only in relation to them, along with reference to the specific aesthetic aims realized in particular works. What is attractive

[5] For a concise account of Wollheim's distinction between general and individual styles, see R. Wollheim, *Painting As An Art*, pp. 26–27. See also R. Wollheim, 'Pictorial Style: Two Views', in Berel Lang, ed., *The Concept of Style*, Philadelphia: University of Pennsylvania Press, 1979.

[6] Jenefer Robinson, 'General and Individual Styles in Literature', *Journal of Aesthetics and Art Criticism* 43, 1984, pp. 147–158. See also her 'Style and Personality in the Literary Work', *Philosophical Review* 94, 1985, pp. 227–247; rept. in Peter Lamarque and Stein Haugom Olsen, eds., *Aesthetics and the Philosophy of Art: The Analytic Tradition: An Anthology*, Oxford: Blackwell, 2003.

about this account of individual style is that it gives substance to act-based definitions of style that conceive style as a *way of doing something*, where that way of doing something expresses an artist's personality, in the sense of values, attitudes, interests, and qualities of mind. A distinctive style, on this account, is precisely the way that these inner states manifest themselves. This notion of style carries over to non-artistic applications. It might apply to the way we dress, or drive, or play games, or make things.

The relation of style to expressiveness is interesting for a number of reasons. It helps to get away from an excessive emphasis given to formal features in stylistics. By emphasizing techniques, methods, motifs, textures, figures, light/shade, or diction, metre, and versification in studies of styles there is a tendency to forget that styles have a *function*, they contribute to meaning and effect, they have a point. We talk about the treatment of a theme in a certain style and it is clearly important in understanding what a work is about, what it seeks to achieve, to grasp the contribution of style to the kind of work that it is. The idea that personality—values, attitudes, interests, aims—can be expressed through stylistic features gives further point to those features.

However, what Walton's *guernica* example shows, going beyond Robinson's Barnett Newman example, is that aesthetic, including stylistic, properties of a work (or action) depend not only on what specific intentions or expressive aims underlie the work (or action) but on a broader class of contextual factors, such as the 'category' into which the work is placed or the tradition to which it belongs. Yet this constraint too must be incorporated into act-based definitions of style. Accordingly, we can now say that *what is being done* in a work (or action) is explicable both in terms of underlying psychological states within the artist (or agent) and in terms of a more general classification of the work (or action) relating it to other works (or actions) of the same kind.

7.3. Two Test Cases: Parody and Forgery

A good way of refining the idea of an act-based definition of style linked to the expressiveness of individual style and to contextual categorization is to see how it fares in two especially problematic cases of sameness and difference of style: namely, parody and forgery, both of which involve the imitation of style. A parodist attempts to imitate and exaggerate individual stylistic features for humorous or satirical ends. The forger attempts to imitate individual stylistic features with the dishonest aim of trying to pass off a work as if it were an original by the artist imitated. The question is: To what extent does, or can, the parodist and forger reproduce the individual style of another artist? I suggest that in one sense they can do it exactly and with great effect. Yet in another deeper sense they fail altogether and are bound to fail; the imitation and the imitated are worlds apart precisely because of the groundedness of individual style in personal expression and aesthetic category.

7.3.1. Parody: Henry James and Max Beerbohm

Henry James developed a quite distinctive individual style in his later novels.[7] This was characterized by the use of increasingly complex syntactic structures, by long dense sentences with fastidious parenthetical qualifications in embedded clauses, by emphases, and inverted commas, also by the use of Latinisms, the juxtaposition of the abstract and the mundane, the formal and the vernacular, and the subtle use of narrative point of view, characteristically employing the limited third-person mode to expose a character's intimate reflections with a degree of external detachment. Some of these features appear in this passage, chosen fairly randomly, from *The Golden Bowl*:

> It appeared thus that they might enjoy together extraordinary freedom, the two friends, from the moment they should understand their position aright. With the Prince himself, from an early age, not unnaturally, Charlotte had made a great point of their so understanding it; she had found frequent occasion to describe to him this necessity, and, her resignation tempered, or her intelligence at least quickened, by irrepressible irony, she applied at different times different names to the propriety of their case. The wonderful thing was that her sense of propriety had been, from the first, especially alive about it. There were hours when she spoke of taking refuge in what she called the commonest tact—as if this principle alone would suffice to

---

[7] For a detailed analysis of this style, see Seymour Chatman, *The Later Style of Henry James*, Oxford: Basil Blackwell, 1972.

light the way; there were others when it might have seemed, to listen to her, that their course would demand of them the most anxious study and the most independent, not to say original, interpretation of signs. She talked now as if it were indicated, at every turn, by fingerposts of almost ridiculous prominence; she talked again as if it lurked in devious ways and were to be tracked through bush and briar; and she even, on occasion, delivered herself in the sense that, as their situation was unprecedented, so their heaven was without stars. " 'Do'?" she once had echoed to him as the upshot of passages covertly, though briefly, occurring between them on her return from the visit to America that had immediately succeeded her marriage, determined for her by this event as promptly as an excursion of the like strange order had been prescribed in his own case. "Isn't the immense, the really quite matchless beauty of our position that we have to 'do' nothing in life at all?—nothing except the usual, necessary, everyday thing which consists in one's not being more of a fool than one can help."

Ian Watt, reflecting the account given earlier of individual style, has suggested that the stylistic features in James's later work, as partly exhibited in this passage, are expressive of James's *interest* in the abstract, his *preoccupation* with what is going on in the consciousness of his characters, and his *attitude* of humorous compassion for them.[8] Here the terms 'interest', 'preoccupation', and 'attitude' refer to the underlying psychological states in the writer that must be invoked in a full explanation of James's style and his aesthetic achievement.

Max Beerbohm wrote two celebrated parodies of James's later style, 'The Mote in the Middle Distance' and 'The Guerdon'. Here is a short passage from 'The Guerdon':

The question, however, was to answer itself, then and there, to the effect that this functionary belonged to whom *he* belonged to; and the converse of this reminder, presenting itself simultaneously to his consciousness, was to make him feel, when he was a few minutes later ushered into the Presence, that he had never so intensely, for general abjectness and sheer situational funk, belonged as now. He caught himself wondering whether, on this basis, he was even animate, so strong was his sense of being a "bit" of the furniture of the great glossy "study"—of being some oiled and ever so handy object moving smoothly on castors, or revolving, at the touch of a small red royal

---

[8] Ian Watt, 'The First Paragraph of *The Ambassadors*: An explication', in Tony Tanner, ed., *Henry James*, London: Macmillan, 1968. Jenefer Robinson cites this description from Ian Watt in 'Style and Personality in the Literary Work', p. 228.

finger, on a pivot. It would be placed questioningly, that finger—and his prevision held him with a long-drawn pang of nightmare—on the cryptic name. That it occurred, this name, almost at the very end of the interminable list, figured to him not as a respite but as a prolongment of the perspirational agony. So that when, at the long last, that finger *was* placed, with a roll towards him of the blue, the prominent family eye of the seated reader, it was with a groan of something like relief that he faintly uttered an "Oh well, Sir, he *is*, you know—and with all submission, hang it, just *isn't* he though?—of an eminence!"[9]

The cumulative effect of the parody is brilliant.[10] The elements mount up to devastating effect: the almost unintelligibly convoluted sentences, the laboured, even pompous phrase-making, 'perspirational agony', 'situational funk', the dogged parentheses, and of course the general bathos of the protagonist's predicament.[11] A successful parody mimics not only surface stylistic features but also those elements of style that lie at a deeper level than mere surface convention. A good parodist must recognize not only *how* the subjects express themselves but also, in a sense, *why* they express themselves in that way. But that understanding must in the end be self-defeating in parody, and self-consciously so. For the function of stylistic features in a parody is, ex hypothesi, quite different from that of the original. And this different function—a combination of exaggeration, humour, mimicry—subverts and mocks those very features it imitates. We laugh at the parody but not at the real thing. The expressiveness in the style of the real thing *works* while in the parody it deliberately fails.

Beerbohm's parody of James is about as good as any parody could be yet if I am right the style in the parody is not identical to the individual style in James's later novels. The surface features are superbly mimicked but the underlying (expressive) processes which serve to make it *James*'s style are absent. The explanation for the surface features is different in the two cases, not merely for the trivial reason that only one is written by James but because the features are functioning

---

[9] Max Beerbohm, 'The Guerdon', in Dwight Macdonald, ed., *Parodies: An Anthology from Chaucer to Beerbohm and After*, London: Faber & Faber, 1964, p. 148.
[10] Chatman, op. cit., discusses the success of the parody.
[11] The parody concerns the conferring of the Order of Merit on James and the confusions of the Lord Chamberlain, Stamfordham (the 'he' of this passage), and the King about James's identity.

differently in the two cases. Furthermore, the categorization of the works is different, obviously so, for only one is a parody conforming to the specific conventions of that genre.

I do not want to make it analytically true that no-one can imitate someone else's individual style, for then again the thesis would be trivialized. There is no reason in principle why two people should not share sufficiently similar psychological dispositions with regard to a work or performance to manifest the same or very similar individual styles in their distinct works or performances. In such cases they must share the same aims (aesthetic or otherwise) and the stylistic features must be conceived as belonging to the same kind of work or action consonant with those aims. The explanation for the surface features will then be the same; the actions and the way of performing the actions will be type-identical.

It might be thought unduly paradoxical to deny that a good parody captures the individual style of what it parodies, especially on what looks like the weak ground that the surface features in the two cases admit of different explanations. The argument seems perversely to miss the point of parody. If this is a consequence of an act-based definition of style then is not the argument a *reductio* of that definition? I think not. But to strengthen the case we need to bring forward another element in parody: make-believe. When we read a parody we make believe or imagine that what we are reading is in the (individual) style of the original. Indeed we make believe that the work is by the author being parodied. To do this we must deliberately set aside known facts about its origin, its real status or genre, the actual aims behind it. Make-believedly the work has the individual style of the original; make-believedly it expresses facets of the author's personality. But in reality neither is true. Because parody exaggerates the features it mimics what is imagined to be the case and what is known to be the case nicely interact (benignly conflict) thereby producing the humorous effect.

7.3.2. *Forgery: van Meegeren and Vermeer*

Some of these points can be clarified and reinforced by turning to the case of forgery. Again we find that the expressiveness in a forged style fails, though in this case not by being deliberately undermined. In a forgery many of the surface features of the copied style are reproduced, often brilliantly, yet, I would argue, once again rarely with the same expressive qualities of the original, precisely because the expression is *imitated*, not *originated*.

Van Meegeren's forgeries of Vermeer are not only among the most celebrated forgeries in modern times but also the most successful. They fooled the art-historical community and even contributed to a redefinition of Vermeer's stylistic development. Van Meegeren's *The Supper at Emmaus* (1937) in Rotterdam is widely regarded as the most successful of all. In composition the painting ingeniously echoes Caravaggio's *Supper at Emmaus*, thereby establishing a much speculated-on Italian connection in Vermeer. In authenticating the painting, the Vermeer scholar Abraham Bredius wrote:

Neither the beautiful signature 'I.V.Meer' . . . nor the *pointillé* on the bread which Christ is blessing, is necessary to convince us that we have here a—I am inclined to say—*the* masterpiece of Johannes Vermeer of Delft. . . . In no other picture by the great master of Delft do we find such sentiment, such a powerful understanding of the Bible story—a sentiment so nobly human expressed through the medium of the highest art.[12]

Here is a modern art critic noting the subtleties of the forgery:

the head of the serving girl, with its clean oval shape, draped hair, and slightly open mouth, reminds us of the heartbreakingly beautiful *Girl in a Turban*. The profile and hair of the disciple on the right recalls Vermeer's *Interior with an Astronomer*. The prominent stitching on the rough garments of the disciples, particularly the shoulder seam of the left-hand figure, brings to mind the homespun garments of *The Milkmaid*. Another resemblance in this picture can be found in the *pointillé* patterns of light on the crusty bread in front of Christ. This is an important point, because *The Milkmaid* is one of the earliest paintings in which the *pointillé* appears and is held by many to be the earliest truly characteristic Vermeer. . . . There is also an atmosphere of serenity and quiet, which is an attempt to convey the emotional quality of Vermeer's paintings. Then, too, van Meegeren made a stab at rendering Vermeer's colors, his ineffable light, and at painting a background wall of the same fascinating subtlety as Vermeer's.[13]

---

[12] Quoted in Hope B. Werness, 'Han van Meegeren *fecit*', in Denis Dutton, ed., *The Forger's Art: Forgery and the Philosophy of Art*, University of California Press, 1983, p. 31.

[13] Hope B. Werness, op. cit., pp. 32–33, 35.

But in the end it just doesn't work. The forgery fails, and it is precisely a failure in style.

The light lacks the limpid and harmonious character of Vermeer's light. And although the colors are the same as those used by Vermeer—the contrast of yellow and blue, the rich brown, terracotta and green—van Meegeren's inability to duplicate Vermeer's handling of light and surface texture makes the color appear murky and lifeless. The window through which the light falls is a simplified geometrical shape which bears no resemblance to Vermeer's luminous, multipaned windows.

Most disquieting of all, perhaps, is the manner in which van Meegeren has chosen to depict this event. Bredius felt that the expressions of the figures in the painting convey emotions—"adoration, mingled with astonishment". He praised the profound understanding of the Bible story. The story of the supper at Emmaus is told in Luke 24:30–31. "When at the table with them, he took the bread and blessed, and broke it, and gave it to them. And their eyes were opened and they recognized him; and he vanished out of their sight." Given this account it is hard to see what moment van Meegeren is attempting to depict. There is a feeling of slightly awkward suspense in the painting, but to see adoration mingled with astonishment or even recognition stretches the imagination. The expressions are generally rather vague. The disciple in profile might have an adoring look, but then he might simply be attentive. At any rate the profile is not a particularly expressive view of the human face. The expressions of the other two visible faces are equally calm and inexpressive.[14]

Significantly, it seems not unreasonable to speculate that these remarks about the stylistic failures of the painting could only have been made against the background knowledge that what is being spoken of is a *forgery*. The very same painting, believed to be a genuine Vermeer, elicited from the Vermeer scholar Bredius (endorsed by others in the artistic community) a quite different description of the painting's stylistic achievements. That of course nicely confirms the thesis at hand. Stylistic features—that is, features of an individual's style—are emergent properties that apply not to an object per se but to an object conceived as a contextualized *work*, whose identity rests on further facts about its nature and provenance, including its expressive aims, the aesthetic function of its salient features, and its artistic category.

[14] Hope B. Werness, op. cit., pp. 36–37.

When Vermeer used the *pointillé* effect in *The Milkmaid* he was experimenting and innovating in an attempt to depict the way that sunlight surrounded by shadows is transformed visually into patches and spots of pure light (an effect later developed by Seurat). Van Meegeren's concern is less to give a naturalistic depiction of light as to furnish a convincing imitation of Vermeer. To explain what van Meegeren is doing, and how well he succeeds, we must make essential reference to his desire for effective deception. To explain what Vermeer is doing we must invoke his aesthetic intentions with respect to the depiction of light, perhaps with further reference to contemporary theories on the matter to which Vermeer was responding. In this regard their actions fall under quite different descriptions even though the observed outcome is similar in both cases.

The appearance of the van Meegeren having the same individual style as the Vermeer stems, not as in the case of parody because of any *make-believe* that it is in that style, but because of a *false belief* about its provenance. Forgery, unlike parody, relies for its success on mistaken facts about origin, intention, and classification. Once the facts are known it becomes increasingly difficult to ignore the actual status of a forgery. At that point different descriptions of the stylistic features seem inevitable. Of course it is always possible to regard a forgery, even when known to be a forgery, *as if* it were a work by the artist forged. In such a case we make believe that the stylistic features have the function and underlying purpose that they would have had in an original. But that does not alter the fact that they do not have those features.

At one level both the Beerbohm parody and the van Meegeren forgery do capture the style of the works they are imitating (on a feature-based definition it might seem they do so precisely). Yet at another level, where *acts* rather than *features* are highlighted, and arguably where *works* rather than *objects* are concerned, they both palpably fail. We laugh at the Beerbohm (and are meant to) but not at James himself. We censure van Meegeren but not Vermeer. The products are not equal to the originals—they cannot stand in their place, they are not part of, and do not contribute to, the oeuvre and its achievement. Of course there are all kinds of reasons for this: forgeries are a kind of dishonesty, parodies a kind of humour. But a more interesting reason is that in both cases the style has been cut away from its expressive grounding, that underlying sentiment that makes it the style it is. The resultant works categorized as actions (or sets of actions) must fall under different descriptions. In a deeper sense, then, in both the parody and forgery the imitations and the works they imitate have quite different aesthetic properties and thus are not really in the same style at all.

7.4. Conclusion

What is the moral of this story? First of all, something important has been confirmed about the identity (sameness and difference) of styles. Identity (or near identity) of surface features is not always sufficient for identity of styles. Further questions about what underlies or explains the surface features—what functions they serve, what expressive aims they realize, what kinds of works they occur in—need to be raised. To imitate a style at this deeper level it is necessary to reproduce as far as possible the conditions that explain and make sense of surface features. What has also emerged in the discussion is something of the nature of parody and forgery, viewed as specific, if problematic, forms of the imitation of style. An account is now forthcoming of the ambivalence commonly felt about parodies and forgeries, that they both do and do not succeed in reproducing the styles they seek to imitate. The surface features might be right but somehow they do not cohere; when we try to describe the artistic achievement we find we cannot do so in terms applicable to the works imitated. Yet these descriptions are essential guides to the presence of an individual style. Finally, we have identified further attitudes characteristic of responses to parody and forgery: in the former *make-believe*, in the latter *mistaken belief*. Of course to make believe that a work is in a particular style, just like falsely believing it to be by a particular artist, is no sure indication that it is in the style it seems to be in.

8

Objects of Interpretation

8.1. Preliminaries

Interpretation takes many forms and applies to many different kinds of objects. In the broadest terms, to interpret something is to make sense of it. The need to interpret arises where meaning is unclear. Interpretation is not merely understanding for I could understand your greeting 'Good morning' without needing to interpret it. I would only need to interpret it if I had reason to believe that you meant something other than a greeting.

Natural events as well as human artefacts and actions can call for interpretation. To the extent that physical symptoms, pulsating stars, earth tremors, and the movements of particles can be said to mean something, and where that meaning is unclear, they are subject to interpretation. But meaning in these cases is what H. P. Grice called 'natural meaning'[1] and the relevant mode of interpretation will be causal explanation. Although we seek to understand the natural phenomena, 'make sense' of them, our enquiry will take a different form from that demanded by puzzling artefacts. For artefacts a different mode of interpretation, and accordingly a different kind of meaning ('non-natural'), is sought.

Notoriously, of course, the appropriate mode of interpretation might itself be unclear. In medieval times natural philosophers sought to read the 'book of nature', marking no distinction between the causal and the purposive. But it is not uncommon in any case to mistake, or be unclear about, the origins of a phenomenon, natural or intentional. The flash in the sky might be a distress signal or a meteorite, the pulsating stars signs of intelligent life or just nuclear

[1] H. P. Grice, *Studies in the Way of Words*, Cambridge: Harvard University Press, 1989.

reactions. *How* we interpret is always determined by *what* we interpret. The form of interpretation is governed by the object of interpretation. These preliminary truisms indicate a number of useful premises for our discussion. The first is that interpretation can apply to, or have as its objects, natural as well as cultural phenomena, albeit on the assumption that the meaning sought in the different cases is itself different.[2] The second is that merely being a human artefact or action is not in itself sufficient to warrant interpretation. Interpretation arises only where meaning is unclear or not obvious, where there is a need to 'make sense' of something.[3] This is one basis for a distinction between interpretation and description. Third, not all interpretation follows the same procedures. Having established that a phenomenon is natural rather than intentional we seek to make sense of it through naturalistic explanation, but that would not be appropriate if we viewed the phenomenon to be of human (or intentionalistic) origin. However, even human phenomena admit of different modes of interpretation. We should not assume in advance that every human artefact or action is subject to the same methods of interpretation: a poem, a dream, eccentric behaviour at a party, evidence at a murder scene, a Rorschach blot, a quatrocentro painting, a Biblical passage, and a judgement of the Supreme Court might all be suitable objects of interpretation but the constraints on how an interpreter might proceed cannot be assumed to be the same in the different cases. Finally, given the intimate relation between the mode of interpretation and its objects, interpretation cannot proceed, certainly cannot be successful, without the prior determination of the *kind of thing* being interpreted.

8.2. Mere Things and Interpretable Objects

These points will need to be filled out in what follows. It might be thought that the first, which allows interpretation of natural as well

[2] Joseph Margolis has suggested that interpretation is limited to cultural phenomena. However, there is nothing in his view that precludes him acknowledging a sense of 'interpret' associated with 'natural meaning'; see 'Reinterpreting Interpretation', in John W. Bender and H. Gene Blocker, eds., *Contemporary Philosophy of Art: Readings in Analytic Aesthetics*, Englewood Cliffs, NJ: Prentice Hall, 1993, p. 455.
[3] The point is rightly emphasized by Annette Barnes, *On Interpretation*, Oxford: Blackwell, 1988, p. 26.

as cultural phenomena, can and should be set aside fairly quickly as undoubtedly the philosophical interest in interpretation lies in the cultural rather than natural sphere, just as the philosophical interest in meaning is in 'non-natural' not 'natural' meaning. But a moment's more reflection on the matter could I believe yield dividends later. The best way to engage the relevant issues is to broach the tricky topic of indiscernibles, which has come to play a prominent role in discussions of interpretation.

The sorts of examples that come immediately to mind are those in which purely natural phenomena have all the appearance of being cultural phenomena (we will be looking at converse cases in a moment). Knapp and Michaels, in their discussion of literary intention, famously propose the case of 'squiggles in the sand' on a beach that spell out two stanzas of a Wordsworth lyric.[4] By the time the second stanza appears, as Knapp and Michaels observe, an onlooker would be struggling to find an explanation:

> Are these marks mere accidents, produced by the mechanical operation of the waves on the sand . . . ? Or is the sea alive and striving to express its pantheistic faith? Or has Wordsworth, since his death, become a sort of genius of the shore . . . ? You might go on extending the list of explanations indefinitely, but you would find, we think, that all explanations fall into two categories. You will either be ascribing these marks to some agent capable of intentions (the living sea, the haunting Wordsworth, etc.) or you will count them as nonintentional effects of mechanical processes. . . . But in the second case—where the marks now seem to be accidents—will they still seem to be words?
>
> Clearly not. They will merely seem to *resemble* words. . . . In one case you would be amazed by the identity of the author—who would have thought that the sea can write poetry? In the other case, however, in which you accept the hypothesis of natural accident, you're amazed to discover that what you thought was poetry turns out not to be poetry at all. It isn't poetry because it isn't language; that's what it means to call it an accident.[5]

---

[4] A similar example is in Kendall Walton, *Mimesis as Make-Believe*, Cambridge: Harvard University Press, 1990, pp. 86-88.

[5] Steven Knapp and Walter Benn Michaels, 'The Impossibility of Intentionless Meaning', in Gary Iseminger, ed., *Intention & Interpretation*, Philadelphia: Temple University Press, 1992, pp. 54-55.

The example is instructive whether or not we concur with Knapp and Michaels' view of literary intention. It shows several things: first, that it makes an obvious and deep difference to how we respond to, and interpret, a phenomenon whether we think it a product of intention (and in general a cultural object) or just a natural occurrence;[6] second, that there are different levels at which 'making sense' of something occurs, from a base level which determines the kind of phenomenon at hand right up to a higher level, indisputably that of interpretation, where, on the assumption that the marks are linguistic and poetic, detailed meanings are sought; third, that mere marks or physical configurations, which might be common between a natural and cultural phenomenon, are not sufficient to determine the appropriate mode of interpretation.

A fourth lesson is perhaps the most important of all, which emphasizes just how bizarre thought-experiments of this kind are. If we had reason to believe that there was no human intention involved, we would be at a total loss to explain how a Wordsworth lyric could appear etched on a beach. However, the crucial philosophical lesson goes beyond mere puzzlement. It tells us that we must not set the puzzling case as the paradigm. It would be wrong to suppose that in every case of written language a first step of interpretation must always be to establish whether the written marks are natural phenomena or intentional signs. *That* question does not arise except in the most improbable scenarios (usually dreamt up by philosophers). We should recall that interpretation is only warranted where there is uncertainty or unclarity about meaning. In standard cases written symbols present no such unclarity so, as I shall put it, interpretation need not, and

---

[6] Walton, in contrast to Knapp and Michaels, seeks to play down the importance of intention in identifying genuine representations. It is enough, he argues, that natural objects should have the *function* of 'serving as props in games of make-believe'. He writes: 'A thing may be said to have the function of serving a certain purpose, regardless of the intentions of its maker, if things of that kind *are typically or normally meant by their makers to serve that purpose*' (Walton, *Mimesis as Make-Believe*, p. 52). But intentions cannot, I believe, be so easily dismissed in the characterization of representations. What is likely to happen in cases of 'naturally occurring stories' is that in effect the marks are intentionally *appropriated* by an observer, rather in the manner of *objet trouvé* art, and made into a representation thereby. Walton is criticized along similar lines in Jerrold Levinson, *The Pleasures of Aesthetics: Philosophical Essays*, Ithaca, NY: Cornell University Press, 1996, pp. 295-297; see also Peter Lamarque, Review of *Mimesis as Make-Believe* by Kendall Walton, *Journal of Aesthetics and Art Criticism* 49, 1991.

should not, go 'all the way down'. Interpretation begins only at the level where genuine alternative hypotheses about meaning present themselves. In the case of a normal apprehension of a Wordsworth lyric—other than as squiggles on a beach—not only do we not need to entertain the hypothesis of intentionless occurrence but there is no occasion to question whether the language is English nor indeed whether the lines are a stretch of lyric poetry (nor would a suitably informed reader doubt the authorship of Wordsworth). In standard cases of confronting a piece of verse, interpretation only becomes an issue at the level of poetic meaning, as a task for literary critics.

The idea that there should be contextually determined levels at which interpretation begins and thus that it is wrong to assume that interpretation in all cases must go all the way down to a bedrock of physical marks, sounds, or movements might seem obvious enough on reflection except that it has been denied in influential circles and its implications not addressed in important debates. Richard Rorty, for example, appeals to a reductive base of 'marks and noises' in the task of ascribing coherence to a text:

> the coherence of [a] . . . text is . . . no more than the fact that somebody has found something interesting to say about a group of marks or noises—some way of describing those marks and noises which relates them to some of the other things we are interested in talking about. (For example, we may describe a given set of marks as words of the English language, as very hard to read, as a Joyce manuscript, as worth a million dollars, as an early version of *Ulysses*, and so on.) This coherence is neither internal nor external to anything: it is just a function of what has been said so far about those marks.[7]

Rorty's discussion is part of an argument that seeks to blur two distinctions: between interpretation and use and between 'finding an object' and 'making it'. Rorty attaches priority to the second item in each case and relates them in supposing that by *using*, for example, marks and noises we thereby *make* an object of enquiry. Objects, for Rorty, like texts *par excellence*, do not present themselves for our attention with their natures already determined but allow themselves to acquire natures only relative to the malleable uses to which they are put.

---

[7] Richard Rorty, 'The Pragmatist's Progress', in Umberto Eco, *Interpretation and Overinterpretation*, Stefan Collini, ed., Cambridge: Cambridge University Press, 1992, pp. 97–99.

The extreme reductionism of Rorty's position is deeply at odds with the view developed in this chapter. However, we can acknowledge a vestigial truth in it, drawing on Rorty's intuition that the line between the predetermined nature of such objects and the properties imputed to them within interpretative practices is indeed not hard and fast. It requires a great deal of stage setting, though, which will need to be presented carefully, to establish the compatibility of that intuition with the apparently contrasting earlier point about the different starting levels of interpretation.[8]

Meanwhile, we should not leave the topic of indiscernibles, even only temporarily, without a reference to Arthur Danto whose invaluable insight has been to show that two ostensibly indiscernible objects (structures, sounds, marks) might have radically different art-related properties, indeed one being a work of art, the other a 'mere real thing'.[9] Significantly, for Danto, what makes the difference between a work of art and its non-art counterpart is an interpretation: 'Indiscernible objects become quite different and distinct works of art by dint of distinct and different interpretations, so I shall think of interpretations as functions which transform material objects into works of art.'[10] Danto's best known example illustrates this well: the nine indistinguishable canvases consisting of unbroken red which, because of different origins, grounded in different interpretations, support distinct works (the Isrealites Crossing the Red Sea, Kierkegaard's Mood, Red Table Cloth, etc.).[11] However, there is a subtle shift here in the notion of 'interpretation', for what makes the red canvases different works are not interpretations offered by art appreciators, third parties, but interpretations originating in the artists themselves. Appreciators are called upon not to interpret 'mere real things', i.e. red canvases, but canvases-with-a-title, objects which have already been 'interpreted', in a different sense, by the artists.

---

[8] For discussion of Rorty's views on this matter, see Peter Lamarque, 'Marks and Noises and Interpretations', *Semiotica* 108–1/2, 1996: 163–175; and *Fictional Points of View*, Ithaca, NY: Cornell University Press, 1996.

[9] The *locus classicus* is Danto, *The Transfiguration of the Commonplace*, Cambridge: Harvard University Press, 1981.

[10] Arthur Danto, *The Philosophical Disenfranchisement of Art*, New York: Columbia University Press, 1986, p. 39.

[11] Danto, *Transfiguration of the Commonplace*, p. 1ff.

It might seem that Danto is committed to a view not unlike Rorty's, which locates the starting point of interpretation at a basic physical level. But that is an illusion based on a blurring of the two notions of interpretation. Danto himself appears to caution against a Rorty-type view: 'Not every artwork . . . is a transform through an interpretation of an *objet trouvé* and with most works of art it takes some trouble to imagine counterparts to them . . . which are not works of art.' 'Still,' he goes on, 'it is always possible, for any artwork you choose, to imagine something indiscernible from it but caused in a way which renders a transformative interpretation inapplicable.'[12] This latter claim recalls Knapp and Michaels' point about the Wordsworthian squiggles, in supposing that we can imagine contexts, however bizarre, in which configurations indistinguishable from, say, Rembrandt's *Night Watch* do not even count as a painting. To that I would reply, yes, perhaps we can, with a suitably ingenious background story, but that fact plays no part in our efforts to interpret the *Night Watch*, when we have no call to entertain deviant causal origins. Nor does it play any part in Rembrandt's own creative process or in an explanation of that process. From the point of view of both an appreciator's and the artist's interpretation, the thought-experiment is idle.

8.3. Works, Kinds and Categories

With this preliminary scene setting in mind, we can consolidate some of the previous remarks and point towards more substantive theses about interpretation. A central thesis, arising out of what has gone before, is this: in standard cases, at least in the sphere of art, interpretation begins at the level of *works*. This thesis will be refined and developed as we proceed, with particular attention to the notion of a 'work'. When we turn attention to a poem, play, or novel we do not begin a process of interpretation by asking about marks or noises or what language is being used or whether this is a human artefact or a quirk of nature. Interpretation gets under way, indeed is made possible, in the light of prior knowledge about what kind of thing, broadly

[12] Danto, *Philosophical Disenfranchisement of Art*, p. 39.

conceived, the object of interpretation is. The enabling assumption is that the work under investigation belongs in a recognizable generic category.[13] There are, of course, non-standard cases and I shall return to them.

A similar point can be made about any of the arts. In musical interpretation we do not begin, again in standard cases, with bare sounds but with musical works bearing familiar features—structure, harmony, instrumentation, key, musical genre—recognition of which is a starting point not a terminus of interpretation. In painting or sculpture we do not need to hypothesize whether the paint arrived on the canvas or the marble found its configuration through purely natural processes or through human intention. Once again in standard cases we assume, prior to interpretation, that these are works (paintings and sculptures) produced intentionally, conforming to broadly defined conventions in a human practice, which will reward a search for further meaning.

It is not just works of art that come to interpreters in recognizable categories. The cases listed earlier, such as the evidence at a murder scene, the Rorschach blot, the Biblical passage, the Supreme Court ruling, become objects of interpretation *under those descriptions*. Interpretation in those cases does not begin further back; in fact it can only proceed in a constructive way once the point of the interpretation is understood.

Of course not all cases are 'standard' in the way described but we must not take the non-standard as the norm for a theory of interpretation. We have looked at some non-standard cases already, like the fantastic scenario of natural occurrences having the appearance of well-formed sentences in a language. But perhaps the more interesting non-standard cases are those involving a choice not between the natural and the intentional but between different categories of the intentional.

Let us begin with linguistic examples. Suppose we come across sets of symbols that we know to be linguistic—products of intentional activity, possessing a meaning, part of a sign system—but have no idea what they mean. Not only do we not know the specific

---

[13] For the relevant idea of a 'category' of art, see Kendall Walton, 'Categories of Art', *Philosophical Review* 79, 1970: pp. 334–367.

meaning but we have no idea of the *kind* of linguistic act that gave rise to them, so no generic category (mere doodle, communicative message, poem, letter, prayer) into which to locate the signs and thereby focus our interpretation. But these rare cases do not pose a challenge to the view advanced. Interpretation is needed—it is like Quinean radical interpretation—and it does indeed have to start further back. However, we have at least *some* categories to constrain us, 'human', 'linguistic', 'intentional'. What is notable is how different such 'radical' cases are from linguistic (far less literary) interpretation normally understood and how difficult it would be to proceed in these conditions.

Suppose, in another example, we do know the language but nothing of the context in which the linguistic signs were produced. We have a mere text or set of sentences. Although competence in the language would allow us to assign a meaning to the sentences, merely understanding the sentences in virtue of understanding the language does not yet count as *interpretation*.[14] To interpret the sentences we need to grasp their point. But how could we do that in the extraordinary circumstance of knowing nothing about the context in which they were produced? After all, even in the case of enigmatic sentences found on a scrap of paper in a bottle adrift on the ocean, a reasonable surmise would be that this is an attempt at communication, a *message*, and as not all texts are messages that already puts a constraint on how to make sense of it.[15] Can interpretation proceed with genuinely contextless texts? Perhaps, in a sense, it can, or at least an attempt at interpretation can be made. What seems clear is that simply *using* the texts, in Rortyan fashion, as we see fit, will make no contribution to the interpretative effort. The focus for interpretation would be towards reconstructing the context in order to establish the kind of text it is, the function it seeks to fulfil.

As this focus is different from that of standard interpretation it might be helpful to make explicit a distinction between the former as *generic interpretation* and the latter, the standard kind, as *meaning-determining interpretation*. Normally generic categorization is taken for granted—we know that the object of our interpretative efforts is a

---

[14] Here I agree with Gregory Currie, 'Work and Text', *Mind* 100, 1991, p. 339.
[15] See Lamarque, *Fictional Points of View*, p. 171.

metaphor, a poem, a political speech, a philosophical argument—and the search for meaning is guided by that starting point. Where we do not have this knowledge our options for meaning-determination are severely restricted. But consider how rare it is to be confronted with a bare set of sentences apparently without context or purpose. Far from being a paradigm of interpretation, as might be imagined by reductive poststructuralists, these non-standard cases of free-floating texts render interpretation virtually impossible.

Generic interpretation, or something like it, as we saw in discussing Danto's examples, is normally carried out by artists, not appreciators. It is the artist who determines the kind of object created. Only occasionally does an appreciator need to interpret at a more basic level as a preliminary to determining meaning. Where a new category of art or style or genre is created—conceptual art, Cubism, performance art, twelve-tone music—and where that category is not fully assimilated into the critical idiom, a first step in interpretation might be the search for an appropriate generic categorization (which in fact might not be available until a later time[16]). But once the conventions of an artistic genre are established their recognition ceases to be a step in interpretation but becomes a background condition for interpretation. In some exceptional circumstances, such as Palaeolithic artefacts (cave paintings, Stonehenge) the principal interpretative issue is forced to remain at the generic level, and will do so until it is resolved what *kind* of works these are.

It might be objected that the distinction between generic and meaning-determining interpretation is not sharp and that finding the correct category for a work will always be a central part of the interpretative process. There is no clear distinction, so the objection runs, between generic and more fine-grained categorization, in the sense that there is no difference in kind between classifying a work as a poem, a speech, or a philosophical treatise, and classifying it as, say, satirical, electioneering, or literary-cum-philosophical. The latter like the former are still categorizations but they are clearly part of meaning-determination and could be further refined as interpretation proceeds. I concede some of the force of this objection but reply that

---

[16] See Jerrold Levinson, *The Pleasures of Aesthetics: Philosophical Essays*, Ithaca, NY: Cornell University Press, 1996, p. 265.

a precise definition of the generic is not needed for my purposes. The key point I hope to establish is simply this: a prerequisite for successful interpretation is knowing the kind of object under interpretation even though in some, non-standard, cases another mode of interpretation (which I have called the generic) is involved in determining what that kind is.

8.4. Interpretative Practices

Behind this point, and, I believe, further substantiating it, is the thought that generic differences (between kinds of objects) relate to differences in practices and that conventions of interpretation, like the objects of interpretation themselves, are practice-dependent. The idea here is the familiar one that procedures for interpretation vary—albeit under a general heading 'making sense of something'—according to the expectations associated with the object of enquiry. Literary interpretation is a different practice from philosophical interpretation, which in turn is different from the interpretation of dreams under psychoanalysis or the interpretation of conversation according to Gricean conversational implicature or indeed the interpretation of evidence at a murder scene.

Jerrold Levinson has pointed to two broad modes of interpretation, which he calls the determinative (or DM = 'does mean') mode and the exploratory (or CM = 'could mean') mode:

> I suggest that behind DM interpreting, in any sphere, lies a spirit that might be qualified as scientific, practical, and knowledge-seeking. Part and parcel of this spirit is a desire for understanding, explanation, discovery, or communication. . . . Behind CM interpreting, by contrast, lies a spirit that might be qualified as ludic, liberational, freedom-seeking. Central to this spirit is a desire for cognitive play, much like that which Kant located at the core of the aesthetic, without a concern for cognitive payoff of a concrete sort, a fascination with possibilities of understanding, explanation, discovery or communication, but no care for their actuality.[17]

---

[17] Jerrold Levinson, 'Two Notions of Interpretation', in Arto Haapala and Ossi Naukkarinen, eds., *Interpretation and Its Boundaries*, Helsinki: Helsinki University Press, 1999, p. 6.

He goes on to show how each of DM and CM interpreting will be more or less appropriate depending on what is being interpreted. In his own examples, a clue in a crossword puzzle, an X-ray or radiograph, a puzzling situation in real life, or a joke more naturally invite DM interpreting, while Rorschach testing, ambiguous figures, and moves in chess invite the CM mode.[18] Levinson rightly points out that CM enquiry is often a useful preliminary to final DM deliverances. The distinction is helpful in sorting broad classes of interpretative practices, but it is possible, as noted, to identify more specific procedures within each class, say, the philosophical, the literary, the historical, the legal.

It is the specific practices of interpretation that lead to another key thesis, closely connected to the first: modes of interpretation and objects of interpretation are, in standard cases, deeply interlinked such that the practices that make the objects possible (in a sense to be explained) also define the conventions of interpretation that apply to them. This interlinking means that the interpretative processes within a practice do not merely identify properties within objects but go some way towards constituting those properties. Thus, in the case of art an object's possessing aesthetic properties, be they expressive, evaluative, or even representational, is made possible only in virtue of the existence of a practice which determines a mode of appreciating such objects.[19] Without conventions underlying what *counts as*, say, expressiveness in music or thematic content in literature, there would be no such properties. These conventions both constitute the properties and dictate the correct mode of their apprehension (through, for example, interpretation).

To marshal further support for this thesis, in conjunction with the first, we must look more closely at the types of 'objects' involved in interpretative practices, especially the notion of a 'work'. As both theses imply that it is works, not texts, that are the (standard)

---

[18] In fact I am inclined to think that Levinson is wrong about the ambiguous figures for those that are deliberately designed as such—the duck/rabbit, the old woman/young woman—have determinate alternatives which should be recognized if the figures are to be correctly understood. We shall be returning later to such figures and their interpretation.

[19] The relativity of modes of appreciation to practices or institutions is a theme in Stein Haugom Olsen, *The End of Literary Theory*, Cambridge: Cambridge University Press, 1987, to which I am much indebted.

objects of interpretation, this latter distinction should be addressed first.

8.5. Text and Work

A text, as I understand it, is an ordered set of sentence-types individuated at least partly by semantic and syntactic properties.[20] Two texts are identical if they have the same semantic and syntactic properties, are in the same language, and consist of the same word-types and sentence-types ordered in the same way.

A literary work, on the other hand, although it is, in Margolis's terms, 'embodied'[21] in a text, is not identical with a text, nor does it possess the same identity conditions. One and the same text might embody two distinct works, perhaps in the manner of Pierre Menard's *Quixote*,[22] or embody no work at all. Literary works are cultural objects, dependent on a practice governed by social conventions concerning the production and reception of texts. As they owe their nature and existence to the practice, should the practice cease (the conventions be lost) literary works themselves would go out of existence, even though the texts remain. Literary works are, like all works of art, Intentional[23] objects, not just in the sense of having content or meaning but as being, broadly conceived, 'objects of thought'. Correspondingly, they possess Intentional properties, like expressive or representational properties, which can be discerned only by those sufficiently well informed about the cultural practice in which the works are embedded. I am inclined also to follow Levinson in supposing that literary works, again like other artworks, are essentially bound to their origins so that a literary work, in his terms, is a

---

[20] See Currie, 'Work and Text', p. 325.
[21] e.g. Joseph Margolis, *Art and Philosophy: Conceptual Issues in Aesthetics*, Atlantic Highlands: Humanities Press, 1980, p. 39f.
[22] Jorge Luis Borges, 'Pierre Menard, Author of the *Quixote*', in *Labyrinths*, Harmondsworth: Penguin, 1971. For discussion, see Chapter 4 'Distinctness and Indiscernibility in the Allographic Arts'.
[23] I follow Margolis (e.g. Joseph Margolis, *What, After All, Is a Work of Art?* University Park: Pennsylvania University Press, 1999, p. 55) in capitalizing the first letter of 'Intentionality' in order to mark a term of art, which I use in essentially the same way as Margolis.

text-as-indicated-in-a-context,[24] although there is room for debate about how finely that context should be specified.[25]

Confusions over terminology bedevil discussions of interpretation so let me emphasize that the use of the terms 'text' and 'work' as just defined is not universally adopted. A similar, but not identical, distinction between 'text' and 'work' was popularized by Roland Barthes in an essay from the 1960s,[26] although his inclination to give priority to text over work (a position followed by Rorty) is the opposite of the stance taken here. Also for Barthes a work is 'concrete', 'occupying a portion of book-space (in a library, for example)' whereas a Text is 'a methodological field';[27] in contrast, in my own usage, both works and texts are abstract entities. What occupies space on a shelf might be an instance or copy of a work but cannot be the work itself for to destroy that copy would not be to destroy the work. Barthes's 'Text' is more like my own 'text', yet perhaps more indeterminate, for a Text is an instance of *écriture* (writing in general) and it is hard to see what semantic constraints operate on it, there being virtually no limits on what a Barthian Text can mean, nor what its identity conditions are.

Joseph Margolis on occasion uses the term 'text' much as I use 'work', although he does not restrict texts to linguistic items and expands the term to encompass any referent of an interpretation,[28] sometimes using the expression 'text or artwork'[29] as if these were interchangeable. Crucially, though, and centrally to his theory, he holds that 'the individuation and identity of artworks are hardly the same as the individuation and identity of the natural or linguistic entities upon which they depend (and which they incorporate)'.[30] So something like the distinction between text and work, as I draw

---

[24] Levinson, *Pleasures of Aesthetics*, p. 195.

[25] In particular it is a matter of controversy whether it is necessary for a work to have just that author, or in general for a work of art to be created by that particular person. See Chapter 3 'Work and Object' and Peter Lamarque, *The Philosophy of Literature*, Oxford: Blackwell, 2009, pp. 79–80.

[26] Roland Barthes, 'From Work to Text', in *Textual Strategies: Perspectives in Post-Structuralist Criticism*, translated and edited by Josué V. Harari, Ithaca, NY: Cornell University Press, 1979.

[27] Barthes, 'From Work to Text', p. 74; Barthes capitalizes the first letter of 'Text'.

[28] Margolis, 'Reinterpreting Interpretation', p. 456.   [29] Ibid., p. 459.

[30] Margolis, *What, After All, Is a Work of Art?*, p. 89.

it, is implied by Margolis, indeed is pivotal to his view, even if his terminology is different.

The text/work distinction is an instance of a broader distinction running across all the arts and indeed other cultural objects, between that which possesses only physical (or 'natural') properties and that which is 'practice-dependent', cultural, and Intentional. In the other arts the distinction arises between, say, sounds (or sound-types) and musical works, canvas-plus-pigment and paintings, pieces of marble and sculptures. The notion is well entrenched in aesthetics. Examples outside aesthetics might include the distinction between bits of printed paper and banknotes, a leather sphere and a soccer ball, a flesh and blood human being and a monarch. In each case we might say that the latter item is 'embodied' in the former but not identical with it, that the latter but not the former depends on cultural factors or human practices, that in different worlds the former could exist unchanged without the latter.

Not all cultural entities call for interpretation (banknotes, monarchs, and sports equipment at best yield to a straightforward DM mode of interpreting, in Levinson's terms), but many such entities, artworks in particular, are the very paradigm objects of interpretation. As Intentional objects they possess meaning, as artworks they can also be expressive, representational, and bearers of other aesthetic properties. But what exactly is the relation between an interpretation and a cultural object of this kind? Does an interpretation bring to light a meaning (or other aesthetic property) that is already part of the nature of the object or does it in some way help constitute that nature? The question is one of the most vexed and difficult in discussions of objects of interpretation and merits careful examination.

8.6. Imputationalism

Both Margolis and Michael Krausz have defended versions of 'imputationalism', the view, in Krausz's words, that 'an interpretation may constitute or impute features of its object-of-interpretation'.[31] This

---

[31] Michael Krausz, *Rightness and Reasons: Interpretation in Cultural Practices*, Ithaca, NY: Cornell University Press, 1993, p. 67. Page references in parenthesis are to this work.

view is contrasted with 'nonimputationalism' according to which 'the character of the object-of-interpretation is understood to be fully autonomous or independent of interpretation as such' (67). Krausz contrasts 'radical' with 'moderate' imputationalism. While the former holds that 'any particular interpretation on a given occasion may fully constitute its object-of-interpretation', the latter allows that 'a given object-of-interpretation may be constituted within webs of interpretation' (94). The radical version postulates a one-to-one relation between interpretations and objects-of-interpretation and thus implies what Krausz calls 'singularism', the thesis that 'for any object-of-interpretation, there is one and only one ideally admissible interpretation of it' (42). Singularism, it should be noted, does not imply radical imputationalism or even the moderate kind, as it does not require that objects-of-interpretation be constituted through interpretation. Krausz himself favours moderate imputationalism and also 'multiplism', the thesis that 'for some object-of-interpretation, there is more than one ideally admissible interpretation of it' (42), while again recognizing that 'multiplism does not require imputational interpretation' (93).

One issue that immediately arises is whether, with the resources he allows himself, Krausz can avoid radical imputationalism and in consequence singularism.[32] The very term 'object-of-interpretation', coined by Krausz,[33] seems question-begging in favour of imputationalism for the hyphens appear to link object and interpretation conceptually: no interpretation, no object-of-interpretation. But if there is this conceptual link, then what is to stop different interpretations generating different objects-of-interpretation?

Krausz runs through a number of examples to illustrate how interpretative imputation works. One of these is the case of the ambiguous line-drawing that can be seen either as a vase or as two facing heads. Interpretation in this case, for Krausz, amounts to assigning salience to different features of the drawing, thus yielding the vase

---

[32] This is a charge pressed by Robert Stecker in 'The Constructivist's Dilemma', *Journal of Aesthetics and Art Criticism* 55:1, 1997: 43–52 and 'The Wrong Reasons: A Response to Michael Krausz', *Journal of Aesthetics and Art Criticism* 55:4, 1997.

[33] Krautz's aim (op. cit., p. 39, fn. 2) in coining this 'term of art' is 'to signal that no particular ontological construal of that which is interpreted is thereby implied. It remains ontologically neutral'.

or the faces. He writes: 'the interpretation—face or vase—prompts one to impute salience to certain features of the presented configuration, which in turn confirms the propriety of interpreting the configuration as a face or vase.' (68) He goes on: 'whether we accept one interpretation over another is not so much a matter of the fit between an interpretation and an autonomous or practice-independent object-of-interpretation, but is rather a matter of the fit between an interpretation and the object-of-interpretation *construed in the light of the interpretation in question*' (68, Krausz's italics). So now we must ask: how many objects-of-interpretation are there in the example? No doubt Krausz would want to reply 'one', in line with his moderate imputationalism, but isn't the answer 'two' forced upon him? 'Interpretations and their objects-of-interpretation', he tells us, 'are taken as packages' (69). Yet as there are clearly two packages here are there not correspondingly two objects-of-interpretation, namely something like 'the figure-seen-as-a-vase' and 'the figure-seen-as-faces'? Further evidence that these two items are distinct is that they might well possess different aesthetic properties: the former could be graceful, curvaceous, elegant, the latter aggressive, confrontational, menacing.

All our intuitions, though, suggest that there is only one object here, the figure, and two interpretations. But has Krausz the resources in his theory to allow this? I think not. Certainly he talks, in the earlier quoted passage, of the 'presented configuration' and it might seem that that is the single object we need. However, the configuration, consisting of the mere lines on the page, is not an 'object-of-interpretation' in Krausz's sense, for it is not an 'intentional object, so construed within a pertinent practice' (120), nor 'partly a function of . . . [an] interpretation' (68). Indeed the line-drawing seems to be just the kind of autonomous and practice-independent entity that is contrasted with an object-of-interpretation. In our terms, it is the equivalent of a 'text' not a 'work'.

Another example of Krausz's fares no better than the vase/face drawing in saving him from a commitment to radical imputationalism. He discusses different interpretations of Van Gogh's *Potato Eaters*, formalist, psychological, Marxist, feminist, under which strikingly different features are made salient. In each case the 'interpretation imputes an object-of-interpretation' (73). A tension emerges, however, in the very account Krausz gives of how many objects-of-interpretation are involved:

> Despite the differences in their imputing interpretations, the resulting objects-of-interpretation . . . are sufficiently similar for the three interpretations to compete. Of course, were one to pluralize the object-of-interpretation—that is, argue that each interpretation is really about another object-of-interpretation, whatever their relation to the physical canvas—the interpretations could not compete. But it seems perfectly natural to say that the formalist and the psychological interpretations do address an object-of-interpretation sufficiently common for the interpretations to compete. (74)

The first sentence clearly implies that there is more than one object-of-interpretation in the Van Gogh example; apart from the fact that the plural is actually used, the objects-of-interpretation could not be described as 'similar' unless they were distinct. The second sentence spells out the consequences of supposing there is more than one object-of-interpretation. The third sentence suggests that these consequences are undesirable and proposes that we postulate a single object-of-interpretation after all. Just to confuse matters further, the implication in that sentence is that this single object-of-interpretation is not identical to any of the earlier three but is a *fourth* one sharing common features, presumably not all, with the others. The result is a dramatic case of multiplying objects-of-interpretation beyond necessity. We should also note, as in the earlier example, that Krausz is not able to fall back on the 'physical canvas' (mentioned in the passage) as the unifying object-of-interpretation for, like the line-drawing, it is not an object-of-interpretation at all, in Krausz's terms.

The problem for Krausz is that he is trying to get by with too few resources, allowing himself nothing more than bare physical objects (configurations, canvases), on the one hand, and objects-of-interpretation, tightly tied to particular interpretations, on the other. What I suggest is needed is a threefold distinction between physical object, work (or cultural artefact), and interpretation.[34]

---

[34] Paul Thom also offers a threefold distinction, between 'interpretation', 'object-as-represented', and 'further object' which is similar to, but not identical with, the one proposed; see Paul Thom, *Making Sense: A Theory of Interpretation,* Lanham, MD: Rowman & Littlefield, 2000. For a discussion, and criticism, of Thom's schema, see Peter Lamarque,

8.7. A Threefold Distinction

More specifically, we need to acknowledge three elements in the interpretative process. The first element involves the physical properties of the item being interpreted: the configuration of the lines in the drawing, the paint and canvas in the Van Gogh, the tones, pitches, and tempo prescribed by musical notation, the sets of sentences comprising a text, the paper, ink, and design of the banknote. Krausz recognizes this element. When he writes that '[i]mputational interpretation involves selecting features of the presented materials with which to fashion an object-of-interpretation' (94), the 'presented materials' are precisely those that belong at this level.

The second element is what I have called a *work*, as defined earlier, or more generally a cultural artefact. We noted that the distinction between text and work has analogues outside art, as in that between the printed paper and the banknote that it embodies, so we should not think of 'work' as restricted to works of art. Works, I have been urging, are the proper objects of interpretation (in cultural, not natural, applications). Some of their identity conditions have emerged already: they are Intentional objects, linked essentially to their origins; they are not numerically identical to their material embodiment (the latter could exist without the former); and their continued existence depends on the existence of the practices within which they acquire their identity. But are they 'objects-of-interpretation' in Krausz's sense? In other words, do they owe their existence and nature to an interpretation or 'web of interpretations'?

The matter is complex but I am inclined to reply in the negative. Certainly they are objects of interpretation (without the hyphens), in the sense that they are the kinds of entities that conventionally invite (and, in the case of works of art, reward) interpretation. Also, as Intentional objects, they are 'objects of thought', not natural kinds, and their continued existence, as the kinds of entities they are, is dependent on the responses of people who reflect on them. But, crucially, they come into being, through an act of *creation* (by an artist, say), not

---

Review of Paul Thom, *Making Sense: A Theory of Interpretation* and Wolfgang Iser, *The Range of Interpretation*, British Journal of Aesthetics, 43, 2003, pp. 80–84.

essentially through an act of *interpretation*. Being an Intentional object might imply, in Margolis's terms, being 'intrinsically interpretable'[35] but it does not imply being created through interpretation. Here we can recall again the discussion of Danto. Some works are created in effect by having an interpretation imposed, by an artist, on an object. This is the 'transformative interpretation' of which Danto speaks. The paradigm case is the *objet trouvé* transformed into a work of art. But not all works come into being that way. Admittedly most artists will have a conception of the work they seek to realize, and that conception is something like an interpretation. But there is an intuitive difference between realizing a conception and supplying an interpretation, certainly in an age where interpretation is viewed as the prerogative of the critic. The artist does have a role in what I earlier called 'generic interpretation', the locating of an object in a *category*, as a *kind* of thing. Although subsequent appreciators might appropriate a work into a category not envisaged by the artist, the original intended category will usually retain a normative authority. Also artists often become interpreters of their own work, in a more substantive 'meaning-determining' way, but that activity is separate from the creation of the work, and arguably an artist's own meaning-determining interpretations have no more authority than, and are subject to the same justificatory criteria as, those of other appreciators.

Perhaps we can conclude this, taking a cautious line: that the coming into being of a work is not dependent on an interpretation other than that which might inform an artist's act of creation. It is a further question whether the continued existence of a work depends on subsequent interpretation. Because works (like all cultural artefacts) are grounded in practices their survival depends on that of the practices themselves and thus minimally the works must continue to 'secure uptake' within an appropriate community of practitioners, and be *recognized*, or recognizable, as the works they are. It is not obvious, though, that this requires *interpretation* in any robust sense.

Our third element covers interpretation in precisely that robust sense that seems to underlie the notion of an object-of-interpretation. At this

[35] Margolis, *What, After All, Is a Work of Art?*, p. 98.

level we move from objects of interpretation (without the hyphens) to Krauszian objects-of-interpretation but we no longer have the concerns about multiplying objects-of-interpretation that seemed to complicate Krausz's theory. We can readily accept that interpretations are productive of entities, their own intentional objects, and we might even think of objects-of-interpretation (in Krausz's sense) as more like products-of-interpretation. Thus, the vase-interpretation produces an intentional object, *the-figure-seen-as-a-vase*, which is distinct from another intentional object, *the-figure-seen-as-two-faces*. Other objects-of-interpretation might include performances of musical works; or productions of plays, say, Olivier's *Hamlet* or Branagh's *Hamlet*; or readings of poems, like (in Krausz's example, p. 77ff.) F. W. Bateson's and Cleanth Brooks's readings of Wordsworth's Lucy Poem; or interpretations of paintings, such as the various approaches to *The Potato Eaters*. Productions or readings or pictorial interpretations, as objects-of-interpretation, have a life of their own. They can be referred to, individuated, compared, evaluated, and have their properties described; they are genuine, if Intentional, individuals. They are distinct from the works to which they refer. Interestingly, they too can become objects of interpretation, as well as objects-of-interpretation, subject to discussion and open to misunderstanding.

Returning to the face/vase drawing, what is the *work* in that case, as distinct from the object-of-interpretation? The answer is the *vase/face ambiguous representation* (designed to fall into that category). It is not identical with the lines on the page, nor is it identical with *the-figure-seen-as-a-vase* or *the-figure-seen-as-two-faces*. If we ask how the two objects-of-interpretation relate to the *work* we can say they both stand for legitimate aspects of the work, in line with conventions governing representations of this kind. An interpretation that generates as an object-of-interpretation *the-figure-seen-as-an-elephant* will be dismissed as fanciful, only tenuously, at best, related to the work, and not sanctioned by the rules of the game.

Working with a threefold distinction between object, work, and object-of-interpretation puts 'imputationalism' in a new light. For now, on the account given, it seems that imputationalism—the view that 'an interpretation may constitute or impute features of its object-of-interpretation'—turns out to be not just true but tautological, even in the 'radical' version that postulates a one-to-one pairing of interpretations and objects-of-interpretation. And if we substitute 'work' for 'object-of-interpretation' in the thesis of 'non-imputationalism', that 'the character of the object-of-interpretation is understood to be fully autonomous or independent of interpretation as such', then it seems that in a slightly qualified form (as in the earlier remarks about an artist's creation) this thesis is true of works.

Krausz might respond in a number of ways to what no doubt he would view as an unduly precipitous dismissal of imputationalism. Thus, he might insist that he has not done away with my central notion of a *work*, lodged between text and object-of-interpretation, for it is already implicit in his notion of the 'unicity' of objects-of-interpretation (120ff.).[36] This 'unicity' or 'commonality', he explains, 'is a function of consensual agreement by pertinent practitioners' (121). He goes on: 'When interpretations impute different properties, they must impute a sufficiently large number of properties in common to warrant the agreement that they are addressing a sufficiently common object-of-interpretation' (ibid.). An obvious thought, then, would be to identify the *work* with this core of common (meaning-based) properties. However, both Krausz and Margolis[37] deny that the common properties themselves must remain constant through the 'career' of an artwork. This leaves them with seemingly insuperable difficulties in identifying an object-of-interpretation that, as it were, rises above the class of all other objects-of-interpretation and stands out as the (intentional) object *that is being interpreted*. In other words they do not seem to have the resources to acknowledge what I have called the *work*.

Margolis suggests that we might look to 'the relative constancy of . . . [the artwork's] physical properties' and 'the norms of interpretive practice'[38] to provide a reasonably stable *denotatum* but insists that the question of how we 'referentially fix' or individuate artworks is

---

[36] I believe the term 'unicity' originated with Margolis who describes it as 'the sense of the integral career of an artwork or cultural entity . . . in virtue of which we are able to assign a relatively stable number and nature to such *denotata*, though their natures change' (Margolis, *What, After All, Is a Work of Art?* pp. 90–91).
[37] Ibid., p. 91. [38] Ibid., p. 91.

separate from the question whether they have fixed natures (which he denies).[39] Krausz suggests that 'objects-of-interpretation are co-created by text and interpreter'.[40] Curiously neither alludes to the artist or the creative act that brings the artefact into being. Yet surely that is the foundation for the identity of works. A work is of necessity that (admittedly Intentional) entity brought into being by the intentional act (or set of acts) of a person, at a time, in a context.[41]

Levinson takes a robust view of this kind and thinks that it sees off the Krauszian problems about constructed objects-of-interpretation:

> There is no difficulty whatsoever with saying that there is just one poem . . . , though there are perhaps numerous interpretations or readings of it—so long as we recognize that the poem is not, of course, the brute text that it comprises but rather the text poetically projected in a specific context anchored to a particular person, time, and place. That anchoring, together with the text's complete orthography, is enough to fix a literary work's identity for all critical intents and purposes, and so there is no need to bring meanings, conceptual complexes, or interpretive guises into it.[42]

This, I believe, is broadly correct but I don't think it is enough to dismiss the interesting core of truth (beyond the merely trivial truth mentioned above) in imputationalism. That is what I shall now try to bring to light using the resources on offer.

Although Krausz struggles with unicity in finding something equivalent to a work, he might well agree with Margolis that it is one thing to 'referentially fix' an artwork, another to determine its nature. Indeed Levinson continues the passage just quoted: 'A poem as I suggest we ontologically construe it will, to be sure, *generate* meanings and conceptual structures under interpretation . . . ; but the poem is not to be *identified*, even partially, with such meanings, concepts, thoughts, or views' (ibid.). But the question inevitably arises: what meaning-based properties 'generated' by a work genuinely belong to it and which are 'imputed' to it by an interpreter? The force of imputationalism is to insist that there is no clear distinction between

---

[39] Margolis, 'Reinterpreting Interpretation', p. 465.
[40] Michael Krausz, 'Rightness and Reasons: A Reply to Stecker', *Journal of Aesthetics and Art Criticism* 55:4, 1997, p. 416.
[41] cf. Robert Stecker, *Artworks: Definition, Meaning, Value*, University Park: Pennsylvania State University Press, 1997, p. 244.
[42] Levinson, *Pleasures of Aesthetics*, p. 197.

what 'belongs' to a work and what is 'imputed' to it, for it is precisely the imputed properties that comprise the changing nature of the work over time. Whatever other doubts there might be about imputationalism, scepticism about a distinction of this kind is what makes, I believe, some version of imputationalism worth holding on to. Showing why takes us back to the close interlinking between interpretation and objects of interpretation within practices, which was one of the theses outlined earlier.

8.8. Properties 'In' and 'Imputed to' an Object of Interpretation

A good place to start is with views that see a clear line between 'in' and 'imputed to'. Robert Stecker, for example, sees a dilemma in the imputationalist's position:

> The problem is to understand how making a claim about an object, even an object-of-interpretation, can give it a property claimed for it. . . . If the claim is true, the object already has the property. If it is false, the object does not have the property. If it is neither true nor false, then what difference can be made by saying that the object has the property, or even by telling a plausible story according to which the object has the property? Before an interpretation is offered, an object may well be indeterminate with respect to a property, but if it is, then such saying or storytelling will not make it determinate, though it may get people to think of the object as determinate.[43]

Krausz's response to Stecker is this: 'The non-radical imputationalist proposal does not urge that the text first does not have a given property and then gets it. Rather, it urges that, upon appropriate imputation, a more determinate object-of-interpretation arises.'[44] But the response is unsatisfactory in a number of respects. First, it makes reference to 'the text' which, in both Krausz's and our own view, is no more than a set of sentences. But a text on its own, independent of context and use, has

---

[43] Stecker, 'The Constructivist's Dilemma', p. 50.
[44] Krausz, 'Rightness and Reasons: A Reply to Stecker', *Journal of Aesthetics and Art Criticism* 55:4, 1997, p. 417.

OBJECTS OF INTERPRETATION 177

no properties of the kind identified through interpretation, although it might have semantic and syntactic properties. Second, Krausz's claim that a 'more determinate object-of-interpretation arises' opens him to the charge of 'pluralizing' (his own term), in other words generating a new and distinct object, thereby contradicting the thesis of imputationalism, which requires that the nature of *one and the same object* (the 'unicitous' object) is determined by imputed interpretations. If Stecker's dilemma is to be met, the solution must lie in the peculiar nature of the objects under interpretation, along with the properties attributed to them, and the form that interpretation takes.

The first move (emphasized in Margolis's somewhat sketchy reply to Stecker[45]) is to note again the Intentional nature of works. With non-intentional objects, such as ordinary medium-sized physical objects, the line between the properties they possess inherently and those that are 'imposed on' them is *reasonably* clear, even if the former are not always known or fully understood.[46] But Intentional objects are *essentially* relational, in the sense that they depend for their existence on human thought-processes and practices. It is not just incidental *how they are taken* but determinative of their natures. Interestingly, Stecker concedes what he calls a 'trivial' version of constructivism (imputationalism): 'When we give a new interpretation of a work, we are thinking of it in a new way and, in virtue of this, the work acquires the property of being thought of in this new way.'[47] He dismisses this as too slight to appeal to full-blooded constructivists and thus 'trivial', I take it, partly because it is all too easy to acquire relational properties of this kind and partly because such properties can have little to do with the *nature* of the thing that acquires them.[48] However, in the context of Intentional objects it would be wrong to dismiss

---

[45] Margolis, *What, After All, Is a Work of Art?* p. 100.
[46] Of course the wider debate in metaphysics between realism and anti-realism shows that even this claim is far from uncontroversial. But any weakening of the distinction between 'inherent in' and 'imposed on' in other contexts is only going to aid an argument that seeks to weaken the distinction in the cultural sphere.
[47] Stecker, 'The Constructivist's Dilemma', p. 44.
[48] Peter Geach famously described the changes that acquiring such relational properties brought about 'mere Cambridge changes', in contrast to genuine changes. The allusion is to philosophers like Russell and McTaggart who held that an object changes just to the extent that a predicate truly applied to it at one time does not apply at another time. (See Geach, *God and the Soul*, New York: Schocken Books, 1969.)

all such relational properties either as trivial or as extraneous to the nature of the objects, for Intentional properties, which characterize Intentional objects, are themselves relational. Aesthetic properties, for example, including expressive, evaluative, and representational properties, are also relational, resting on the responses of qualified perceivers (see Chapter 5 'Aesthetic Essentialism'). Of course merely being thought about or perceived by a person is not sufficient to bring about a meaningful change in a work. But attributing aesthetic properties to a work or, to take Krausz's paradigm of interpretation, assigning salience to features of it, might do so, if constrained, again in Krausz's terms, by the 'consensual agreement by pertinent practitioners'.

Stecker might reply to this that the relational properties of works that matter (*par excellence* its aesthetic properties) will be those that the work has, as it were, at the outset and to the extent that interpretation brings them to light it *discovers* rather than *imputes* them. This at least is the line taken by Levinson:

> It is not *artworks* that, in the crucial sense, change over time, it is rather *us*. We think more, experience more, create more—as a result are able to find more in artworks than we could previously. But these works are what they are, and remain, from the art-content point of view, what they always were. It is not their content that changes over time, but only our access to the full extent of that content, in virtue of our and the world's subsequent evolution. The latent and unnoticed must not be confused with the newly acquired and superadded; later history may *bring out* what *was* in earlier art, but it does not progressively *bring about* that there is *now* more in it.[49]

While I am sympathetic to Levinson's attempt to defend a fairly substantial notion of a work (and work-content) independent of subsequent interpretation I think he is hard put to confine all relevant interpretative properties within the work at the moment of its initial realization, and I do not think that he establishes an unbridgeable line between 'inherent in' and 'imputed to'. He admits, for example, that what he calls 'future-oriented artistic attributes', such as 'influentiality . . . , seminality, importance, pivotalness, revolutionariness,

---

[49] Levinson, *Music, Art & Metaphysics: Essays in Philosophical Aesthetics*, Ithaca: Cornell University Press, 1990, pp. 180–181.

fecundity'⁵⁰ are difficult to accommodate to his view. He toys with the idea that instead of *making* the influentiality, future events rather *disclose* what is already present in a work. But it seems highly implausible (if not metaphysically suspect) to suppose that a relation with future contingencies can be part of a work's very nature at the time of its inception. His alternative is to exclude future-oriented attributes from his general thesis, separating out these attributes from what he calls *art-character*, the latter 'compris[ing] *all* of what an artwork means or conveys' (211). The concession, though small, is significant for the imputationalist, for here is a class of familiar properties of works—influence, fecundity, etc.—that are central to the art-critical enterprise and are acknowledged by the staunchest anti-imputationalist to be acquired by works in the course of their 'careers', as products of interpretation.

There are other examples as well. Levinson makes a strong case for showing that later works in an artist's oeuvre may 'augment or affect the *meaning* of earlier ones'.⁵¹ Admittedly he explains this by suggesting that an artist's oeuvre can count as a single work, 'a single artistic act' (245). Given that an artist's output might span fifty or more years, possibly including radical personal and cultural changes, the postulation of a single act could only be a theoretician's fiction. Nor could Levinson assert the theory of just some but not all oeuvres, for it is hard to see how there could be any non-arbitrary or non-question-begging criteria for demarcating the two classes. Nevertheless, proffered explanation apart, the idea itself seems to be plausible, and its implications are congenial to the imputationalist cause in allowing us to accept that an object-of-interpretation (an early work) can change its nature in the light of later interpretation, that it is 'incomplete' and seemingly 'indeterminate' in its original form.

Another artistic property that causes difficulty for Levinson is that of style, particularly in the case of works that pioneer a new style or genre category that 'arguably does not fully exist until other works are subsequently created that serve to stake out the boundaries of the category involved'.⁵² He gives the examples of film noir, twelve

⁵⁰ Ibid., p. 208.   ⁵¹ Levinson, *Pleasures of Aesthetics*, p. 245; his italics.
⁵² Levinson, *Pleasures of Aesthetics*, p. 265.

tone music, sculptural assemblage, and mannerist painting. Until the arrival of later works, which develop or consolidate the style, it is not just that we do not *know* what style the pioneering work belongs in but that the style simply does not exist at the time the work was created. This was the kind of case considered earlier to show that interpretation sometimes cannot take the generic or categorial level for granted. Levinson offers a number of ways round the problem but one of them takes us back to Krausz and the idea of making an object-of-interpretation more determinate:

> one might grant that art content can become more *determinate* over time, through gradual emergence in concrete fashion of a work's historically correct categories of interpretation, while insisting on a real difference between that kind of focusing and wholesale alteration in art content. (ibid., Levinson's italics)

The final clause is a gesture to distance the view from imputationalism but the use of 'wholesale' suggests nervousness on that score. Can imputationalism be defended in terms of the indeterminacy of works or their added determinacy over time through interpretation? Prima facie this does not look especially promising for the imputationalist. For one thing it suggests a very linear view of the development of a work as if it consisted in the gradual accumulation of more determinate features; yet it seems to be compatible with imputationalism that a work should lose features as well as gain them. There is also Stecker's objection to the effect that if a work is inherently indeterminate in certain specifics (like the number of Lady Macbeth's children), then no amount of subsequent interpretation is going to change that fact, unless presumably the interpretation shows that what initially seemed to be an indeterminacy was in fact no such thing. Stecker's point, though, faces the obvious charge of begging the question.

8.9. Works and Indeterminacy

The idea of indeterminacy is worth pursuing, I suggest, for it takes us right back to our earlier discussion about the relation of interpretation and particular kinds of objects. Not all cultural objects have indeterminacy. Margolis is not right to suppose that indeterminacy is an inevitable concomitant of Intentionality.[53] Having the value of five cents is an Intentional property but it is perfectly determinate that a nickel possesses that property. In fact we can say that it is an *intrinsic* property of the *nickel* (not the piece of metal) that it has the value five cents. Similarly, within a game of soccer kicking the ball between the goal posts, while in play and without incurring a penalty, is an action that has the determinate Intentional property of scoring a goal. Determinacies of a similar kind are to be found in all cultural objects, including art. That *The Potato Eaters* depicts human beings sitting round a table is a determinate, Intentional, fact about a work. Of course it is true that the mere physical object embodying the nickel, just like the mere action of kicking the ball or the canvas per se of the picture, does not *independently of a complex Intentional structure* have the cited Intentional property. It is only given a rule-governed practice that the Intentional properties are made possible. But that does not impugn their determinacy. Indeed it might be one reason why we are not called upon to *interpret* a nickel or a soccer goal or the ostensible subject of a painting.

But is the value of the nickel 'in' the coin or 'imputed to' it? The answer seems to be *both*, once we acknowledge the special status of the Intentional object. Having the value of five cents becomes an *intrinsic* quality of the 'work' (the coin) in virtue of having the value *imputed to* it within the practice or 'institution'. This is a clear-cut case where the very conventions of the practice dictate what it is to have a particular quality and also how we are to identify that quality (recognizing salient features of the metal's design and appearance).

What about properties of works of art that are subject to interpretation, which do seem to have indeterminacies, making the question of what is 'in' and 'imputed to' even more pressing? Consider the example of Dostoevsky's *Crime and Punishment* where a long-standing critical crux has been trying to make sense of the conflicting motives behind Raskolnikov's crime. Numerous psychological and political

---

[53] He makes this supposition when he claims: 'Intentional attributes are not determinate . . . when compared with what is usually taken to be the determinate nature of physical or non-Intentional attributes' (Margolis, *What, After All, Is a Work of Art?* p. 58) or that 'Intentional properties are determinable . . . but not antecedently determinate' (p. 73).

interpretations have been offered and it is sometimes even suggested that the novel fails for not presenting a unified character. Here is one, not untypical, reading:

> The whole point of the book lies precisely in the process by which Raskolnikov moves from one explanation of the crime to another, and in so doing discovers the truth about the nature of the deed he has committed. . . . Why, for example, does Dostoevsky begin his narrative just a day before the actual commission of the crime, and convey Raskolnikov's *conscious* motivation in a series of flashbacks? One reason, of course, is to obtain the brilliant effect of dramatic irony at the close of Part I. For the entire process of reasoning that leads to Raskolnikov's theory of the altruistic Utilitarian crime is only explained in detail in the tavern-scene, where Raskolnikov hears his very own theory discussed by another student and a young officer; and this scene is the last important one before the crime is committed. . . . Temporarily, the tavern-scene and the murder itself are at the very opposite ends of a single time-sequence; but they are telescoped together deftly by Dostoevsky's narrative technique. . . . The purpose of [the] juxtaposition and telescoping of the time-sequence is obviously to undermine Raskolnikov's *conscious* motivation for the reader. The hypnotic hysteria in which he kills the old pawnbroker could not reveal more clearly, in an objective, dramatic fashion, that Raskolnikov's crime is not being committed according to his altruistic, Utilitarian theory. . . . Each step, then, in the *backward* process of revealing Raskolnikov's conscious, altruistic motive . . . is accompanied by another episode moving *forward* in time that undercuts it.[54]

A number of observations can be made about this passage. First, it is paradigmatically a *literary* interpretation, proceeding on the assumption that the work is *literary* (and fictional), not, for example, a work of biography or empirical psychology. The ways that thematic developments are connected to individual episodes and narrative techniques are features unique to the practice of literary reading. Second, the reading assigns salience, to use Krausz's term, to narrative elements—time-sequencing, flashbacks, juxtapositioning of scenes—to help establish interpretative points. Third, the property attributed (in this passage by implication) to Raskolnikov as a coherent, unified character, albeit with tension in his motivation, is a property (broadly

---

[54] Joseph Frank, 'The World of Raskolnikov', in *Crime and Punishment*, by Feodor Dostoevsky, edited by George Gibian, New York: W.W. Norton & Co., 1975, pp. 567–569.

an aesthetic property) that again emerges only *through an interpretation* or *under a description*. It makes no sense to say that the *text* possesses that property, any more than it makes sense to say that the text is aesthetically coherent. This is the vestigial truth behind Rorty's position.

Are the saliences described in the passage 'in' the work, from its very inception, or 'imputed to' it in an interpretation? Again, as with the case of the nickel—although here with the added background of indeterminacy—the answer is *both*. Every element in a work, given the kind of work it is, has potential saliency but the aesthetic function of elements like the time-sequences and flashbacks is determinable only relative to an interpretation. Margolis is right that at this level the insistence on bivalent truth-values—either truth or falsity of interpretative statements—is gratuitous. Instead we look at consequences: what follows from assigning salience in this way, of making these connections? Does a more or a less coherent work emerge? Does it draw together more elements or does it make some unaccountable? These questions themselves are already grounded in a conception of a literary work. The search for thematic unity, coherence of characterization, connectedness of episode, symbolic or figurative meaning, narrative functions fulfilling aesthetic ends, is at the heart of the practice of literary interpretation. It is not a merely contingent fact that works of literature should yield such a search, for literary works are defined within a practice that dictates the expectation of this reward. We must conclude, then, that so close is the linking of work and mode of interpretation that there is an inevitable blurring of what is 'in' a work, or part of its inherent nature, and what is 'imputed to' it through interpretation. That is the insight of imputationalism.

8.10. A Sketch of Two Models for the 'Incompleteness' of Works

Let me end by sketching two further kinds of models for explaining the indeterminacy of works: that of fictional characters, whose properties are incomplete, and that of metaphors, whose meanings are open-ended. They are not incompatible.

There are several parallels between the ontological status of fictional characters and that of literary works. Both, arguably, are abstract entities, created artefacts, cultural objects, dependent on originating texts, sustained in existence by Intentional acts and attitudes, and subject to interpretation.[55] They are also both 'incomplete', if only in the formal sense that there are some predicates which can justifiably neither be asserted nor denied of them. There are many 'facts' about fictional characters (including the hoary example of whether there is a mole on Sherlock Holmes's back) that remain permanently indeterminate, there being no principles of inference which warrant acceptance or rejection.[56] On the other hand there are many psychological or motivational properties, which, although indeterminate, in the sense that they are not explicitly ascribed to a character in the narrative, nevertheless appear warranted *relative to an interpretation*, or under a perspective, which itself might fall within consensually defensible bounds;[57] Raskolnikov's motives might be one example of such a property.

Often when fictional works are dramatized for stage or film, decisions have to be made about details, physical as well as psychological, which are indeterminate in the original narrative work. The same is true for pictorial renderings. What we have then in the case of fictional characters are objects-of-interpretation (in the sense of products-of-interpretation) comparable to those associated with interpreted works (like Branagh's *Hamlet*). The question arises whether such an object-of-interpretation retains the identity of the character or creates a new character. On reflection, it turns out that character-identity is no less elusive than work-identity. The necessity of origins, at whatever strength, holds for both, but on the matter of *content* it seems reasonable to suppose there is some degree of tolerance in property-ascription. Thus, in the case of fictional characters, we can say (1) that some more or less stable *core* of characteristics must be

[55] For an illuminating account of these and other parallels, see Amie Thomasson, *Fiction and Metaphysics*, Cambridge: Cambridge University Press, 1999, p. 139ff. Also, Chapter 9, below.
[56] Currie labels as 'narrative interpretation' the investigation of what is 'true in' a story and recognizes that 'one kind of interpretive disagreement is about whether some aspect of the story is indeterminate or not' (Currie, 1993, p. 415, n. 5).
[57] Lamarque, *Fictional Points of View*, p. 64.

shared by representations of the *same character*[58] but (2) that there is room for alternative supplementations of the character in drawings or other works that add new properties (under suitable constraints of consistency, coherence, and the like) without jeopardizing the basic identity. In the case of minor unspecified indeterminacies, particularly trivial details (like the presence of moles, the number of hairs on the head, and so on), it will often *make no difference* what form the supplementation takes—imaginatively, pictorially, conceptually—as long as it coheres with the core properties.

If this is a plausible story—albeit very roughly sketched—for the identity of fictional characters and if characters share important ontological features with works then the parallel offers further support to the imputationalist case about properties imputed to works. One other factor should be introduced here, namely that character-identity is often thought of, or treated as, *interest-relative* (see Chapter 9 'How to Create a Fictional Character'). In other words rather than thinking there are absolute criteria for sameness of character perhaps we need to take into account the interests behind our talk of characters. From the point of view of literary history, for example, fairly loose criteria might be acceptable, whereby the Faust-character or the Christ-character can be seen to be cropping up in different guises across time and even cultures. But a careful student of Thomas Mann might insist on the uniqueness of Faust in Mann's treatment and its deep divergences from that of, say, Christopher Marlowe. So from the perspective of literary history, the Goethe and Marlowe characters are the same; from that of work analysis they are different. Again there might be a fruitful analogy between characters and works with regard to such interest-relative identity and this analogy again might be congenial to the imputationalists.

The other model is that of metaphor, where the indeterminacy is not that of incompleteness or 'missing facts' but of meaning. There are accounts of the semantics of metaphor that hold that any meanings discoverable in a metaphor must already be present within the literal meanings of the component terms, making the process of

[58] Ibid., p. 49.

interpretation that of eliciting these semantic features somewhat in the manner of disambiguation.[59] Such a view, which might parallel extreme 'realist' theories of cultural objects, is open to many objections.[60] But a more familiar dispute among theorists of metaphor is between those who ascribe some special metaphorical meaning or content to a metaphor, a product of interaction, transference, comparison, or other mechanisms, and those, usually followers of Donald Davidson, who reject the idea of metaphorical meaning altogether. In favour of the former it can be said that they acknowledge the structured and rule-governed nature of metaphor and seek to show in systematic ways how metaphorical meaning is generated and can be recovered; the anti-content school acknowledges the more unruly aspects of metaphor, its appeal to the imagination, its non-reliance on propositional content, its causal powers. Perhaps there are echoes of Levinson's DM and CM interpreting in these positions.

But the real lessons from metaphor that I believe bear on literary (or artistic) interpretation lie in a conception of metaphor that brings together the rule-governed and the imaginative aspects. Rather than thinking of metaphor as a kind of assertion, or vehicle of truth, or propositional content, it is more illuminating to think of it as an act of a certain kind, embedded in a practice. The act is not assertion but exhortation, an encouragement to pursue comparisons imaginatively, conceptually, propositionally, or imagistically. There might be context-specific aims in any given metaphorical utterance—to convey a thought, to say something true, to advance an argument—but the core of a metaphor has the force more of an invitation to *do* something than to *believe* something.

Clearly much more needs to be said to flesh out the theory[61] but whether or not the theory is sustainable about metaphor it yields an instructive model for literature and art. The idea that literary (and artistic) works also invite a kind of imaginative exploration, at least in relation to those aspects which are indeterminate and thus subject to

---

[59] Perhaps the clearest account of such a view is in L. J. Cohen, 'The Semantics of Metaphor', in A. Ortony, ed., *Metaphor and Thought*, Cambridge: Cambridge University Press, 1979.

[60] Peter Lamarque and Stein Haugom Olsen, *Truth, Fiction, and Literature: A Philosophical Perspective*, Oxford: Clarendon Press, 1994, pp. 354–355.

[61] See Lamarque and Olsen, *Truth, Fiction, and Literature*, Chapter 14.

interpretation, takes us away from the paradigm of semantic content. Artistic works, unlike certain other cultural objects (coins, judicial rulings), are precisely the kind of objects that invite an imaginative and exploratory response, the seeking of new saliences, the forging of connections. That is part of their practice-dependent nature, just as it is with metaphor. This is not to say that every imaginative response is warranted by the work—some will perhaps create their own objects-of-interpretation with a separate identity. But it shows that what is *in* the work, as part of its nature, given to it by the very practice that makes it a work, is an invitation to *impute* things to it. If interpretation is making sense of something then we should not lose sight of the creative connotation of 'making'.

9

How to Create a Fictional Character

9.1. The Issues

If you hold an eliminativist view of fictional characters, in other words if you hold that fictional characters have no reality whatsoever and that apparent reference to them can be eliminated, then presumably you hold that no-one does or ever could create a fictional character. I take this to be one implication of the eliminativist theories of philosophers like Bertrand Russell, Nelson Goodman, and Kendall Walton. Of course these philosophers need not deny that authors engage in creativity. According to the different theory on offer, it could be admitted that authors create things like sentences, descriptions, stories, Pickwick-pictures, props in games of make-believe. But it could not be admitted that they create fictional characters, because, on these views, there are no such things.

Even among theorists who do admit some kind of being to fictional characters, it is not universally agreed that fictional characters are created. On Meinongian theories, for example, which see fictional characters as instances of non-existent objects, two factors count against the characters being created: the first is that they cannot be brought into existence (a requirement, it would seem, for creation[1]) because they do not exist, they are *non-existent* objects, the second is that as non-existent *objects* they are eternal and timeless. There are other views that take fictional characters to be timeless, and thus uncreated: the view that they are unactualized possibilities, for example, or the view that they

---

[1] In fact not everyone does accept this point about creation; it is explicitly rejected, for example, by Harry Deutsch in 'The Creation Problem', *Topoi* 10, 1991, pp. 209–225, as part of an argument for a modified Platonism about fictional characters.

are kinds or sets of properties. However, a different strand of realist theories of fictional characters, originating with Kripke,[2] and developed recently by Nathan Salmon[3] and Amie Thomasson,[4] does allow for the literal creation of characters, as abstract artefacts. The idea is that fictional characters are not just created entities but essentially created, coming into existence only as a result of the mental and physical acts of an author and enjoying the same kind of existence as other abstract artefacts such as theories, laws, governments, and literary works.

I will not be summarizing the now substantial literature on the ontology of fiction but I do want to address some of the intriguing and difficult metaphysical questions that arise. To grasp the nature of creativity in fiction we need a reasonably secure conception of fictional characters themselves and their identity conditions. After all, if I create a fictional character and it turns out—as it inevitably will—to have features in common with other fictional characters, just how creative have I been? Have I produced something new or just a variant on something old? Did Shakespeare *create* his central characters or just rework those of his sources? How similar can characters become yet remain distinct? How, for that matter, do you count characters? If an author writes 'A crowd of a hundred people gathered outside', and says nothing more about the crowd, has he created a hundred characters? It might seem obvious that he has not but it is not clear exactly why not. What conditions must obtain for a character to be introduced in a narrative?

But I don't want to get stuck on the metaphysics of fiction, interesting as it is. There are clearly literary considerations, too, about the creation of fictional characters. The literary approach can seem curiously at odds with the metaphysical enterprise and each can have the effect of undermining the other. Character has been an unpopular and discredited conception for a generation of literary critics, and even for a short period, that of the Nouveau Roman of the 1950s and 1960s, among authors themselves. Why is that? To what extent does this reaction depend on a certain conception of character and indeed of character-based criticism? There seems to be an irresolvable tension

---

[2] Saul Kripke, *Reference and Existence: The John Locke Lectures for 1973* (unpublished).
[3] Nathan Salmon, 'Nonexistence', *Nous* 32:3, 1998, pp. 277–319.
[4] Amie Thomasson, *Fiction and Metaphysics*, Cambridge: Cambridge University Press, 1999.

between realist assumptions about characters as persons-in-fictional-worlds and literary assumptions about characters fulfilling narrative roles. Yet there is no metaphysical reason why these two aspects shouldn't co-exist. More on that later.

9.2. Metaphysics and Character-Identity

Let us turn first to the ontological question of character creation. How important is it to preserve the intuition that fictional characters are literally created? Certainly we talk as if they were. We attribute part of the genius of Dickens to the creation of, say, Nicholas Nickleby and David Copperfield or the genius of P. G. Wodehouse to the creation of Jeeves and Bertie Wooster. But everyone, eliminativists, Meinongians, possibilists, have their own story about how to accommodate this intuition of creativeness so the artefactualists cannot win the argument on this alone. We need to probe deeper to see what hangs on the issue, clarifying, among other things, exactly what a story-teller needs to do—on any account—to bring a character to the light of day.

Let me lay out my own metaphysical stall then I will elaborate and set it in context. In the expression 'fictional character' it is helpful to assign different roles to the two terms. Not all characters are fictional and character, in its general sense, is an abstract concept, designating a type, a more or less specific set of characteristics realizable in individuals. To say that a character is *fictional* is not to say something about its existence but something about its origins, namely, that it originates in fiction, in a narrative of a certain kind.[5]

It can be misleading, I believe, to attend too early in a metaphysical enquiry to the complex fictional characters of the nineteenth-century realist novel, where a remarkable experiment took place in trying to depict in immense detail the inner life and motivation of fictional personages rather than merely their outward action and speech. We get a quite different perspective if we focus instead, at least to begin with, on, say, the simple characters of the folktale. In his classic

---

[5] For more details on this view of fictional characters, see my *Fictional Points of View*, Ithaca, NY: Cornell University Press, 1996, esp. Chapter 2, and also Peter Lamarque and Stein Haugom Olsen, *Truth, Fiction, and Literature*, Oxford: Clarendon Press, 1994, Chapter 4.

study of the fairy tale, Vladimir Propp outlines the distinct roles that characters, or character-types, perform in different tales. Take, for example, the villain who enters at a set point in the narrative (never right at the beginning but usually, as Propp describes it, when an 'interdiction is violated'). 'His role', Propp writes, 'is to disrupt the peace of a happy family, to cause some form of misfortune, damage, or harm. The villain(s) may be a dragon, a devil, bandits, a witch, or a stepmother, etc.'.[6] With characters of this simplicity, interesting and important observations arise about character-identity. There is clearly a sense in which *the same character*, e.g. the villain, occurs in different stories, even though taking different forms. So to add to my first two suggestions, namely that fictional characters (a) are types, and (b) originate in fictional narratives, I add a third, that (c) they possess an identity which is, as I shall put it, interest-relative.

9.3. Interest-Relative Identity

Let me develop this latter idea a bit further. The suggestion is that there is no absolute answer to the question of whether two fictional characters are the same, only an answer relative to the discourse-based interests of those raising the question. Relative to a study of the morphology of the folktale, there are a comparatively small number of recurrent characters—the villain, the donor, the magical helper, the dispatcher, the hero, the false hero, etc. These crop up over and over and it is important to identify the same character, or role, in different manifestations. However, relative to a study of individual stories, different characters fulfilling these roles can be identified and distinguished—the dragon, the witch, the stepmother, and so forth.

One way of looking at this interest-relativity of character-identity is by pairing sets of essential and inessential, or contingent, properties. For the morphologist, interested in identifying the same 'villain' character across works, being a villain is deemed an essential property, while being a dragon or witch inessential. On the other hand, for those concerned with individual story analysis, or story identity, both being

---

[6] Vladimir Propp, *Morphology of the Folktale*, Austin, TX: University of Texas Press, 2nd edition, 1968, p. 27.

a villain and being a dragon become essential while no doubt some more minor points of detail remain merely contingent. It should not be assumed that a norm of character-identity is that maximal type to which all relevant narrative detail is deemed essential. Take sequences of novels—the Holmes stories, the Palliser novels, the Jeeves stories. It seems entirely acceptable to say that the very same Holmes or the very same Jeeves would have existed even if only one novel had been written in each series. It is not essential to Jeeves that he perform all the rescue missions described in the total oeuvre, so not all of the properties of the Jeeves-character are essential to it.

Yet another way of viewing the matter might be in terms of the nesting of character-types. Each character—and this holds for characters of any degree of complexity—can be broken down into character-types from the most general to the highly specific. Judgements of sameness or difference will be relative to the appropriate level of specificity in this hierarchy of types. Relative to literary history, very broad identity claims might be made about characters: to take the familiar example, the same Dr Faustus crops up in works by Christopher Marlowe, Johann Wolfgang von Goethe, and Thomas Mann, where the essential identity criteria reside in a small cluster of Faust-characteristics.[7] But relative to an analysis of the individual works (and authors) the characters differ as the identity conditions become more demanding and the set of essential characteristics expands. Again, the amateur detective character-type is exemplified by Sherlock Holmes, Hercule Poirot, Miss Marple, and Lord Peter Wimsey. Are they the same character? Relative to some interests, yes; relative to most, no, because the set of essential characteristics is normally taken to be fuller than just the single trope of inspired-amateur-detective. The same goes for the character-type unhappily-married-adulterous-and-doomed-woman: Emma Bovary, Thérèse Raquin, and Anna Karenina are the same type (thus the same character) under a broad cultural perspective, different of course under other, more refined, perspectives.

Note that the four (fictional) amateur detectives or indeed the three (fictional) doomed women do not stand to the character-type in the way that, say, Tony Blair, John Major, and Margaret Thatcher stand

---

[7] The case is discussed in my *Fictional Points of View*, p. 49; see also, Nicholas Wolterstorff, *Works and Worlds of Art*, Oxford: Clarendon Press, 1980, pp. 148–149.

to the type British Prime Minister. For the latter, unlike the former, are *instances* of the type and do not owe their identity to it. We could identify the three individuals independently of the type they instantiate and the type is not essential to them (which is not to say that they might not instantiate some types, like human being, essentially). It would be absurd to suppose that under any description, or relative to any interests, these three people are the same, even though the same description truly applies to them. But it is quite different for characters, at least on the hypothesis that they are abstract entities. Although characters per se can have instances in the real world, *fictional* characters cannot because even were someone to instantiate the Emma Bovary type in the real world she would not *be* Emma Bovary, lacking the fictional origins. We might of course describe her as *an* Emma Bovary, using the name as a general term. In any case, if Emma Bovary, as a character, is a type no human being could be Emma Bovary because no human being can be (as opposed to instantiate) a type.

Now we can return to the creation question. A number of significant points begin to emerge. First there is an inverse relation between the generality of character specification and the creativity attributable to the story-teller. The unadorned characters *amateur detective, adulterous wife*, or plain *villain* are not the products of creative acts. The reason is that at this level of generality the characters or types are well known. No special imaginative effort is required to bring the concepts to mind. We would call these stock or stereotypical characters should they be introduced in a narrative with only limited further specification. If creativity is linked to specificity then specificity must be linked to narrativity for it is only through narrative detail that characterization can develop. So we have a nice dovetailing of creativity with narrativity.[8]

There is obviously a literary angle on the relation between creation and narration, to which I will return, but there is a metaphysical angle as well. I suggested earlier that what makes a character fictional is its being anchored to a fictional narrative in which it originates. One metaphysical motivation for this is what might be called the

---

[8] For an account of narrative, see my 'Narrative and Invention', in Cristopher Nash, ed., *Narrative in Culture*, London: Routledge, 1990, and 'On Not Expecting Too Much from Narrative', *Mind & Language*, 19, 2004, pp. 393–408. In the present context very little theoretical sophistication is presupposed in the concept as used. Narrative, in this sense, implies any 'story-telling', that is, tensed discourse where events are suitably related.

Levinson point, after Jerrold Levinson's well-known discussion of the ontology of musical works.[9] There is a telling, though not entirely straightforward, analogy between the ontology of music and the ontology of fictional characters.

Levinson sought to resist a certain kind of Platonism about music, defended by philosophers like Nicholas Wolterstorff, Peter Kivy, and Julian Dodd, which sees musical works as eternal sound-structures discovered but not created by composers.[10] Levinson offers an impassioned defence of the importance of creation in art, and in musical composition in particular. 'There is a special aura', he writes, 'that envelops composers, as well as other artists, because we think of them as true creators.'[11] But the argument from creativity, as Levinson realizes, is not decisive against musical Platonism and it cannot be decisive either against Meinongians or possibilists or those who see characters merely as eternal types. After all, those philosophers who deny that fictional characters are created have, as I suggested earlier, their own accounts of creativity. Wolterstorff, for example, proposes that although authors merely 'select', but do not create, the 'person-kinds' (as he puts it) that are the components of fictional worlds, perhaps 'a person-kind is not properly called a "character" until some work has been composed of whose world it is a component'.[12] Terence Parsons takes a similar line, suggesting that while characters cannot be brought into existence, 'we might say, I suppose, that the author makes them *fictional* objects, and that they were not fictional objects before the creative act'.[13] The arguments seem ad hoc, resting on decisions about how we might use the terms 'character' and 'fictional'. For the artefactualist, taking the Levinson line, fictional characters are *essentially* created. Their origins in intentional acts are *necessary* to their identity. Although I think that is right it needs careful refinement, especially if we accept the interest-relativity of characters.

---

[9] See Jerrold Levinson, 'What a Musical Work Is', and 'What a Musical Work Is, Again', in *Music, Art & Metaphysics*, Ithaca, NY: Cornell University Press, 1990.

[10] Wolterstorff, *Works and Worlds of Art*, pp. 62–73 and Peter Kivy, 'Platonism in Music: Another Kind of Defense', *American Philosophical Quarterly* 24, 1987, pp. 245–252; and Julian Dodd, *Works of Music: An Essay in Ontology*, Oxford: Oxford University Press, 2007. For criticisms of Dodd and a defence of Levinson, see Robert Howell, 'Types, Indicated and Initiated', *British Journal of Aesthetics* 42, 2002, pp. 104–127.

[11] 'What a Musical Work Is', p. 67.

[12] Nicholas Wolterstorff, *Works and Worlds of Art*, pp. 144–145.

[13] Terence Parsons, *Nonexistent Objects*, New Haven: Yale University Press, 1980, p. 188.

This is where Levinson's second argument against musical Platonism comes in. The argument, I think, applies only obliquely, but intriguingly, to fictions. This is the argument that musical works must be essentially grounded in a historical context (indeed to a specific creative act), as two identical sound-structures 'selected' at different times would have different aesthetic and artistic properties. Here is an example from Levinson: 'Brahms's Piano Sonata op. 2 (1852), an early work, is strongly *Liszt-influenced*, as any perceptive listener could discern. However, a work identical with it in sound-structure, but written by Beethoven, could hardly have had the property of being Liszt-influenced. And it would have had a visionary quality that Brahms's piece does not have.'[14] Levinson invites us to conclude that the Piano Sonata is *essentially* by Brahms and an identical sound-structure written by Beethoven would be a different work in virtue of having different properties.

How might that apply in the fiction case? Well, suppose that the character of Bertie Wooster miraculously manifested itself, via a suitable narrative, in the early nineteenth century. Would we say that the character had different properties in this context—given its different historical and contextual relations—and thus was not strictly the *same character* as appeared in the twentieth century? But we have seen that that question—about identity—admits of no absolute answer and will rest partially on the degree of specificity demanded of the characterization. There seems no reason why the type *feckless upper-middle-class man of leisure* should not exist in the 1820s, indeed there are many instances of it. Even the more specific type *feckless upper-middle-class man of leisure named Bertie Wooster, with a butler named Jeeves, a best friend Bingo Little, and an elderly aunt of whom he is terrified* does not yet depend on a precise historical or cultural context. In fact there is no reason why nearly all the internal, or constitutive, properties of Bertie Wooster, up to quite a high level of specificity, should not have been characterized a hundred years before P. G. Wodehouse wrote his novels. Of course whether they could have been characterized in the Middle Ages, say, is more problematic given some of the historically determined features of the characterization. But could not a futuristic Wooster narrative have appeared in the 1420s?

[14] 'What a Musical Work Is', pp. 70–71.

The crucial application of the Levinson test lies not with the internal, or what Parsons calls 'nuclear', properties of a character, in other words properties like *being a man of leisure, being a detective, being a villain*, but with the external, relational or 'extra-nuclear' properties. Extra-nuclear properties are those that apply literally to a character, as an abstract entity. Nuclear properties might serve to constitute or delineate a character but they cannot literally be *possessed* by a character for an abstract entity cannot be a man or a villain. *Being essentially created* is an extra-nuclear property, as is *being created in the twentieth century* or *being conceived by P. G. Wodehouse*.

What Levinson's argument forces us to address is the question whether, or to what extent, character-identity rests with extra-nuclear as well as nuclear properties. For Levinson facts about origin affect musical work-identity because they affect aesthetic or artistic properties. Undoubtedly something similar is true for literary works. The Bertie Wooster novels would not be the same *works*, i.e. would not retain their work-identity, even as word-for-word facsimiles, if they had appeared in the Middle Ages or even just a hundred years earlier.[15] As with Pierre Menard's *Don Quixote* the works would have, for example, different stylistic and meaning properties given the different cultural settings. At least some of these differences will manifest themselves as differences in extra-nuclear properties of the Wooster-character itself. For does not the character possess culture-specific properties: being a humorous comment on post-First World War upper-middle-class life, expressing nostalgia for an age of wealth and leisure, being a satire on class attitudes in 1920s Britain, and so on. To the extent that these properties are held to be essential to the Wooster-character then that character could not be identical with the nineteenth-century manifestation—and Levinson's argument would go through for fiction.

But should extra-nuclear properties count in the identity conditions of characters? Of course some will be shared by all fictional characters: including, if it is one of their properties, being created. But what about historically specific properties? Again much will depend on the level of specificity. Many different characters can parody the follies of 1920s England or symbolize decadence or call to mind a lost age.

[15] For more on indiscernibles and work-identity, see Chapters 3, 4, and 8.

The question really becomes whether narrative-specific extra-nuclear properties are in the identity conditions of fictional characters. But there will be no general answer to that given the interest-relativity of character-identity. In other words it will depend on what demands are placed on the delineation of a character and what ends are thereby served. The matter soon becomes an issue for the literary critic for whom, as we shall see, literary properties of characters assume more importance than they do on metaphysical accounts. But we should note that if characters can be distinct merely in virtue of narrative-specific properties, i.e. appearing in this narrative rather than that, then borrowed and barely altered characters become new characters (in their new setting) and the creation of characters, the bringing of new ones into existence, is all too easily achieved.

We cannot quite leave the matter there for it brings us back once again to the relation between fictional characters and fictional narratives. Nearly everyone, from eliminativists to artefactualists, recognizes some connection between characters and narratives. For eliminativists there is nothing more to characters than the narratives that describe them, for Meinongians and possibilists characters have their essential being independently of narratives but narratives are the principal means by which we come to know them. For artefactualists, like Salmon and Thomasson, fictional characters are created through the creation of narratives. As Thomasson sees it, the existence of the former is dependent on the continued existence of the latter, with the implication that characters can go out of existence when their grounding narratives are lost or there are no longer competent readers for them or no appropriate memories of them.[16]

Although I think fictional characters are dependent on narratives for their existence—in much the way that Thomasson describes—the closeness of the dependence will vary according to the specificity of the characterization. *Fictional* characters (although not characters per se) are, I suggest, what Levinson has called 'initiated types', that is, those that 'begin to exist only when they are initiated by an intentional human act of some kind'.[17] However, I do not share Thomasson's view that they are essentially tied to, or (in her terms) 'rigidly dependent

---

[16] Amie L. Thomasson, *Fiction and Metaphysics*, pp. 10–11.
[17] 'What a Musical Work Is', p. 81.

on', a particular author and a particular narrative. It seems to me that it is not essential to the Sherlock Holmes-character that it was created by Conan Doyle and certainly not essential to the villain-character in the Russian folktales that it was the product of a particular individual's intentional acts. But the matter gets complicated, again, as we reach more and more specific levels of characterization or, as I have put it, place increasingly demanding conditions on character-identity. The historical and cultural conditions in which a character is initiated are probably always essential to it, even in simple cases like the folktale villain; I say 'probably' because we might have to admit a level of abstraction where a stock character is truly universal or ahistorical. As we refine the conditions and identify a character more and more closely with a particular literary work we will anchor it more and more tightly to the facts of its origin.

Could Emma Bovary have originated in a different novel? Even a novel by a different author? By Zola, perhaps, Baudelaire, Proust, even? There is no determinate answer because there are no determinate, non-relative criteria for the identity of the Emma Bovary-character. Note that this position can be maintained even if you hold, as seems plausible, the necessity of origins for (some) literary works.[18] Even granting the Levinson and Thomasson view that the novel *Madame Bovary* is essentially by Flaubert, we should leave room in principle for the possibility of the Bovary-character's appearing, even originating, in another novel, perhaps by another author, just as most of Shakespeare's main characters appear in antecedent texts.

9.4. Characters and Individuation

To create a fictional character you need to create a narrative in which the character appears. Characters must be tied, if not to a particular

[18] In Chapter 3 'Work and Object' I argue that whether or what origins are essential to a work's identity will depend on what is required for an appropriate response to, or experience of, the work. An adequate appreciation of Beethoven's Third Symphony requires knowledge that it is *by Beethoven* but for less complex or iconic works such knowledge (of origins) might not be required for full appreciation.

narrative, then to some narrative or other. But what is involved in creating a character through a narrative? Suppose a narrative simply states 'Three men entered the room'. Have three characters thereby been created? The question recalls the case of the hundred-strong crowd. According to John Searle all that is needed to create a fictional character is to 'pretend to refer to a person'.[19] Have we pretended to refer to three persons? Even if so, we have not, I suggest, created three characters. The reason is that we have not provided conditions for individuation. A minimal requirement for character creation is that means are provided for distinguishing one character from another. Even a narrative that consists only of the sentence 'A man and a woman entered the room' has satisfied this base condition. Here are two characters distinct from one another in virtue of possessing different properties.

What even this impoverished narrative allows—another crucial feature of character initiation—is something akin to *indexicality*. A reader of the narrative or someone reporting it can refer to *that* character—the man—as opposed to *that* character, the woman. Yet it would be wrong to suppose, in line with an earlier point, that because only general terms, 'a man', 'a woman', are used in the narrative then any individual satisfying those predicates automatically instantiates them in this context. The narrative is not about just *any* man or *any* woman, in spite of its failing to provide more specific information. A deep referential opacity follows from the intentionality of fiction.[20] This reinforces the idea of fictional characters being essentially grounded in narratives. Each fictional narrative invites its readers to make believe or imagine that the character descriptions are instantiated by some unique individual or that the fictional proper names refer uniquely. Of course individuation is normally secured by the use of proper names. But proper names are not a condition for character creation. Once a fictional character is individuated within a narrative it can become an object of reference in non-fictional

---

[19] John Searle, *Expression and Meaning*, Cambridge: Cambridge University Press, 1979, pp. 71–72.
[20] The point is developed in Lamarque and Olsen, *Truth, Fiction, and Literature*, Chapters 5 and 6.

contexts, as happens when well-known characters take on a life of their own as cultural paradigms.

What I will call individuation-via-indexicality is one way in which mere free-floating or universal character-types are distinguishable from *fictional* characters in spite of an apparent co-extensionality. The villain character or the amateur detective or even the Emma Bovary-character can exist independently of any narrative and could be multiply instantiated but *that* villain, *that* detective, and *that* Emma Bovary are products of this or that narrative. They are created because they are grounded.

It is common to associate the creation of fictional characters with the imagination. But while fictional characters do rest on the intentional acts of those who write fictional narratives there is no necessity that they be objects of the imagination. Of course they might be, in the case of complex creations, but where imagination is needed is in the reader's response in making believe that an individual instantiates the character.[21] It is obvious, though, that in novels or dramas of any complexity a reader's response to character and the implied conception of character-identity rests on much more than this limited imaginative exercise. That brings us squarely to the literary dimension of character. Before we turn to that, let me briefly summarize the metaphysical story so far.

If we reject, as I think we must, the eliminativist programme—for which there seem no satisfactory candidates[22]—and admit the reality of fictional characters as abstract entities, then the most promising metaphysical picture is this: that fictional characters are initiated types, grounded in acts of story-telling, i.e. fictional narratives, although not essentially bound to any one, even if tied to a reasonably determinate historico-cultural context. Their identity is interest-relative depending on the demands placed on their identity conditions, which in turn determine the extent of their essential properties. As *characters* per se,

---

[21] The importance of the imagination in *responses* to fiction is a common element in the theories of Kendall Walton, *Mimesis as Make-Believe*, Cambridge, MA: Harvard University Press, 1990, Gregory Currie, *The Nature of Fiction*, Cambridge: Cambridge University Press, 1990, and Lamarque and Olsen, *Truth, Fiction, and Literature*.

[22] For a survey of such theories, see my 'Fiction', in Jerrold Levinson, ed., *Handbook of Aesthetics*, Oxford: Oxford University Press, 2002.

and thus types, they are not created, for sets of properties exist just to the extent that the properties themselves exist, an existence which in the case of universals like *being a detective, being a villain,* seems to be timeless. However, as *fictional* characters they are created, to the extent that their grounding narratives are created, and to the extent that they can be individuated in a quasi-indexical manner by pointing to the source narrative. So even a minimal fictional character, whose only properties are *being a bald man,* is created just in case it makes sense to say of the character that he is *that* bald man. The distinction between the character per se (in this case *being a bald man*) and the *fictional* character (*that* bald man in the story) is akin to the distinction offered by Levinson between a 'sound-structure *simpliciter*' (which he, and others, hold can pre-exist acts of composition) and a 'sound-structure-as-indicated-by-X-at-*t*' (which comes into being through an act of composition).[23]

[23] Levinson includes in his identity conditions of a musical work the 'performing means structure' essentially associated with the work, e.g. being performed on instruments of a particular kind. Is there anything parallel in the case of fictional characters? Is there, for example, any medium-specificity for character-identity? It might seem obvious that characters like Bertie Wooster or Nicholas Nickleby can retain their identity when realized in different media: the *very same* Wooster can appear in drawings, movies, cartoons, and sculptures. Perhaps, though, the matter is not always so clear-cut. Might it not be that a cartoon-character, such as Mickey Mouse, is *essentially* a cartoon-character, so that were a human being to act out the character on stage or in the movies we should say that this is a *rendering* or *version* of Mickey Mouse but, in some sense, not 'the real thing'? Another problematic factor is the degree of specificity that different media afford. To portray a character on stage or in a movie is to present the character with a plenitude of (at least physical) properties, such that the height, weight, dimensions, movements, etc. of the character are all perforce made explicit and determinate. In a literary narrative a writer can be more selective about what details to reveal or imply. Although audiences of stage or cinema are quite sophisticated in discriminating merely contingent properties associated with the human actor and properties genuinely attributable to the fictional character, nevertheless visual media always have the capacity to be more specific in the delineation of character than purely literary media. One consequence of this is that the indexicality requirement I have described in character-identity conditions is far more easily fulfilled in visual than in literary media. If the narrative mentioned earlier, 'Three men entered the room', fails to create three characters in its literary form because of the failure of individuation, it might well do so in a visual form. But this asymmetry has an unexpected knock-on effect. It seems to imply that the visual narrative and the written narrative cannot be identical narratives, for one contains individuated characters which do not appear in the other. To produce the *same* narrative, with its radical indeterminacy, would require quite radical and unfamiliar visual effects. Perhaps this reinforces the notion that dramatizations of literary works are not

9.5. The Literary Dimension

The literary dimension of fictional characters casts a somewhat different light on the question of their creation. For over fifty years there has been a deep scepticism about the importance of character in literary studies and the relevance of character-centred criticism. Partly this has been methodological, urging a change of emphasis towards more formal properties of texts, but partly also, more recently, epistemological. The post-modernist attack on character has been motivated by a general anti-humanism that seeks to undermine notions like the self, the subject, autonomy, human nature.[24] By a curious reversal, rather than seeing fictional characters as human beings, post-modernists have come to see human beings as more like fictional characters: diffuse, uncentred, lacking unity, constructs of discourses. Jean-François Lyotard offers a plausible version:

each [self] exists in a fabric of relations that is now more complex and mobile than ever before. Young or old, man or woman, rich or poor, a person is always located at 'nodal points' of specific communication circuits, however tiny these might be. Or better: one is always located at a post through which various kinds of messages pass.[25]

Other versions are more extreme in denying the autonomous self:

The notion of the "self"—so intrinsic to Anglo-American thought—becomes absurd. It is not something called the self that speaks, but language, the unconscious, the textuality of the text.[26]

However, whatever one makes of this view of the *self*, it can hardly serve to dislodge the concept of fictional character, given that it takes

---

only difficult in practice but, in some sense, impossible in principle. I am grateful to Paisley Livingston for inviting me to reflect on these matters.

[24] I discuss the matter further in *Fictional Points of View*, Chapter 1.

[25] Jean-François Lyotard, *The Postmodern Condition: A Report on Knowledge*. Trans. Geoff Benington and Brian Massumi, Minneapolis: University of Minnesota Press, 1984, p. 15.

[26] Alice A. Jardine, *Gynesis: Configurations of Woman and Modernity*, Ithaca, NY: Cornell University Press, 1985, p. 58. Similar views can be found in Hélène Cixous, 'The Character of "Character" ', *New Literary History* 5, 1975, pp. 383–402.

the phenomenon of fiction as a kind of paradigm.[27] The very ideas of existing in a 'fabric of relations' or speaking through the 'textuality of the text' applies par excellence to fictional characters and should be the starting point for any serious consideration of literary character.

The literary dimension of character creation begins, as the metaphysical dimension ended, with the embeddedness of fictional characters in narratives. But literary creativity moves well beyond the initiation of types and introduces complex questions of literary value. My own focus will be restricted to the role and nature of narrative detail in relation to literary characters. On the metaphysical story the accumulation of detail in characterization is explicable in terms of the increasing specificity of character-types. The more properties attributed to a character the fuller the type and perhaps the richer the imaginative possibilities it affords. But literary creativity does not increase merely in proportion to the piling up of detail or the specificity of characterization. A character does not get richer, deeper, or more interesting in virtue of having more detail ascribed to it. In formulaic narratives like the Holmes or Wooster stories the large number of specific incidents accumulated through the series serves little to develop either character. That is why I suggested that there is a great deal of non-essential or contingent detail about such characters that has no bearing on character-identity. Holmes's identity as a character would not have been affected if there had been, say, no 'Adventure of the Blue Carbuncle'.

But with literary fiction things are different or at least attention towards detail is differently directed, and this for three reasons: first, details of characterization are seen as having an aesthetic function; second, characterization acquires an evaluative (including moral) dimension as well as a purely descriptive one; and third, characterization, and the development of character, is subject to interpretation, introducing another layer of indeterminacy.

These are large issues but I hope enough can be said in a few paragraphs to throw at least some light on the literary, rather than

[27] For a more detailed argument on these lines, see *Fictional Points of View*, Chapters 1 and 12.

merely metaphysical, demands on character creation. Literary creativity is explicable not just through clichéd notions of rounded characters and psychological depth, for literary value resides in the integration of many facets of a narrative, not least the way that formal textual features, subject matter, and broader thematic content cohere.[28] The metaphysical picture suggests that detail simply adds to a store of information about a fictional world. The literary picture suggests, in contrast, that much detail performs a functional, not factual, role.[29] Take this literary critical analysis of certain details in *Our Mutual Friend* (the critic is J. Hillis Miller):

> To see a Veneering dinner party reflected in "the great looking-glass above the sideboard," to see the vain Bella admiring herself in her mirror, or to see Fledgeby secretly watching Riah's reflection in the chimney-glass is to witness a concrete revelation of the way the lives of such people are self-mirroring. . . . Mirroring brings to light the vacuity of people whose lives are determined by money. Each such character is reflected in the blankness of the glass, and can see others only as they are mediated by the reflected image.[30]

Here narrative detail is assigned an aesthetic function, drawing out a motif in the novel, thus connecting diverse episodes with each other, rather than merely adding information. Or rather it does both: Bella's vanity, part of her identity as a character, is reinforced by her preening in front of a mirror, but the mirror shows us something broader about the novel's themes.

Detail alone is not enough to bring originality to a character. The critic Marvin Mudrick famously attacks Jane Austen's creative achievement in the characterization of Darcy in *Pride and Prejudice*. For Mudrick, 'she borrows him from a book; and, though she alters and illuminates everything else, she can do nothing more with him than fit him functionally into the plot'. He becomes 'the conventionally generous and altruistic hero . . . fall[ing] automatically into the grooves prepared . . . by hundreds of novels of sentiment

---

[28] For a detailed defence of this conception of literature, see my *The Philosophy of Literature*, Oxford: Blackwell, 2009.

[29] On tensions between the logical and the literary interest in character, see *Fictional Points of View*, Chapter 4.

[30] J. Hillis Miller, 'Afterword', in Charles Dickens, *Our Mutual Friend*, New York: Signet, 1964, pp. 905–906.

and sensibility'.[31] Here, if Mudrick is right, is a different kind of lack of specificity, not a dearth of factual detail but a failure, as one might say, of embeddedness. Darcy, on this account, is no more than a character-type, contributing little to the 'fabric of relations' that makes the novel distinct and valuable.

I have not said much about the linguistic aspect of character creation. From the metaphysical point of view, as emphasized by Thomasson, characters come into being through the performative acts of authors, rather as marriages, contracts, and promises also depend on performatives.[32] The literary perspective, on the other hand, highlights not merely the representational or descriptive aspect of these acts but the full utilization of linguistic resources. The creative achievement is fundamentally a linguistic one and we praise writers for what they can do with language. Obviously vividness and clarity of description aid vividness and clarity of characterization. But at a literary level something more interesting is going on. For literary description embodies not just facts but values, attitudes, and figurative meanings. The critic Dorothy van Ghent in her discussion of *Tess of the d'Urbervilles* stresses what she calls Hardy's 'symbolic use of natural particulars'. She writes:

> the chattering of the birds at dawn after the death of Prince [Tess' horse] and the iridescence of the coagulated blood, the swollen udders of the cows at Talbothays and the heavy fertilising mists of the late summer mornings and evenings, the ravaged turnip field on Flintcomb-Ash and the visitation of the polar birds. All of these natural details are either predictive or interpretive or both, and prediction and interpretation of events through analogies are the profession of magic. When a piece of blood-stained butcher paper flies up in the road as Tess enters the gate of the vicarage at Emminster, the occurrence is natural while it is ominous; it is realistically observed, as part of the "given", while it inculcates the magical point of view.[33]

In such an atmosphere of symbolic meaning, a curious phenomenon occurs in literary characterization, which complicates the metaphysical account: nuclear properties, those belonging to a character as *person*

---

[31] Marvin Mudrick, 'Irony as Discrimination: *Pride and Prejudice*', in Jane Austen, *Pride and Prejudice*, Donald J. Gray, ed., New York: Norton, 1966, pp. 403, 405.
[32] Thomasson, *Fiction and Metaphysics*, p. 13.
[33] Dorothy van Ghent, 'On *Tess of the d'Urbervilles*', in Thomas Hardy, *Tess of the d'Urbervilles*, ed. Scott Elledge, ed., New York: Norton, 1979, p. 437.

in a world intermix with extra-nuclear properties, those possessed by characters as *abstract constructs*. When Alec d'Urberville appears, in the episode of the planting fires, with a pitchfork among flames, he is both a human being fighting a fire and also a symbol of evil: both a person, we might say, and an artefact of fiction. It does not seem quite enough to say that the one is make-believe, the other a real, if abstract, entity, for on the literary perspective the two are not so obviously distinguishable.

Finally, the constructedness of character is emphasized by the role of interpretation. On the metaphysical story, character-identity is relative to demands made on the inclusiveness of the set of essential properties. There is not always a determinate answer to whether two characters are the same or different. A comparable indeterminacy is a consequence of divergences among literary interpretations. At the simple level of imaginative supplementation of fiction there are always alternative, well-grounded ways of filling in missing detail. But again more interestingly the very identity of a character, in the sense of what essential properties belong to the character, might depend on more global interpretative judgements. With characters like Raskolnikov, Hamlet, or Meursault, where the central crux concerns motivation, part of the literary creativity resides in setting up a narrative context in which competing but plausible interpretations can foreground deep, diverging facets of human nature. In one of the more insightful passages in his book *Faultlines*, Alan Sinfield remarks tellingly:

> Character criticism depends in actuality not on unity but on superfluity—on the *thwarting* of the aspiration to realize unity in the face of material resistance. That is why 'stereotypical' characters, who do have a certain unity, are thought unsatisfactory, and why when characters gain an appearance of unity through closure at the end of the text they become suddenly uninteresting. . . . Hamlet tantalizes traditional critics: they cannot get him to add up without surplus. But this is not because there is insufficient subjectivity in the text for them to work on, but because there is too much. The text overloads the interpretive system.[34]

Under the literary gaze fictional characters—or those with literary stature—assume an increasingly fragile constitution. They come to

---

[34] Alan Sinfield, *Faultlines: Cultural Materialism and the Politics of Dissident Reading*, Oxford: Clarendon Press, 1992, p. 65.

look indeed more and more like the post-modernist version of the self. Indeterminate, deeply implicated in textual and narrative strategies, the product of interpretation at nearly every level, imbued not only with human qualities but also with symbolic and value-laden properties, perspectival in nature,[35] ascribed functional and teleological roles, sometimes naturalistic, sometimes self-consciously artefactual, it is surprising that they retain their remarkable capacity to engage the imagination, to steer us into the make-believe of a world containing real human beings. Perhaps the greatest creative achievement of the writer is to perform a conjuring trick of such a startling kind, as Theseus says, giving to 'airy nothing/A local habitation and a name'.

[35] On this notion, see Lamarque and Olsen, *Truth, Fiction, and Literature*, Chapter 6.

10

Art, Ontology, and the End of *Nausea*

The final sections of Jean-Paul Sartre's novel *Nausea*[1] are often deemed to be its weakest part and even a failure in so far as they attempt to offer a putative 'solution' to the crisis of being. Such, for example, is the view of Iris Murdoch and a similar lukewarm reception is found in the commentaries by Anthony Manser and Arthur Danto.[2] However, little attention has been directed at the implied ontology of art in these closing passages or their relation to Sartre's writings on the imagination. It is these issues I shall address in this chapter and in the light of the discussion I shall propose at least a tentative reassessment of the literary achievement of the novel.

Before starting, I should emphasize that my approach will be primarily philosophical rather than literary. My principal aim is to try to extract a coherent philosophical view about art and ontology from the novel. Only to the extent that this succeeds will it be possible to argue that the novel hangs together better, from a literary point of view, than has sometimes been supposed. Such a methodology is justifiable, if at all, only in novels, such as *Nausea*, which carry overt philosophical themes.

---

[1] Jean-Paul Sartre, *La Nausée,* Paris: Gallimard, 1938. Translated as *Nausea* by Robert Baldick, Harmondsworth: Penguin Books, 1965. All quotations are from this latter edition.
[2] Iris Murdoch writes: 'The interest of *La Nausée* does not lie in its conclusion, which is merely sketched in; Sartre has not developed it sufficiently for it even to pose as a solution to the problem' (*Sartre: Romantic Rationalist,* Cambridge: Bowes and Bowes, 1953, p.16). See also Anthony Manser, *Sartre: A Philosophic Study*, London: Athlone Press, 1966, pp. 17–18; Arthur C. Danto, *Sartre*, London: Fontana, 1975, p. 40.

10.1. A Sense of the Ending

At the very end of the novel the protagonist Antoine Roquentin decides, albeit without great resolve, to write a book: not, he tells us, a history book, which he has attempted already and abandoned. '[H]istory talks about what has existed—an existent can never justify the existence of another existent.' He continues:

> Another kind of book. I don't quite know which kind—but you would have to guess, behind the printed words, behind the pages, something which didn't exist, which was above existence. The sort of story, for example, which could never happen, an adventure. It would have to be beautiful and hard as steel and make people ashamed of their existence. (252)

The context for this decision rests in two crucial episodes prior to it. The immediate trigger is his hearing for the last time his favourite jazz tune 'Some of These Days' played on a scratchy record in the seedy cafe in Bouville (Mudville) where he has spent much of his time in the past months. Roquentin's response to that tune lies at the heart of his ontological reflections. I shall return to that later. The wider context is Roquentin's increasing alienation from the world around him, both the social world—the town's bourgeoisie who he despises, the eccentrics, like the autodidact, who cross his path, and even his ex-girlfriend Anny—and the physical world of nature and artefact which induces in him bouts of nausea. This alienation reaches its climax in the revelation, as he sees it, of the absurdity and superfluousness of existence, which overwhelms him when staring at the root of a tree in the municipal park.

> Absurdity was not an idea in my head, or the sound of a voice, but that long dead snake at my feet, that wooden snake. Snake or claw or root or vulture's talon, it doesn't matter. And without formulating anything clearly, I understood that I had found the key to Existence, the key to my Nausea, to my own life. In fact all that I was able to grasp afterwards comes down to this fundamental absurdity. (185)

If we analyse this revelation—the episode in the park—in more detail we notice that there are three elements in Roquentin's conception of the existence of natural objects. These elements, which will come into play when we offer the contrast with works of art, are: the *viscous*, the *absurd* or superfluous, and the *contingent*.³

First of all, the viscous is a picturesque image that Sartre frequently uses to characterize the appearance of things when conceptual or verbal differentiation is loosened or when, as he puts it in an earlier passage, 'things have broken free from their names' (180). In the park episode he writes: 'the root, the park gates, the bench, the sparse grass on the lawn, all that had vanished; the diversity of things, their individuality, was only an appearance, a veneer. This veneer had melted, leaving soft, monstrous masses, in disorder . . .' (183). The viscous stands for the unstructured disordered appearance of being, as directly perceived when the mind is in a purely passive state void of conceptual thought.

Secondly, the absurdity or superfluousness of things alludes, in Sartre's sense, to their lack of meaning or intrinsic purpose: 'We were a heap of existents inconvenienced, embarrassed by ourselves, we hadn't the slightest reason for being there, any of us, . . .' (184). Also involved is the idea that *l'être en-soi*, bare thinginess, is beyond explanation; it eludes definition. '[T]he world of explanations and reasons is not that of existence' (185). Roquentin contrasts the existence of the root with that of a circle: 'a circle is not absurd, it is clearly explicable by the rotation of a segment of a straight line around one of its extremities. But a circle doesn't exist either. That root, on the other hand, existed in so far as I could not explain it' (185–186). Roquentin's claim that a circle does not exist picks up resonances later when he asserts that works of art likewise do not exist, although as we shall see the non-existence of art and that of mathematical figures is not of the same kind. A circle is merely an abstract entity brought into being by definition; it escapes absurdity because a mathematical explanation could capture all there is to know about it, while a brute object or existent, like the root, has a particularity, a haecceity, which cannot be rationalized and is thus, in Roquentin's terms, absurd or without meaning.

[3] Here I am indebted to Ronald Aronson's *Jean-Paul Sartre—Philosophy in the World*, London: NLB, 1980, pp. 65–66.

ART, ONTOLOGY, AND THE END OF *NAUSEA* 211

Thirdly, there is the contingency of existents, related but not reducible to the other elements. Roquentin uses the word himself:

> The essential thing is contingency. I mean that, by definition, existence is not necessity. To exist is simply *to be there*; what exists appears, lets itself be *encountered*, but you can never *deduce* it. There are people, I believe, who have understood that. Only they have tried to overcome this contingency by inventing a necessary, causal being. But no necessary being can explain existence. (188)

Contingency in the natural world is a radical lack of necessity; everything could have been different, nothing in existence can be deduced from first principles. Danto, rightly, compares Sartre's view in this respect to that of Hume.

The revelations about existence in Roquentin's confrontation with the root can be directly related to the passage about the jazz tune which, as I said, is the immediate occasion for Roquentin's resolution to write a book. It is in this passage that we find a clear sketch of an ontology of the artwork. An important theme of the passage is the contrast between the kind of existence (or strictly non-existence) of the work of art and that of natural objects like the root. Thus, it is immediately apparent that there is an explicit rejection in the former of all three of the elements—the viscous, the absurd, and the contingent—that characterized the latter.

The novel contains two episodes relating to the jazz tune, one near the beginning, one at the end; on both occasions Roquentin notices that on listening to the music his nausea disappears. A prominent aspect of the phenomenon is what he calls 'hardness'; there is a solidity or structure not just to the sounds but to the composition itself which contrasts with the viscous quality of objects which brings on his nausea. 'When the voice sounded in the silence, I felt my body harden and the Nausea vanished. All of a sudden: it was almost painful to become so hard, so bright. At the same time the duration of the music dilated, swelled like a water spout. It filled the room with its metallic transparency, . . .' (38). We recall that when Roquentin describes his own projected book he says: 'it would have to be beautiful and hard as steel.' Elsewhere he describes the melody as 'slim and firm' (248). It is the precision of the notes, following inexorably one from another, structured, clear, and determinate that impresses Roquentin. 'Four notes on the saxophone. They come and go, they seem to say: "You must do like us, suffer in strict time." Well, yes! Of course I would be glad to suffer that way, in strict time, without any complacency, without any self-pity, with an arid purity' (247).

The contrast with the absurd and the contingent comes in the purposefulness and inner necessity of the music. This comes out in the earlier passage:

> Another few seconds and the Negress will sing. It seems inevitable, the necessity of this music is so strong: nothing can interrupt it, nothing which comes from this time in which the world is slumped; it will stop of its own accord, on orders. If I love that beautiful voice, it is above all because of that: it is neither for its fullness nor its sadness, but because it is the event which so many notes have prepared so far in advance, dying so that it might be born. (38)

The primary contrast with physical objects, however, which explains the lack of viscousness, absurdity, and contingency in the music, lies in the remarkable claim that the work of art itself does not exist. Speaking of the song, Roquentin writes:

> It does not exist. It is even irritating in its non-existence; if I were to get up, if I were to snatch the record from the turn-table which is holding it and if I were to break it in two, I wouldn't reach *it*. It is beyond—always beyond something, beyond a voice, beyond a violin note. Through layers and layers of existence, it unveils itself, slim and firm, and when you try to seize it you meet nothing but existents, you run up against existents devoid of meaning. It is behind them: I can't even hear it, I hear sounds, vibrations in the air which unveil it. It does not exist since it has nothing superfluous. . . . It *is*. (248)

Part of the point here is the thought, familiar in aesthetics, that a musical work is not identical either to the medium in which it is exhibited, in this case the gramophone record, or even the sounds produced in a particular performance. The actual song is distinct from the sounds I hear on an occasion. Roquentin constantly emphasizes the distance between the work and the physical manifestation; it is 'beyond', 'behind', 'far away' and, in the case of his own projected book, 'above existence'. The work is also outside time: 'behind the existence which falls from one present to the next, without a past, without a future, behind these sounds which decompose from day to day, peels away and slips towards death, the melody stays the same, young and firm, like a pitiless witness' (249). Arthur Danto interprets Sartre—or at least Roquentin—here as making the point that the song 'Some of These Days' is 'like Keats's Grecian Urn, a thing of beauty and a joy forever because, whatever might happen to it, nothing can happen to the figures it shows, logically frozen in the postures and gestures given them by the artist, eternally young and perpetually loving'.[4] There is no doubt a parallel but the contrast Danto identifies is that between the contents of the physical world and that of a fictional world. But Roquentin is not locating the song in a fictional world nor is he referring to any representational content of the song, e.g. in the words sung. His point is strictly about the ontological status of the work itself; it is the work that does not exist, quite apart from the characters that are depicted in it. Even when he turns to a literary work—as in his own project—it is not the remoteness of the representational content that interests him but that of the work itself 'behind the printed word, behind the pages'.

Of course it is one thing to say that a musical work, or any allographic work, is not identical with its physical manifestations—the score, a performance, a record—and quite another to claim that the work does not exist at all. Is this then merely a literary hyperbole in the mouth of a fictional character? No, Roquentin here speaks for Sartre, as he does in the entire discussion of the status of art in *Nausea*. This is clear if we turn to Sartre's philosophical writings, notably those on the imagination. It is surely no coincidence that two years before publishing *La Nausée* Sartre published a book on the imagination and a second book on the topic appeared a year after the novel. In fact it is in the latter book, *L'Imaginaire*, of 1939, translated as *The Psychology of Imagination*, that Sartre gives his most extended discussion of the imagination and art. The connections are telling, not only for making sense of Roquentin's remarks but ultimately, I think, for making sense of, even redeeming, the novel.

[4] Danto, *Sartre*, p. 39.

10.2. Consolidating a View on the Ontology of Art

Towards the end of *The Psychology of Imagination* Sartre discusses the mode of existence of Beethoven's Seventh Symphony. 'The Seventh Symphony', he writes, 'is in no way *in time*. It is therefore in no way real. It occurs *by itself*, but as absent, as being out of reach. . . . It is not only outside of time and space—as are essences, for instance—it is outside of the real, outside of existence.'[5] It should not, though, he tells us, be thought of as 'existing in another world, in an intelligible heaven'. He rejects Platonism. A work of art is not an abstract entity like a circle; it does not rest on a definition, nor is it an object of intellectual thought. So how does art exist? What kind of being does it have? The answer in brief, for Sartre, is that it exists in the imagination, or more strictly as an object of the imagination (or the imagining consciousness, as he calls it). A work of art has much the same status as an image but, as he emphatically insists, an image is not a picture or object in the mind, it is not something we perceive, it is rather a mode of consciousness, a kind of intentionality. As all consciousness has an object that is distinct from it, the objects of imagination are themselves distinct from consciousness. In spite of first appearances, Sartre is not an idealist; he is not claiming that works of art exist as ideas in the mind.

To consolidate these points we must proceed carefully. First of all, why should he say that works of art are unreal or do not exist? The answer is that Sartre takes reality or existence to be that which is perceivable. This, however, is not equivalent to the idealist view that to be is to be perceived. Sartre is a direct realist about perception; he believes we directly perceive material things distinct from consciousness. He rejects as the 'illusion of immanence' the Berkeleyan and empiricist view that the immediate objects of perception are ideas in the mind. In fact it is his direct realism about perception that leads him to conclude that we do not perceive works of art. At best we only perceive what he calls their 'material analogue'.

---

[5] Jean-Paul Sartre, *The Psychology of Imagination*, New York: Carol Publishing Group, 1991, p. 280. Page references will be given in parenthesis from this edition.

About the Seventh Symphony he says: 'I do not hear it actually, I listen to it in the imaginary' (280); this echoes Roquentin's remark about the jazz tune: 'I can't even hear it, I hear sounds, vibrations in the air which unveil it' (*Nausea*, p. 248). The point is not restricted to the multiple arts, music and literature, but extends to singular arts like painting. Sartre thinks that paintings—that is, representational paintings—act much like images; to reveal their content requires an act of imaginative consciousness. He writes of a portrait of Charles VIII:

> As long as we observe the canvas and frame for themselves the esthetic object "Charles VIII" will not appear. It is not that it is hidden by the picture but because it cannot present itself to a realising consciousness. It will appear at the moment when consciousness, undergoing a radical change in which the world is negated, will itself become imaginative. . . . And since this Charles VIII, who is an unreality so long as he is grasped on the canvas, is precisely the object of our esthetic appreciations . . . , we are led to recognize that, in a picture, the ethetic object is something *unreal*. (274)

The 'radical change' that Sartre mentions is in effect the change from perception to imagination. All we can perceive is the paint and canvas; only when we shift to an imaginative consciousness can we bring to mind what he calls the 'ethetic object', in effect the work of art itself. Incidentally, the claim that strictly we do not perceive works of art reinforces the earlier view from Roquentin that art is 'hard as steel', lacking the viscous quality of objects; for the viscous is essentially connected to the way that objects appear to perception.

Works of art, for Sartre, are both objects of the imagination and products of the imagination. How does he avoid idealism, identifying art with ideas in the mind? The answer is partly that consciousness is always directed beyond itself. But more interestingly it lies in the fact that the intentional objects of imaginative consciousness are always grounded in properties of physical objects, the material analogue created by the artist. When we look at a canvas or listen to a symphony imaginatively the object of our reflection is an imaginative transformation of the colours or sounds we perceive. The colours and sounds as intentional objects of the imagination are not mental entities, ideas, but the perceived colours and sounds interpreted or given meaning. Admittedly, to sustain this sharp distinction between perception and imagination, Sartre requires a limited and essentially passive view of perception. Perception, on this account (here Sartre diverges from Husserl, who in other respects he is following), is no more than the raw stimulus of a sense by a physical presence. While this might be far too narrow a view of perception, it has a consequence which on independent grounds is of some interest. Sartre thinks it is always wrong, i.e. misleading, to describe objects of pure perception—this bare stimulus—in aesthetic terms. This is an example he offers:

Some reds of Matisse, for instance, produce a sensuous enjoyment in those who see them. But we must understand that this sensuous enjoyment, if thought of in isolation—for instance, if aroused by a color in nature—has nothing of the esthetic. It is purely and simply a pleasure of sense. But when the red of the painting is grasped, it is grasped, in spite of everything, as a part of an unreal whole [in other words in the imagination] and it is in this whole that it is beautiful. For instance it is the red of a rug by the table.   (276)

Sartre is led by this line of thought to the remarkable conclusion that 'the real is never beautiful. Beauty is a value applicable only to the imaginary and which means the negation of the world in its essential structure' (281). The idea seems to be that aesthetic properties never adhere in natural objects, being in-itself, but only in intentional objects of the imagination. He is surely right in this at least to the extent that aesthetic properties are relational properties dependent in part on intentional states. Once the intentional object is constituted then we can say that aesthetic properties not only belong to it but, in some cases, do so essentially. In another work, Sartre writes: 'To be terrible is a *property* of this Japanese mask, an inexhaustible, irreducible property which constitutes its very nature, and not the sum of our subjective reactions to a piece of carved wood.'[6]

Sartre, then, is not an idealist about art, nor a subjectivist, nor, as we have seen, is he a Platonist giving to art the status of mathematical objects. He believes that aesthetic properties genuinely (i.e. objectively) inhere in works of art but works of art are never coextensive with physical objects and therefore never merely objects of passive perception. They are intentional objects of the imagination.

---

[6] Jean-Paul Sartre, *Situations* I, p. 34; quoted in Eugene F. Kaelin, *An Existentialist Aesthetic*, University of Wisconsin Press, 1966, pp. 70–71.

Apprehending physical properties—sounds, colours, shapes, spoken or written words—might be necessary for reflection on works of art but it is never sufficient. Works of art are not simply out there in the world with a brute existence like the root in the park. They are not objects of perception at all, nor strictly objects of thought (like the circle), but objects of the imagination which acquire intentional properties (e.g. aesthetic and representational properties) only as such, these properties never being inherent in the physical analogues created by the artist.

10.3. A Literary Judgement

Now we can pull some of the threads together and return to the novel. The charge often made against the novel is that it is 'escapist'—the end is unsatisfactory, it is claimed, because in it Roquentin resolves to leave the real world altogether and immerse himself in the world of the imagination, in art. Danto speaks of the 'hyperaesthetic, precious view of art' and points out how remote it seems from Sartre's later view of the 'engagement' needed in literature.[7] But the charge of escapism or aestheticism is not entirely just. Sartre—via Roquentin—is at pains to reject an elitist, elevated, consoling view of art. He chooses not one of the great works of art to illuminate his theme but a cheap sentimental tune 'Some of These Days'. He mocks those who seek easy consolation from art:

> To think there are idiots who derive consolation from the fine arts. Like my Aunt Bigeois: 'Chopin's *Preludes* were such a help to me when your poor uncle died.' And the concert halls are full to overflowing with humiliated, injured people who close their eyes and try to turn their pale faces into receiving aerials. They imagine that the sounds they receive flow into them, sweet and nourishing, and that their sufferings become music, like those of young Werther; they think that beauty is compassionate towards them. The mugs. (246)

Roquentin's objection to this bourgeois view of fine art is that it is purely passive. After all, it is the passivity of perception—of all

---

[7] Danto, *Sartre*, p. 40.

kinds—that reveals the world to be viscous and absurd. The escape from passivity through the active imagination is the very opposite of escapism (which is usually the flight from activity). Nor is art a release from suffering—as the bourgeoisie hope. Roquentin sees the command of the music as 'suffer in strict time', something he is glad to accept 'without any complacency, without any self-pity, with an arid purity'. Art offers rigour, purity and necessity, not a passive indulgence or a consolation. As for the creation of art, Roquentin stresses the very opposite of inspiration by the Muses; he fantasizes about the Jewish composer writing 'Some of These Days', in the sapping heat of a New York summer, in poverty, drunkenness, failed love, desperate to make a few bucks by cranking out another melody.

Yet he thinks that both the composer and the singer, by bringing into being this minor 'miracle', are 'saved'. Why? Because 'they have cleansed themselves of the sin of existing' (251). What does Sartre/Roquentin mean by that? He certainly does not mean, as is sometimes supposed, that art is a panacea, a salvation for us all. It is only the creators of art who are saved and that, I suggest, precisely because they have created a structure for the imagination (note how different this is from pure fantasy) and in doing so have overcome the passivity of perception.[8] Through the imagination they have transformed the world; they have produced meaning where otherwise there was none; they have created something timeless and universal where before there was only the ephemeral and the contingent. We are surely invited to recognize a strikingly positive aspect to artistic creativity. When finally Roquentin resolves to create an imaginative work himself he is not depicted as escaping from reality, giving up, or retreating into quietism but rejecting passivity and absurdity. The ending is an affirmation of hope; Roquentin senses while reflecting on the creators of the song 'something I didn't know any more: a sort of joy' (251). His aim in taking up writing is not to offer consolation but 'to make people ashamed of their existence' (252). There seems to me a commitment

---

[8] Iris Murdoch explains the salvation to which Roquentin aspires entirely in terms of what it can do for his conception of his own life: 'through the book he will be able to attain to a conception of his own life as having the purity, the clarity and the necessity which the work of art created by him will possess' (op. cit., p. 18) which she calls 'a very thin and unsatisfactory conclusion'. But I think her view, which does not mention the role of the imagination, is far too restricted.

here, an involvement, an activeness against a prevailing passivity, which is not acknowledged by those who see the ending of the novel as a cop-out, a sterile aestheticism.

So what about a final literary judgement? By emphasizing and trying to expound the ontology of art underlying the closing passages in the novel I have hoped to show how these passages fit consistently and integrally into the wider themes. If we take a central theme to be the nature of existence, or strictly what it is to be a centre of consciousness surrounded by existents, then the ending carries on the theme and in some sense resolves it by looking 'beyond existence' to the world of the imagination. On my reading the novel ends on an optimistic note, exalting the imagination above the nauseous presence of brute objects and the self-deceptions of complacent humanity. The resolution is not in passivity but in activity, not in retreat but in a kind of engagement. We cannot ignore either the self-reflective nature of the work. What we have been reading is itself a work of the imagination. Perhaps it is co-extensive with the work that Roquentin resolves to produce: something 'beautiful and hard as steel', that can 'make people ashamed of their existence'. The novel instantiates the very theme it promotes and the hope that its ending promises.

11

On Perceiving Conceptual Art

In a recent graduation exhibition at a British art school a work was displayed that consists of a man bearing two full-length sandwich boards on which is printed, in large Times Roman type: 'This is not "Art" in itself but a means of creating it.' I have not seen the display, only a photograph of it on a flier sent to me by the art school.[1] But it has some paradigmatic features of the kind of conceptual art that I want to consider. It uses language as its central medium; it is a reflection on the status of art; it involves a mildly witty self-referential paradox; it is partially a performance work in that the man carrying the boards is standing outside at the edge of a park; and finally my description captures, I believe, enough to give you a pretty clear idea of the essence of the work itself. In fact the work is not especially original. There have been numerous efforts along similar lines, raising similar questions. There is, for example, a well-known work by Keith Arnatt from 1972, entitled *Trouser-Word Piece*, which consists of a photograph of the artist also holding a sandwich board on which is written 'I'm a Real Artist'; next to the photograph is a long quotation from the philosopher J. L. Austin stating that it is not the word 'real' itself but the negative of 'real' that, in Austin's memorable phrase, 'wears the trousers'.[2]

What interests me about the art school piece is less what it tells us about art than—to put it in stark terms—what the word 'This' refers to in its legend 'This is not "Art" in itself but a means of creating it'. We might suppose that 'This' refers to the work itself. But what is the

---

[1] This was a Press Release from the Nottingham Trent University's School of Art & Design, April 2004.
[2] See Tony Godfrey, *Conceptual Art*, London, Phaidon, 1998, p. 172.

work? Is it the sentence? If so, is it the sentence-token as it appears on the sandwich board, or the sentence-type, as instantiated just now in my description? Or is it the sentence and the board and the man holding it? Again, if the work is the whole ensemble then is it the ensemble-type or this one specific token? If I were to reproduce the sentence on a sandwich board of my own have I produced the *same* work? Or an *instance* of the work? Or a distinct but visually indiscernible work?

These are familiar questions on the ontology and identity conditions of art and of course Arthur Danto has shown how such questions become especially pressing in the case of conceptual art.[3] Note that to pursue the question—as I want to—about what counts as a *work* in talking of conceptual art—and what counts as the same or distinct works—is not equivalent to asking what counts as *art*. I am not concerned here with the question whether conceptual art really is art or not, in any honorific sense, but I am concerned with the, to my mind more interesting, question of what the identity conditions are for objects or performances of this avowedly odd kind. I think that until we have some better idea of this we are not able to get much of a handle on what it means to appreciate the work so described *as a work*. Can I, for example, do full justice to this work and appreciate it as intended merely by thinking of it? Or by talking of it as I have just now? Or by reproducing a version of my own? Or by changing it in various ways (e.g. the layout of the words)? Or do I have to go to the art school to see it for myself?

11.1. The Issues in Question

My discussion will be focused on perception, with the broad question in mind whether or not the kind of conceptual art just exemplified is essentially *visual* art, whether the objects are necessarily objects of perception, and with more specific questions centring on exactly how perception, art, and the aesthetic are related. The starting point is whether it even makes sense to suppose that art could be both non-perceptual and non-aesthetic. It would be ill-advised to try to *define*

[3] Arthur Danto, *The Transfiguration of the Commonplace*, Cambridge, MA: Harvard University Press, 1981.

conceptual art or over-generalize, since conceptual art takes many different forms, yet it seems to be at least an aspiration of some such art, or a direction towards which it tends, to be both non-perceptual and non-aesthetic. The emphasis on ideas is a common feature and this is often associated with giving low priority to material form, to what is perceptible. Lucy Lippard writes: 'Conceptual art . . . means work in which the idea is paramount and the material form is secondary, lightweight, cheap, unpretentious and/or "dematerialized" '.[4] Sol LeWitt goes further: 'What the work of art looks like isn't too important. It has to look like something if it has physical form. No matter what form it may finally have it must begin with an idea. It is the process of conception and realization with which the artist is concerned.'[5] Here too is Mel Bochner:

> A doctrinaire Conceptualist viewpoint would say that the two relevant features of the 'ideal Conceptual work' would be that it have an exact linguistic correlative, that is, it could be described and experienced in its description, and that it be infinitely repeatable. It must have absolutely no 'aura', no uniqueness to it whatsoever.[6]

Three questions immediately present themselves: Can there be art that is non-perceptual? Can there be art that is non-aesthetic? Can something be aesthetic but not perceptual? It might be hoped that answers to these questions might cast light on what kinds of works are works of conceptual art.

11.2. Conceptual Art and Literary Art

The first question, 'Can there be art that is non-perceptual?', seems to yield an obvious Yes, citing the case of literature and poetry. This then encourages the thought that such conceptual art that de-emphasizes

---

[4] Lucy Lippard, *Six Years: The Dematerialization of the Art Object from 1966 to 1972*, Berkeley: University of California Press, 1997, p. vii.

[5] Sol LeWitt, 'Paragraphs on Conceptual Art', *Artforum*, summer, 1967; quoted in Lucy Lippard, *Six Years*, p. 29.

[6] Mel Bochner, 'Mel Bochner on Malevich: An Interview' (with John Coplans), *Artforum*, June 1974, p. 62; quoted in Roberta Smith, 'Conceptual Art', in Nikos Stangos, ed., *Concepts of Modern Art*, London: Thames & Hudson, 1994, p. 259.

the perceptual and gives prominence to language and description might be assimilated to the literary arts. But this calls for more careful examination.

First of all, is it clear that literary works are non-perceptual? After all, our access to them must ultimately be through the senses; we read by scanning a text with our eyes or following it with our fingers in Braille, or hearing a spoken version with our ears. Does that make literature perceptual after all? No, because our senses give us perceptual access to a text and a text is not identical with a work. Texts are ordered strings of sentence-types but any perceptual instantiation of the sentence-types, in a particular font or size or in a particular pattern of sounds, is merely contingent to the identity of the work. And texts so defined are not identical with works because two identical strings might be different works. Or, put another way, any one string of sentence-types might yield or make possible more than one literary work. Different tokenings might be open to different interpretations or might be construed as works of different kinds. Our perceptual access to works through texts is not sufficient to determine what works the texts give us access to.

Of course one notable exception to this principle among literary works is the rather special case of concrete poetry where the configuration of the words on a page is essentially, not merely contingently, related to what the work is.[7] It might well be that some concrete poetry is quite close in kind to some conceptual art but this hardly helps establish that conceptual art is not essentially perceptual for the perceptual appearance of concrete poetry is essential to its identity.

More interesting is the role of ideas in literary art and conceptual art. It might seem that on this level the two come closest together. But, to anticipate, I don't think the analogy is very strong. How do ideas inform literary works? Obviously the question affords no simple answer. Wherever there are meanings there are ideas and wherever there is language there is meaning. I think the most promising analogies revolve round the notion of a *theme* in a literary work. One

---

[7] For examples see Emmett Williams, ed., *An Anthology of Concrete Poetry*, New York: Something Else Press, 1967. For an argument that concrete poetry is not literature, see Louise Hanson, 'Is Concrete Poetry Literature?' *Midwest Studies in Philosophy* XXXIII, 2009, pp. 78–106.

of the aims of literary interpretation is to elicit themes, that is ideas or conceptions, which can be seen to give coherence and interest to the work's ostensible subject, be it poetic image or narrative event.[8] The theme of Shakespeare's sonnet 65 ('Since brass, nor stone, nor earth, nor boundless sea, / But sad mortality o'ersways their power') is easy to discern: the inescapability of time and the sadness of mortality with a hint that love might attain a kind of immortality through the written word, perhaps in the form of the sonnets themselves. The beauty and power of the poem lie in the way that the apparent hopelessness of the ravages of time is expressed and developed, tempered at the end by a glimmer of hope. The images are mixed—from the military ('the wrackful siege of batt'ring days') to the mercenary ('Time's best Jewel from Time's chest lie hid')—but they cohere round the ever-present central theme. What is typical of a literary work is that an idea in the form of a theme—either individual concepts such as mortality or passing time, or a proposition such as 'poetry sustains love through the ravages of time'—is developed out of and gives coherence to specific detail at the subject level.

It is hard to see any exact parallel in the case of conceptual art. Certainly something like thematic ideas come to be associated with some works but the crucial features of the literary case are typically missing or blurred: the fine interplay between thematic description and subject description, the essentially linguistic development of the theme, the notion of detail cohering round a theme, even the requirement that themes in literary works centre on matters of universal interest. In conceptual art where there is an informing thematic idea—often, as in our earlier example, about the boundaries between art and non-art—it is only loosely, perhaps metaphorically, connected to the specific item displayed, be it a performance, a sequence of numbers, a disparate collection of objects, an empty frame, lights turned on and off, a beach hut, a pile of clothes, or, as above, a provocative sentence. These basic conceptions might prompt reflective thinking of a thematic kind but the close integration of subject and theme in the literary case is missing, the way the subject matter both enhances and defines thematic content. Such complexity that is realized in conceptual art is, as we might say, external not internal to the work.

[8] See my *The Philosophy of Literature*, Chapter 4.

A closer parallel between ideas in conceptual art and literary ideas might be with the poetic conceit, familiar in metaphysical poetry, such as John Donne's famous comparison of absent lovers with the legs of a compass or his finding sexual connotations in a flea bite. In a conceit the poet works a seemingly mundane idea into a metaphor of ever-growing elaboration. Again, though, such elaboration occurs within the poem through image and description and its success rests on a sense of completeness and resolution: as Donne himself says, 'the whole frame of the Poem is a beating out of a piece of gold'.[9] Poetic language, like the language of fiction, allows for this 'beating out', for details to emerge through precision of expression. Although conceptual art might use snippets of language to set up something comparable to a poetic conceit it does not use linguistic resources to follow through. If it did it would become poetry. Any following through is left to the ingenuity of the spectator.

But this makes the claim that ideas are paramount a site of potentially serious weakness in conceptual art. For ideas are only of interest when they are articulated, worked out, when something is done with them. Literature and philosophy show two paradigmatic and radically different ways in which ideas can be worked out, either through the unification of a subject round a literary theme or through theory building, hypothesis testing, and intellectual analysis. Conceptual art sometimes aspires to both the literary and the philosophical but all too often, in having the resources only to suggest rather than develop ideas, it falls well short of both.

As to the thought that a *description* of the ideas in conceptual art might do just as well as the work itself—that the essence of the work could be captured in a description—this too distances it from literature, even if it brings it nearer to philosophy. For merely describing the themes of a novel or a poem could be no substitute for reading the work itself. To suppose that it might be not only raises the spectre of Cleanth Brooks's 'heresy of paraphrase'[10] but more crucially it eliminates what I can only describe as the 'experience', very broadly conceived, of reading and appreciating literature.

---

[9] Quoted in Helen Gardner, ed., *The Metaphysical Poets*, Harmondsworth: Penguin, 1966, p. 22.
[10] Cleanth Brooks, 'The Heresy of Paraphrase', in *The Well Wrought Urn: Studies in the Structure of Poetry*, London: Methuen, 1968, pp. 157–175.

It is this appreciative experience, which in different forms characterizes responses to all art, that I want to take up. I think it is a mistake for conceptual art to associate itself too closely either with the literary or the philosophical. To stress the dominance of ideas is to encourage the wrong—and misleading—analogies. I think to understand what is unusual and of interest in conceptual art it is best to hang on to something like the notion of appreciative experience and to recover at least some role for the visual aspects of conceptual art thus returning us inevitably to perception.

Of course conceptual artists see themselves as breaking away from traditional forms of visual art—centred on the revered art-object, the easy consolations of the aesthetically pleasing experience, the false reverence of the art gallery, and so on—but in producing objects that can be seen, however fleeting or insubstantial, they force us to confront facts of perception, in a way that is seldom relevant to literature or philosophy. Rather than trying to make conceptual art non-perceptual (setting aside the clear, but I think unusual, cases where that is literally true), it might be better to admit a perceptual level but somehow make it subservient to the conceptual. I hope to sketch out a way in which this might be possible, drawing on a range of separate but interrelated factors: the role of conceptualization in the perception of all art, the distinction between perceiving a work and perceiving a mere physical object, and the peculiar, perhaps unexpected, role of the aesthetic in all this.

11.3. Conceptual Art and the Aesthetic

Let us begin with the aesthetic. Much conceptual art sets itself resolutely against the aesthetic—it revels in being non-aesthetic or deliberately anti-aesthetic. It rebels against the idea that art must be pleasing, easy to look at, beautiful, and ordered and unified. It seeks out the ugly, the repulsive, the ephemeral, the shocking, as well as cheap materials, kitsch, the banal, the boring, the ordinary, objects that are commonplace. For many critics and spectators it is precisely this self-conscious turning against the aesthetic that makes the art-credentials of conceptual art so suspect. In turn conceptual artists themselves emphasize the dominance of ideas over the perceptual to reinforce their remoteness from the aesthetic. But both these reactions rest on false assumptions. The critics are assuming that art is necessarily aesthetic, the artists that the aesthetic is necessarily perceptual. The artists' assumption is wrong given, once again, the existence of literature or poetry. Literature is a non-perceptual art open to aesthetic description. Nor need the aesthetics of literature be limited to what might be described as its sensuous aspects—fine writing, mellifluous prose, elegant phrases, vivid images, and so forth—or indeed to formal features, like structure, organization, and unity. All these count as aesthetic, of course, but they are also features that occur in all kinds of writing and do not capture what is distinctive about imaginative literature, more narrowly conceived. To do that we need a conception of what it is to read and value a text from a literary point of view: a distinction again between text and work. Taking a literary interest in a text—as opposed to a philosophical or historical or sociological interest—is to attend to its aesthetic features in a deeper sense of asking how the sensuous and formal aspects are used to achieve some literary purpose. Mellifluous prose is not a literary virtue if one is trying to portray a dialogue between teenage street gangs. An aesthetic appraisal of literature must take into account the consonance of means to ends. And, coming full circle, literary ends typically centre on the development of themes, the shaping of a subject matter round some cohering vision, be it of moral, political, or broadly human concern. If the subject matter depicts destruction, fragmentation, or loss of identity in the service of a vision of a fractured and desolate world then beauty and harmony are unlikely to be the best means to achieve this.

It is no good, then, for conceptual artists to try to reject the aesthetic simply by stressing idea over perception. Literature is non-perceptual but amenable to aesthetic ends. But the lesson from literature, this time, is one that conceptual artists might do well to embrace. First, it shows that the aesthetic need not be confined to the beautiful, the sensuous, or the formally unified. The wider conception of seeking consonance of means to ends is compatible with the use of local detail that might be quite at odds with traditional but limited ideas of the aesthetic. There is a difference between the non-aesthetic and the anti-aesthetic. Non-aesthetic means an absence of aesthetic qualities, anti-aesthetic suggests the presence of negative aesthetic qualities. It is an aesthetic judgement to remark on the effective use of anti-aesthetic elements, such as ugliness, repulsiveness, kitsch, the shocking, etc. These means might be consonant with desired artistic ends.

Whether this implies the logical inescapability of the aesthetic in art I am not sure. It does not seem to be part of the *concept* of art that it demands aesthetic appraisal. I don't think P. F. Strawson is right to say that 'it would be self-contradictory to speak of judging something *as a work of art*, but not from the aesthetic point of view'.[11] But if the aesthetic includes, as I am suggesting, appraisal of the effectiveness of means to ends and if, as also seems the case, a work, in contrast to a text or mere object, is an essentially purposive conception then it is hard to see in principle how any work could be genuinely non-aesthetic even if it employs anti-aesthetic means.

The second lesson to draw from the literary case highlights the distinctiveness of works over texts and concerns the idea of a distinctive kind of attention or interest directed at a text (or object more generally). The thought that written texts are open to different kinds of reading, and that there is something distinctive about a literary interest in a text, invites a parallel distinction in the case of conceptual art between what Danto calls the work and the 'mere real thing'. Conceptual art from the earliest days of the ready-mades has long established this distinction as pivotal and, aided by philosophical interpreters like Danto, this is perhaps one of the greatest contributions of conceptual art. I have argued for this distinction elsewhere in the book so shall largely take it for granted now so as to move to the next stage and reflect on how it bears on perception. That Tracey Emin's bed or beach hut or Damien Hirst's medicine bottles or Duchamps' snow shovel become in some sense 'transfigured' by being put on show and invite a different kind of attention when removed from their original contexts is now a commonplace even if it remains problematic to say exactly what their new status is. Whether and how this affects how they are perceived is the matter at issue.

---

[11] P. F. Strawson, 'Aesthetic Appraisal and Works of Art', in Peter Lamarque and Stein Haugom Olsen, eds., *Aesthetics and the Philosophy of Art: The Analytic Tradition: An Anthology*, Oxford: Blackwell, 2003, p. 239.

11.4. Experiencing Conceptual Art as Conceptual Art

I spoke earlier of a kind of appreciative experience associated with the reading of literature, an imaginative reflection on the ways that subject details are consonant with thematic ends. Perception in the case of the visual arts offers something analogous. The two can be brought together by the admittedly vague term 'experience'. There are important common features, I maintain, in the experience of all the arts, literature included, and one of the binding elements can be described as an experience of art *as art*. Experience in this sense is informed by knowledge about the kinds of objects being experienced. Few would deny that experience, perceptual or imaginative, is permeable to background knowledge. What I know affects what I experience.

The permeability of experience (and perception) to belief plays a crucial part in the perception of all visual art.[12] Kendall Walton has shown how perceptions of a work's aesthetic qualities can vary according to the category to which the work is thought to belong. My concern is how perceptions are affected at a more fundamental level, the level at which a work is distinguished from a mere object. And I wish to propose a principle, which I shall call the Empiricist Principle, which bears on this in relation to experience.[13]

Empiricist Principle
If there is a difference between a work and a 'mere real thing' or object (including a text) then that difference must yield, or be realizable in, a difference in experience.

There is a corollary principle, as follows:

Distinctness Principle
If a and b are distinct works then the experience of a is different from the experience of b, when each is experienced correctly.

---

[12] Richard Wollheim describes the 'central phenomenological feature of seeing-in' as 'its permeability to thought'. See 'On Pictorial Representation', in Lamarque and Olsen, 2003, p. 403.
[13] See Chapter 6 'Aesthetic Empiricism' for similar principles.

Note that 'experience' here includes but is not restricted to perceptual experience—it covers also the appreciative experience of reading literature as literature. This is not necessarily *aesthetic* experience in the way that is standardly understood. What is a difference in experience? It is a difference in either or both of phenomenology (being pleasant, disturbing, vivid) or intentional content. Content here must be intentional not merely causal, internalist not externalist. What matters for the identity of an experience in this context is not what causes it but what it is *thought* to be of. If the art school piece is a work and not just the tokening of a sentence—if the word 'This' refers to a work—then there must be an experience, broadly conceived, of the *work* distinct from the experience of (merely) reading the sentence. The sentence-type itself, *qua* sentence-type, is not yet a work. If there is no such experience then according to the Empiricist Principle there is no distinction between the work and the mere object and thus, I take it, no work of conceptual art. There must be something that counts as perceiving (or experiencing) conceptual art *as conceptual art*. I conjecture that something like this principle provides a rationale for printing the sentence on a sandwich-board. Or take an even more difficult case: John Cage's *4′33″*. If there is no experiential difference between attending a 'performance' of John Cage's work and simply listening to ambient sounds for a period of *4′33″* then there is no 'work'. Likewise there is no 'work' if Cage's instruction collapses into a mere hypothesis or supposition, such as: suppose a performer sat in silence at a piano for *4′33″*. That might be an idea that underpins the work but it is not yet a work.

But why accept the Empiricist Principle and its corollary, the Distinctness Principle? After all, they seem to fly in the face of well-known examples from Arthur Danto. Danto sought to show that two objects might be perceptually indiscernible but distinct as works or distinct because one is a work, the other a mere real thing. He famously said that 'to see something as art requires something the eye cannot descry'.[14] But I don't think either principle does contradict Danto's examples. His red square canvases might well be perceptually indiscernible in the sense that perception alone is not able to tell them apart. But that is compatible with their yielding different

---

[14] Arthur Danto, 'The Artworld', in Lamarque and Olsen, 2003, p. 32.

experiences—and perceptions—once the works have been identified as distinct, for example, by the use of titles. Seeing one red square as the Israelites Crossing the Red Sea and another as Kierkegaard's Mood are arguably different experiences. They have different intentional contents and quite possibly a different phenomenology.

But why stress perception at all in the case of conceptual art when the whole point, we are told, is that the idea is paramount and it is not important what the object looks like? Well, we have seen that an idea per se is not yet sufficient for a work, until something is done with it, and we have also seen that if conceptual art aligns itself too closely to non-perceptual art then it comes to seem impoverished next to literature and philosophy. In presenting objects or performances as vehicles for ideas conceptual art seems to offer something not available to these other forms of expression. The ideas can still be paramount but the ideas must inform the perception of the objects and performances.

So what is it to perceive a work of conceptual art as conceptual art and not as a mere object? I suggest it is, at least partially, a perception of saliencies and significance. The objects literally *seem* in appearance to be different from what they are. The bottles, the branches, the bricks, the clothes, the on and off lights, if they are to succeed in becoming *works* distinct from the things themselves, must invite a kind of perception which makes salient particular aspects and suggests significance for them. If they fail to generate this kind of experience they have failed as art precisely because they have failed to distinguish themselves from the things that are their constitutive base. Being a work—certainly being a work of art—must make a difference and the difference, I suggest, must be realizable either in the phenomenology or the intentional content of an experience, broadly conceived.

Of course experience of art does not take place in a cultural vacuum. A complex array of institutional and cultural conditions must be in place to make possible the apprehension of conceptual art as conceptual art. The frisson that always accompanies such art arises partly because the requisite conditions have not been widely assimilated, partly perhaps because they only have a tenuous hold in the first place. For those who can only perceive the objects in themselves, the works are literally invisible and thus non-existent. These works are a strange kind of cultural entity, dependent both for their creation and survival on a system of conventions, attitudes, and values. As such they have a precarious existence but it has been a central theme of this book that all works of art are similarly grounded in human practices and owe their survival to contingent facts about cultural and historical conditions.

11.5. Normativity

An objection to this whole picture, though, at least for the case of conceptual art, might rest on the issue of normativity. To perceive conceptual art as conceptual art, just as to attend to a text as literature, must have a normative element. In effect it must allow for success or failure. Not just any experience is sufficient to differentiate work from object or art from non-art. But how many times are we told by conceptual artists that there are no norms of response to their work, that any response is fine by them? However, that attitude, when not disingenuous, itself becomes a norm: subjective responses are correct, the search for any single or true interpretation is incorrect. Pure permissiveness of response, though, makes the notion that ideas are paramount difficult to sustain. For a response that takes an object at face value and finds in it no ideas would seem not to count as a response to conceptual art *as conceptual art*. Objects that cannot generate—or more seriously are not intended to generate—any reflection on ideas can hardly count as conceptual art. In this there is no escaping normativity.

I have tried to take seriously the thought that there is something sui generis about conceptual art, that reductive accounts that try to assimilate such art into pre-existing categories—the philosophical, the literary, the visual—are inadequate. Instead, I suggest, we should see conceptual art of the paradigmatic kind as offering a curious hybrid of experience having parallels with, but not reducible to, the cerebral reflection of ideas in philosophy, the apprehension of themes or conceits in literature, and the perception of sculpture and painting. To prioritize any one of these is in many cases to miss what is distinctive. Of course this balancing act puts great demands on conceptual art which are not always fulfilled or not fulfilled very rewardingly. But my point is that there must be something that counts as apprehending the works *as works* rather than merely as the objects or performances they seem to be and that this must be realizable in some broad sense experientially. Does it follow that one can only properly apprehend the works by being in their presence? Does the so-called acquaintance principle apply?[15] No. I think often the requisite experience can be had by attending to a photograph, say, or a copy. Ontologically, I suspect most such works are types, allowing for multiple instantiations, rather than unique particulars. (As Bochner says they are 'infinitely repeatable'.) As for identity conditions, the kinds of conceptual works I am thinking of are not mere ideas, mentalistically defined, accessible contingently through different media. There is an inescapable visual dimension, a physical medium which acts as a vehicle for the transmission of ideas. There is even an aesthetic dimension if we allow the consonance of means to ends under this heading. If our art school artist had his sandwich boards stolen I believe he could produce exactly the same work by drafting it all again. But I do not think I produced an instance of the work when earlier I used (or strictly mentioned) the sentence 'This is not "Art" in itself but a means of creating it'. The sentence-type is not enough—the work is more contextualized than that. Like so many works of conceptual art there is salience in the vehicle—the sandwich-board, the typeface—and perceiving the ensemble, however deliberately un-aesthetic, and perceiving it as a work, are integral to the apprehension it demands.

[15] Malcolm Budd, 'The Acquaintance Principle', *British Journal of Aesthetics*, vol. 43, no. 4, October 2003, pp. 286–292; also Paisley Livingston, 'On an Apparent Truism in Aesthetics', *British Journal of Aesthetics*, vol. 43, no. 3, July 2003, pp. 260–278.

Bibliography

The items listed below are those cited in the notes.

Aronson, Ronald, *Jean-Paul Sartre—Philosophy in the World*, London: NLB, 1980.
Baker, Lynne Rudder, 'Why Constitution is Not Identity', *Journal of Philosophy* XCIV, 1997, pp. 599–621.
—— *Persons and Bodies: A Constitution View*, Cambridge: Cambridge University Press, 2000.
Barnes, Annette, *On Interpretation*, Oxford: Blackwell, 1988.
Barthes, Roland, 'From Work to Text', in *Textual Strategies: Perspectives in Post-Structuralist Criticism*, translated and edited by Josué V. Harari, Ithaca, NY: Cornell University Press, 1979.
Beerbohm, Max, 'The Guerdon', in Dwight Macdonald, ed., *Parodies: An Anthology from Chaucer to Beerbohm and After*, London: Faber & Faber, 1964.
Bell, Clive, *Art*, New York: Chatto & Windus, 1949.
Bender, John W., 'Realism, Supervenience, and Irresolvable Aesthetic Disputes', *Journal of Aesthetics and Art Criticism* 54, 1996, pp. 371–382.
—— 'Aesthetic Realism 2', in Jerrold Levinson, ed., *Oxford Handbook of Aesthetics*, Oxford: Oxford University Press, 2003.
Bochner, Mel, 'Mel Bochner on Malevich: An Interview' (with John Coplans), *Artforum*, June 1974.
Borges, Jorge Luis, *Labyrinths*, Harmondsworth: Penguin, 1971.
Brady, Emily and Levinson, Jerrold, eds., *Aesthetic Concepts: Essays After Sibley*, Oxford: Oxford University Press, 2001.
Brennan, Andrew, *Conditions of Identity*, Oxford: Clarendon Press, 1988.
Brooks, Cleanth, 'The Heresy of Paraphrase', in *The Well Wrought Urn: Studies in the Structure of Poetry*, London: Methuen, 1968.
Budd, Malcolm, *Values of Art: Pictures, Poetry and Music*, London: Allen Lane, The Penguin Press, 1995.

—— 'The Acquaintance Principle', *British Journal of Aesthetics* 43, 2003, pp. 286–292.

Burke, Michael B., 'Copper Statues and Pieces of Copper: A Challenge to the Standard Account', *Analysis* 52, 1992, pp. 12–17.

Carlson, Allen, 'Environmental Aesthetics', in B. Gaut and D. M. Lopes, *Routledge Companion to Aesthetics*, London: Routledge, 2001.

Carroll, Noël, 'Essence, Expression, and History', in Mark Rollins, ed., *Danto and His Critics,* Oxford: Blackwell, 1993.

Cavell, Stanley, *The Claim of Reason,* Oxford: Oxford University Press, 1979.

Chatman, Seymour, *The Later Style of Henry James*, Oxford: Basil Blackwell, 1972.

Cixous, Hélène, 'The Character of "Character" ', *New Literary History* 5, 1975, pp. 383–402.

Cohen, L. J., 'The Semantics of Metaphor,' in A. Ortony, ed., *Metaphor and Thought*, Cambridge: Cambridge University Press, 1979.

Cohen, Ted, 'Aesthetic/Non-Aesthetic and the Concept of Taste: A Critique of Sibley's Position', *Theoria* 39, 1973, pp. 113–152.

Collingwood, R. G., *The Principles of Art*, Oxford: Clarendon Press, 1938.

Currie, Gregory, *An Ontology of Art*, Basingstoke: Macmillan, 1989.

—— 'Supervenience, Essentialism and Aesthetic Properties', *Philosophical Studies* 58, 1990, pp. 243–257.

—— *The Nature of Fiction*, Cambridge: Cambridge University Press, 1990.

—— 'Work and Text', *Mind* 100, 1991, pp. 325–340.

Danto, Arthur C., 'The Artworld', *Journal of Philosophy* 61, 1964, pp. 571–584; reprinted in Peter Lamarque and Stein Haugom Olsen, eds., *Aesthetics and the Philosophy of Art: The Analytic Tradition: An Anthology*, Oxford: Blackwell, 2003.

—— *Sartre,* London: Fontana, 1975.

—— *The Transfiguration of the Commonplace*, Cambridge, MA: Harvard University Press, 1981.

—— *The Philosophical Disenfranchisement of Art,* New York: Columbia University Press, 1986.

—— 'Responses and Replies', in Mark Rollins, ed., *Danto and His Critics*, Oxford: Blackwell, 1993.

Danto, Arthur C., 'The Art World Revisited', in *Beyond the Brillo Box: The Visual Arts in Post-Historical Perspective,* Berkeley, CA: University of California Press, 1998.

Davies, David, 'Aesthetic Empiricism and the Philosophy of Art', *Synthesis Philosophica* 15, 2000, pp. 49–64.

—— *Art as Performance,* Oxford: Blackwell, 2003.

—— 'Against Enlightened Empiricism', in Matthew Kieran, ed., *Contemporary Debates in Aesthetics and the Philosophy of Art,* Oxford: Blackwell, 2006.

Deutsch, Harry, 'The Creation Problem', *Topoi,* vol. 10, 1991, pp. 209–225.

Dickie, George, 'The New Institutional Theory of Art', *Proceedings of the 8th International Wittgenstein Symposium* 10, 1983, pp. 57–64; reprinted in P. V. Lamarque and S. H. Olsen, eds., *Aesthetics and the Philosophy of Art: The Analytic Tradition: An Anthology,* Oxford: Blackwell, 2003.

Dilworth, John, 'A Representational Theory of Artefacts and Artworks', *British Journal of Aesthetics* 41, 2001, pp. 353–370.

Dodd, Julian, 'Musical Works as Eternal Types', *British Journal of Aesthetics* 40, 2000, pp. 424–440.

—— *Works of Music: An Essay in Ontology,* Oxford: Oxford University Press, 2007.

Eco, Umberto, *Interpretation and Overinterpretation,* Cambridge: Cambridge University Press, 1992.

Feagin, Susan, *Reading with Feeling,* Ithaca, NY: Cornell University Press, 1996.

Fine, Kit, 'The Problem of Non-Existents I. Internalism', *Topoi* 1, 1982, pp. 97–140.

—— 'The Non-Identity of a Material Thing and Its Matter', *Mind* 112, 2003, pp. 195–234.

Foucault, Michel, 'What is an Author?' in William Irwin, ed., *The Death and Resurrection of the Author,* Westport, CT: Greenwood Press, 2002.

Frank, Joseph, 'The World of Raskolnikov', in *Crime and Punishment,* by Feodor Dostoevsky, edited by George Gibian, New York: Norton, 1975.

Gardner, Helen, ed., *The Metaphysical Poets,* Harmondsworth: Penguin, 1966.

Geach, Peter, *God and the Soul,* New York: Schocken Books, 1969.

Ghent, Dorothy Van, 'On *Tess of the d'Urbervilles,*' in Thomas Hardy, *Tess of the d'Urbervilles,* Scott Elledge, ed., New York: Norton, 1979.

Gibbard, Allan, 'Contingent Identity', *Journal of Philosophical Logic* 4, 1975, pp. 187–221.

Godfrey, Tony, *Conceptual Art,* London: Phaidon, 1998.

Goodman, Nelson, *Languages of Art,* Indianapolis: Bobs-Merrill, 1968.

——— 'When is Art?' in David Perkins and Barbara Leondat, eds., *The Arts and Cognition,* Baltimore: Johns Hopkins University Press, 1977.

——— *Ways of Worldmaking,* Brighton: Harvester Press, 1978.

——— and Elgin, Catherine, 'Interpretation and Identity: Can the Work Survive the World?' in Eileen John and Dominic Lopes, eds., *Philosophy of Literature: Contemporary and Classic Readings: An Anthology,* Oxford: Blackwell, 2004.

Goldman, Alan, 'Realism About Aesthetic Properties', *Journal of Aesthetics and Art Criticism* 51, 1993, pp. 31–37.

Graetz, H. R., *The Symbolic Language of Vincent Van Gogh,* New York: McGraw Hill, 1963.

Graham, Gordon, 'Aesthetic Empiricism and the Challenge of Fakes and Ready-Mades', in Matthew Kieran, ed., *Contemporary Debates in Aesthetics and the Philosophy of Art,* Oxford: Blackwell, 2006.

Grice, H. P., *Studies in the Way of Words,* Cambridge: Harvard University Press, 1989.

Hanson, Louise, 'Is Concrete Poetry Literature?' *Midwest Studies in Philosophy* XXXIII, 2009, pp. 78–106.

Hopkins, Robert, 'Aesthetics, Experience, and Discrimination', *Journal of Aesthetics and Art Criticism* 63, 2005, pp. 119–133.

Howell, Robert, 'Types, Indicated and Initiated', *British Journal of Aesthetics* 42, 2002, pp. 104–127.

Ingarden, Roman, 'Artistic and Aesthetic Values', *British Journal of Aesthetics* 4, 1964, pp. 198–213.

Janaway, Christopher, 'Borges and Danto: A Reply to Michael Wreen', *British Journal of Aesthetics* 32, 1992, pp. 72–76.

——— 'What a Musical Forgery Isn't', *British Journal of Aesthetics* 39, 1999, pp. 62–71.

Jardine, Alice A., *Gynesis: Configurations of Woman and Modernity,* Ithaca, NY: Cornell University Press, 1985.

Jones, Peter, *Philosophy and the Novel,* Oxford: Oxford University Press, 1975.

Johnson, Mark, 'Constitution is Not Identity', *Mind* 101, 1992, pp. 89–106.

Kaelin, Eugene F., *An Existentialist Aesthetic*, Madison WI: University of Wisconsin Press, 1966.
Kant, Immanuel, *Critique of Judgement*, trans. James Creed Meredith, Oxford: Clarendon Press, 1952.
Kim, Jaegwon, *Supervenience and Mind,* Cambridge: Cambridge University Press, 1993.
Kivy, Peter, 'Platonism in Music: Another Kind of Defense,' *American Philosophical Quarterly* 24, 1987, pp. 245–252.
—— *New Essays on Musical Understanding,* Oxford: Clarendon Press, 2001.
Knapp, Steven, and Michaels, Walter Benn, 'The Impossibility of Intentionless Meaning', in Gary Iseminger, ed., *Intention & Interpretation*, Philadelphia: Temple University Press, 1992.
Krausz, Michael, *Rightness and Reasons: Interpretation in Cultural Practices,* Ithaca, NY: Cornell University Press, 1993.
—— 'Rightness and Reasons: A Reply to Stecker,' *Journal of Aesthetics and Art Criticism* 55, 1997, pp. 415–417.
—— *Limits of Rightness,* Lanham, MD: Rowman & Littlefield Publishers, Inc., 2000.
Kripke, Saul, *Reference and Existence: The John Locke Lectures for 1973,* (Unpublished).
Lamarque, Peter, 'Narrative and Invention', in Cristopher Nash, ed., *Narrative in Culture*, London: Routledge, 1990.
—— Review of *Mimesis As Make-Believe* by Kendall Walton, *Journal of Aesthetics and Art Criticism* 49, 1991, pp. 161–166.
—— 'Style and Thought', *Journal of Literary Semantics* 21, 1992, pp. 45–54.
—— *Fictional Points of View*, Ithaca, NY: Cornell University Press, 1996.
—— 'Marks and Noises and Interpretations', *Semiotica* 108–1/2, 1996, pp. 163–175.
—— 'Aesthetic Value, Experience, and Indiscernibles', *Nordisk estetisk tidskrift* 17, 1998, pp. 61–78.
—— 'The Aesthetic and the Universal', *Journal of Aesthetic Education* 33, 1999, pp. 1–17.
—— 'Fiction', in Jerrold Levinson, ed., *Handbook of Aesthetics*, Oxford: Oxford University Press, 2002.
—— Review of Paul Thom, *Making Sense: A Theory of Interpretation*, *British Journal of Aesthetics* 43, 2003, pp. 80–84.
—— 'On Not Expecting Too Much from Narrative', *Mind & Language* 19, 2004, pp. 393–408.

—— 'Palaeolithic Cave Painting: A Test Case for Trans-Cultural Aesthetics', in Thomas Heyd and John Clegg, eds., *Aesthetics and Rock Art*, Aldershot: Ashgate, 2005, pp. 21–35.

—— *The Philosophy of Literature*, Oxford: Blackwell, 2009.

—— and Olsen, Stein Haugom, *Truth, Fiction and Literature: A Philosophical Perspective*, Oxford: Clarendon Press, 1994.

Levinson, Jerrold, 'What a Musical Work Is', *Journal of Philosophy* 77, 1980, pp. 5–28; reprinted in Peter Lamarque and Stein Haugom Olsen, eds., *Aesthetics and the Philosophy of Art: The Analytic Tradition: An Anthology*, Oxford: Blackwell, 2003.

—— 'Zemach on Paintings', *British Journal of Aesthetics* 27, 1987, pp. 278–283.

—— *Music, Art & Metaphysics*, Ithaca, NY: Cornell University Press, 1990.

—— 'Being Realistic About Aesthetic Properties', *Journal of Aesthetics and Art Criticism* 52, 1994, pp. 351–354.

—— *The Pleasures of Aesthetics: Philosophical Essays*, Ithaca, NY: Cornell University Press, 1996.

—— 'Two Notions of Interpretation', in Arto Haapala and Ossi Naukkarinen, eds., *Interpretation and Its Boundaries*, Helsinki: Helsinki University Press, 1999.

—— 'Aesthetic Properties, Evaluative Force, and Differences of Sensibility', in Emily Brady and Jerrold Levinson, eds., *Aesthetic Concepts: Essay After Sibley*, Oxford: Oxford University Press, 2001.

Lessing, Alfred, 'What is Wrong with a Forgery?' in Denis Dutton, ed., *The Forger's Art*, Berkeley: University of California Press, 1983.

LeWitt, Sol, 'Paragraphs on Conceptual Art', *Artforum*, Summer, 1967.

Lippard, Lucy, *Six Years: The Dematerialization of the Art Object from 1966 to 1972*, Berkeley: University of California Press, 1997.

Livingston, Paisley, 'Counting Fragments, and Frenhofer's Paradox', *British Journal of Aesthetics* 39, 1999, pp. 14–23.

—— 'On an Apparent Truism in Aesthetics', *British Journal of Aesthetics* 43, 2003, pp. 260–278.

Lubin, Albert, *Stranger on the Earth: A Psychological Biography of Vincent Van Gogh*, Holt, Rinehart, and Winston, 1972.

Lyotard, Jean-François, *The Postmodern Condition: A Report on Knowledge*, trans. Geoff Benington and Brian Massumi, Minneapolis: University of Minnesota Press, 1984.

Manser, Anthony, *Sartre: A Philosophic Study*, London: Athlone Press, 1966.
Margolis, Joseph, 'Works of Art as Physically Embodied and Culturally Emergent Entities', *British Journal of Aesthetics* 14, 1974, pp. 187–196.
—— *Art and Philosophy: Conceptual Issues in Aesthetics*, Atlantic Highlands, NJ: Humanities Press, 1980.
—— 'Art Forgery, and Authenticity', in Denis Dutton, ed., *The Forger's Art*, Berkeley: University of California Press, 1983.
—— 'Reinterpreting Interpretation', in John W. Bender and H. Gene Blocker, eds., *Contemporary Philosophy of Art: Readings in Analytic Aesthetics*, Englewood Cliffs, NJ: Prentice Hall, 1993.
—— 'Farewell to Danto and Goodman', *British Journal of Aesthetics* 38, 1998, pp. 353–374.
—— *What, After All, Is a Work of Art?*, University Park: Pennsylvania University Press, 1999.
Matravers, Derek, 'Aesthetic Concepts and Aesthetic Experiences', *British Journal of Aesthetics* 36, 1996, pp. 265–277.
Meiland, Jack W., 'Originals, Copies and Aesthetic Value', in Denis Dutton, ed., *The Forger's Art*, Berkeley: University of California Press, 1983.
Meyer, Leonard B., 'Forgery and the Anthropology of Art', in Denis Dutton, ed., *The Forger's Art*, Berkeley: University of California Press, 1983.
Miller, J. Hillis, 'Afterword', in Charles Dickens, *Our Mutual Friend*, New York: Signet, 1964.
Mudrick, Marvin, 'Irony as Discrimination: *Pride and Prejudice*', in Jane Austen, *Pride and Prejudice*, Donald J. Gray, ed., New York: Norton, 1966.
Murdoch, Iris, *Sartre: Romantic Rationalist*, Cambridge: Bowes and Bowes, 1953.
Nussbaum, Martha, *Love's Knowledge: Essays on Philosophy and Literature*, Oxford: Oxford University Press, 1990.
Olsen, Stein Haugom, *The End of Literary Theory*, Cambridge: Cambridge University Press, 1987.
Olson, Eric T., 'Material Coincidence and the Indiscernibility Problem', *Philosophical Quarterly* 51, 2001, pp. 337–355.
Parsons, Terence, *Nonexistent Objects*, New Haven: Yale University Press, 1980.

Pereboom, D., 'On Baker's *Persons and Bodies*', *Philosophy and Phenomenological Research*, 64, 2002, pp. 615–622.

Pettit, Philip, 'The Possibility of Aesthetic Realism', in Eva Schaper, ed., *Pleasure, Preference, and Value: Studies in Philosophical Aesthetics*, Cambridge: Cambridge University Press, 1983.

Pollock, Griselda, 'Van Gogh and the Poor Slaves: Images of Rural Labor as Modern Art', *Art History* 11, 1988, pp. 407–432.

Predelli, Stefano, 'Goodman and the Wrong Note Paradox', *British Journal of Aesthetics* 39, 1999, pp. 364–375.

—— 'Musical Ontology and the Argument from Creation', *British Journal of Aesthetics* 41, 2001, pp. 279–292.

Propp, Vladimir, *Morphology of the Folktale*, Austin, TX: University of Texas Press, 2nd edition, 1968.

Rea, M., 'Lynne Baker on Material Constitution', *Philosophy and Phenomenological Research*, 64, 2002, pp. 607–614.

Ridley, Aaron, 'The Philosophy of Medium-Grade Art', *British Journal of Aesthetics* 36, 1996, pp. 413–423.

Robinson, Jenefer, 'Style and Significance in Art History and Art Criticism', *Journal of Aesthetics and Art Criticism* 40, 1981, pp. 5–14.

—— 'General and Individual Style in Literature', *Journal of Aesthetics and Art Criticism* 43, 1984, pp. 147–158.

—— 'Style and Personality in the Literary Work', *Philosophical Review* 94, 1985, pp. 227–247; reprinted in Peter Lamarque and Stein Haugom Olsen, eds., *Aesthetics and the Philosophy of Art: The Analytic Tradition: An Anthology*, Oxford: Blackwell, 2003.

—— *Deeper than Reason: Emotion and Its Role in Literature, Music, and Art*, Oxford: Oxford University Press, 2005.

Rorty, Richard, 'The Pragmatist's Progress', in Umberto Eco, *Interpretation and Overinterpretation*, Stefan Collini, ed., Cambridge: Cambridge University Press, 1992.

Russell, Bertrand, *Logic and Knowledge*, R. C. Marsh, ed., London: Allen and Unwin, 1956.

Salmon, Nathan, 'Nonexistence', *Nous* 32, 1998, pp. 277–319.

Sartre, Jean-Paul, *La Nausée*, Paris: Gallimard, 1938. Translated as *Nausea* by Robert Baldick, Harmondsworth: Penguin Books, 1965.

—— *The Psychology of Imagination*. New York: Carol Publishing Group, 1991.

Savile, Anthony, *The Test of Time: An Essay in Philosophical Aesthetics*, Oxford: Clarendon Press, 1982.

—— 'The Rationale of Restoration', *Journal of Aesthetics and Art Criticism* 51, 1993, pp. 463–474.

Scruton, Roger, *Art and Imagination*, London: Methuen, 1974.

—— *The Aesthetics of Music*, Oxford: Oxford University Press, 1997.

Searle, John R., *Expression and Meaning*, Cambridge: Cambridge University Press, 1979.

—— *The Construction of Social Reality*, Harmondsworth: Allen Lane, 1995.

Sibley, Frank, 'Aesthetic Concepts', *Philosophical Review* 68, 1959, pp. 421–450 (rept. in *Approaches to Aesthetics*).

—— 'Aesthetic and Nonaesthetic', *Philosophical Review* 74, 1965, pp. 137–193 (rept. in *Approaches to Aesthetics*).

—— *Approaches to Aesthetics: Collected Papers on Philosophical Aesthetics*, J. Benson, B. Redfern, and J. Roxbee Cox, eds., Oxford: Oxford University Press, 2001.

—— 'Why the *Mona Lisa* May Not Be a Painting', in Sibley, *Approaches to Aesthetics*, 2001.

Sinfield, Alan, *Faultlines: Cultural Materialism and the Politics of Dissident Reading*, Oxford: Clarendon Press, 1992.

Smith, Roberta, 'Conceptual Art', in Nikos Stangos, ed., *Concepts of Modern Art*, London: Thames & Hudson, 1994.

Stecker, Robert, *Artworks: Definition, Meaning, Value*, University Park: Pennsylvania State University Press, 1997.

—— 'The Constructivist's Dilemma', *Journal of Aesthetics and Art Criticism* 55, 1997, pp. 43–52; reprinted in Peter Lamarque and Stein Haugom Olsen, eds., *Aesthetics and the Philosophy of Art: The Analytic Tradition: An Anthology*, Oxford: Blackwell, 2003.

—— 'The Wrong Reasons: A Response to Michael Krausz', *Journal of Aesthetics and Art Criticism* 55, 1997, pp. 418–420.

—— *Interpretation and Construction: Art, Speech, and the Law*, Oxford: Blackwell, 2003.

Strawson, P. F., *Freedom and Resentment and Other Essays*, London: Methuen, 1974.

—— 'Aesthetic Appraisal and Works of Art', *The Oxford Review* 3, 1966; reprinted in Peter Lamarque and Stein Haugom Olsen, eds., *Aesthetics and the Philosophy of Art: The Analytic Tradition: An Anthology*, Oxford: Blackwell, 2003.

Thom, Paul, *Making Sense: A Theory of Interpretation,* Lanham, MD: Rowman & Littlefield, 2000.

Thomasson, Amie L., *Fiction and Metaphysics,* Cambridge: Cambridge University Press, 1999.

—— 'The Ontology of Art', in Peter Kivy, ed., *Blackwell Guide to Aesthetics* Oxford: Blackwell, 2003.

—— 'The Ontology of Art and Knowledge in Aesthetics', *Journal of Aesthetics and Art Criticism,* 63, 2005, pp. 221–229.

Thompson, Judith Jarvis, 'The Statue and the Clay', *Nous* 32, 1998, pp. 149–173.

Tormey, Alan, 'Critical Judgments', *Theoria* 39, 1973, pp. 35–49.

Walton, Kendall L., 'Categories of Art', *Philosophical Review,* 79, 1970, pp. 334–367; reprinted in Peter Lamarque and Stein Haugom Olsen, eds., *Aesthetics and the Philosophy of Art: The Analytic Tradition: An Anthology,* Oxford: Blackwell, 2003.

—— *Mimesis As Make-Believe,* Cambridge: Harvard University Press, 1990.

Watt, Ian, 'The First Paragraph of *The Ambassadors*: An Explication', in Tony Tanner, ed., *Henry James,* London: Macmillan, 1968.

Wedeking, G., 'Critical Notice: Lynne Rudder Baker, *Persons and Bodies*', *Canadian Journal of Philosophy* 32, 2002, pp. 267–290.

Werness, Hope B., 'Han van Meegeren *fecit*', in Denis Dutton, ed., *The Forger's Art: Forgery and the Philosophy of Art,* Berkeley: University of California Press, 1983.

Wiggins, David, *Sameness and Substance,* Cambridge, MA: Harvard University Press, 1980.

Williams, Emmett, ed., *An Anthology of Concrete Poetry,* New York: Something Else Press, 1967.

Wollheim, Richard, 'Pictorial Style: Two Views', in Berel Lang, ed., *The Concept of Style,* Philadelphia: University of Pennsylvania Press, 1979.

—— *Art and Its Objects,* Cambridge: Cambridge University Press, 2nd edition, 1980.

—— *Painting As an Art,* Cambridge, MA: Harvard University Press, 1987.

—— 'Danto's Gallery of Indiscernibles', in Mark Rollins, ed., *Danto and His Critics,* Oxford: Blackwell, 1993.

—— 'On Pictorial Representation', *Journal of Aesthetics and Art Criticism* 56, 1998, pp. 217–226; reprinted in Peter Lamarque and Stein Haugom

Olsen, eds., *Aesthetics and the Philosophy of Art: The Analytic Tradition: An Anthology*, Oxford: Blackwell, 2003.

Wolterstorff, Nicholas, *Works and Worlds of Art*, Oxford: Clarendon Press, 1980.

Wreen, Michael, 'Once is Not Enough?', *British Journal of Aesthetics* 30, 1990, pp. 149–158.

Zangwill, Nick, 'Art and Audience', *Journal of Aesthetics and Art Criticism* 57, 1999, pp. 315–332.

—— 'In Defence of Moderate Aesthetic Formalism', *Philosophical Quarterly* 50, 2000.

—— 'Aesthetic Functionalism', in Brady and Levinson, eds., *Aesthetic Concepts: Essays After Sibley*, 2001.

—— 'Aesthetic Realism 1', in Jerrold Levinson, ed., *Oxford Handbook of Aesthetics*, Oxford: Oxford University Press, 2003.

Zemach, Eddy, 'No Identification Without Evaluation', *British Journal of Aesthetics* 26, 1986, pp. 239–251.

—— *Real Beauty*, University Park, PA: Penn State University Press, 1997.

Zimmerman, D., 'Theories of Masses and Problems of Constitution', *Philosophical Review* 104, 1995, pp. 53–110.

Index

Aronson, Ronald 210 n 3, 234

Baker, Lynne Rudder 49, 50, 65 n 16, 66 n 17, 234
Barnes, Annette 154 n 3, 234
Barthes, Roland 166, 234
Beerbohm, Max 145, 146, 147, 151, 234
Beethoven, Ludwig van 34, 44, 67, 72, 102, 195, 198 n 18, 214
'Moonlight' Sonata, 57, 60, 66, 70,
Bell, Clive 13, 125, 126, 136, 234
Bender, John W. 21, 22 n 28, 25 n 32, 108, 109, 234, 240
Bochner, Mel 222, 233, 234
Borges, Jorge Luis 87–92, 94 n 32, 165 n 22, 234
'Pierre Menard, Author of the Quixote', 87–92, 94 n 32, 165, 196
Brady, Emily xiii, 21 n 25, 71 n 25, 234
Brahms, Johannes
German Requium 81
Piano Sonata op. 2 195
Violin Concerto in D Major op. 77 101
Bredius, Abraham 149–150
Brennan, Andrew 71 n 26, 234
Brooks, Cleanth 173, 225, 234
Budd, Malcolm xii, 72 n 30, 110 n 26, 233, 235
Burke, Michael B. 66 n 17, 235

Cage, John 230
Carlson, Allen 24 n 30, 235
Carroll, Noël xii, 13, 235
Cavell, Stanley 113, 235
Cervantes, Miguel de 87–92
Chatman, Seymour 145 n 7, 147 n 10, 235
Cixous, Hélène 202 n 26, 235

Cohen, L. J. 186 n 59, 235
Cohen, Ted 23, 235
Collingwood, R. G. 8, 38, 51, 52 n 32, 54, 235
Currie, Gregory xii, 2 n 1, 53 n 35, 58 n 1, 67 n 18, 72 n 28, 79 n 2, 81, 89 n 25, 91 n 29, 93, 99 n 7, 100 n 9, 108 n 23, 122–3, 127, 133, 161 n 14, 165 n 20, 184 n 56, 200 n 21, 235

Danto, Arthur C. xii, 11–15, 16, 20, 28, 30, 61, 67 n 18, 77 n 41, 81, 87–90, 93, 99, 100 n 8, 104–5, 128–9, 132, 138, 158–9, 162, 172, 208, 211, 213, 217, 221, 228, 230, 235–6
Davidson, Donald 186
Davies, David 2 n 1, 8–9, 19, 38 n 7, 40 n 8, 9, 11, 53 n 35, 122 n 3, 123, 127, 133–4, 236
Descartes, René 12
Deutsch, Harry 37, 38 n 6, 48 n 22, 188 n 1, 236
Dickens, Charles 190, 204 n 30
Our Mutual Friend 204
Dickie, George 14, 37, 236
Dilworth, John 73 n 32, 236
Dodd, Julian 9 n 7, 33 n 1, 65 n 14, 194, 236
Donne, John 225
Dostoevsky, Fyodor
Crime and Punishment 181–2
Duchamp, Marcel 12, 14–15, 17, 61 n 6, 64, 84, 228
Dvořák, Antonín
Piano Quintet in A Major op. 81 101

Eco, Umberto 107, 157 n 7, 236
Emin, Tracey 228

Feagin, Susan 103 n 14, 236
Fine, Kit 47, 48 n 22, 50
Flaubert, Gustave
  Madame Bovary 198
Foucault, Michel 34–5, 36, 236
Fra Angelico 110
  Lamentation over the Dead Christ 101, 112, 114, 118
Frank, Joseph 182 n 54, 236

Gardner, Helen 225 n 9, 236
Geach, Peter 177 n 48, 236
Ghent, Dorothy Van 205, 236
Gibbard, Allan 61 n 5, 237
Godfrey, Tony 220 n 2
Goethe, Johann Wolfgang von 185, 192
Goodman, Nelson xii, 16 n 20, 45–6, 58 n 2, 74, 80–1, 89–91, 93–4, 103 n 13, 126 n 13, 140, 188, 237
Goldman, Alan xii, 108 n 23, 112 n 29, 237
Graetz, H. R. 30 n 36, 237
Graham, Gordon 18, 19, 122 n 2, 237
Grice, H. P. 153, 163, 237

Hanson, Louise 223 n 7, 237
Hardy, Thomas 101, 205
Hirst, Damien 228
Hopkins, Robert 16 n 20, 126 n 13, 127 n 13, 237
Howell, Robert 65 n 15, 194 n 10, 237
Hume, David 12, 21, 137, 211

Ingarden, Roman 47, 51, 54, 237

James, Henry 145–7
Janaway, Christopher 8 n 18, 92 n 30, 237
Jardine, Alice A. 202 n 26, 237
Jones, Peter 25 n 33, 237
Johnson, Mark 237

Kaelin, Eugene F. 216 n 6, 238
Kafka, Franz 23, 36

Kant, Immanuel 12, 16, 17, 18, 21, 80, 102, 125, 126, 132, 135, 136, 163, 238
Kim, Jaegwon 99 n 7, 238
Kivy, Peter 10 n 8, 81, 194, 238
Knapp, Steven 155, 156, 159, 238
Krausz, Michael xiii, 25 n 32, 29 n 35, 31 n 37, 167–71, 173–8, 180, 182, 238
Kripke, Saul 27, 114, 189, 238

Leibniz's Law 47, 48, 50 n 26, 61, 62, 91
Levinson, Jerrold x, xii, xiii, 21–3, 25 n 31& n 33, 40 n 10, 47, 53 n 35, 58 n 2, 64 n 12, 65 n 14 & n 15, 71 n 25, 72 n 28, 75 n 36, 77 n 39, 79 n 3, 80–4, 85 n 19, 86 n 20, 90, 91, 93, 97, 99 n 7, 108 n 23, 112, 120 n 36, 156 n 6, 162 n 16, 163, 164, 165, 166 n 24, 167, 175, 178–80, 186, 194–8, 200 n 22, 201, 238–9
Lessing, Alfred 125, 126, 239
LeWitt, Sol 38, 222, 239
Lippard, Lucy 222, 239
Livingston, Paisley xiii, 35 n 3, 110 n 26, 202 n 23, 233 n 15, 239
Lubin, Albert 30 n 36, 239
Lyotard, Jean-François 202, 239

Mann, Thomas 185, 192
Manser, Anthony 208, 240
Margolis, Joseph 25 n 32, 47–8, 53 n 35, 58 n 1, 61 n 6, 61 n 8, 77 n 41, 105, 106 n 19, 115, 122 n 1, 154 n 2, 165–7, 172, 174, 175, 177, 180–1, 183, 240
Marlowe, Christopher 185, 192
Matravers, Derek 110 n 26, 240
Meiland, Jack 125, 240
Meinong, Alexius 188, 190, 194, 197
Meyer, Leonard B. 75 n 36, 240
Michaels, Walter Benn 155, 156, 159, 239
Michelangelo 42, 67
  David 66
Miller, J. Hillis 204, 240

Mona Lisa 59, 60, 70–1, 73, 79 n 2
Mozart, Wolfgang Amadeus 36, 37, 139,
Mudrick, Marvin 204, 205, 240
Munch, Edvard 140
Murdoch, Iris 208, 218 n 8, 240

Newman, Barnett 141–2, 144
Nussbaum, Martha 103 n 14, 240

Olsen, Stein Haugom 37 n 4, 77 n 40, 124 n 9, 125 n 12, 143 n 6, 164 n 19, 186 n 60 & n 61, 190 n 5, 199 n 20, 200 n 21, 207 n 35, 228 n 11, 229 n 12, 230 n 14, 240
Olson, Eric T. 64 n 13, 66 n 17, 240

Parsons, Terence 194, 196, 240
Pereboom, D. 49 n 24, 241
Pettit, Philip 108–10, 241
Picasso, Pablo
  'Guernica' 129, 131–2, 138
Piero della Francesca 101
Pollock, Griselda 30 n 36, 241
Pollock, Jackson 41
Predelli, Stefano 48 n 22, 103 n 13, 241
Propp, Vladimir 191, 241
Puccini, Giacomo
  La Bohème 102

Quine, W. V. O. 7, 161

Rea, M. 49 n 24, 241
Ridley, Aaron 110 n 26, 241
Robinson, Jenefer 103 n 14, 141–4, 146 n 8, 241
Rorty, Richard 157–9, 161, 166, 183, 241
Russell, Bertrand 8, 177 n 48, 188, 241

Salmon, Nathan 189, 197, 241
Sartre, Jean-Paul xi, 52, 54, 208, 210, 211, 213–18, 241
Savile, Anthony xii, 74 n 34, 115, 116 n 35, 242

Schubert, Franz 36–7
Scruton, Roger xii, 76, 77 n 39, 109, 110, 242
Searle, John R. 5 n 2, 69 n 21 & n 22, 71, 199, 242
Shakespeare, William 102, 189, 198
  Hamlet 57
  King Lear 114
  Merchant of Venice 16–17
  Sonnet 65: 224
Sibley, Frank xii, xiii, 20, 21 n 25, 23, 59 n 3, 71 n 25, 79 n 2, 98–100, 106, 108–11, 120, 121, 142, 242
Sinfield, Alan 206, 242
Smith, Roberta 222 n 6, 242
Stecker, Robert xii, 25 n 31, 51 n 28, 168 n 32, 175 n 40 & n 41, 176, 177, 178, 180, 242
Stevenson, Robert Louis 36
Strawson, P. F. 79 n 2, 97, 228, 242
Süssmayr, Franz Xaver 37

Thom, Paul 170 n 34, 243
Thomasson, Amie L. 7 n 3, 10 n 8, 69 n 20, 184 n 55, 189, 197, 198, 205, 243
Thompson, Judith Jarvis 61 n 7, 63 n 9, 243
Titian
  Diana and Actaeon 74, 75 n 34
Tolstoy, Leo 102
Tormey, Alan 110 n 26, 243

Valéry, Paul 36
Van Gogh, Vincent 30 n 36
  Potato Eaters 29, 169–71
Van Meegeren, Han 18, 80, 105, 111, 134 n 20, 149–51
Vermeer, Jan 18, 80, 105, 111, 134 n 20, 149–51

Walton, Kendall L. xii, 15, 20, 22, 23, 67 n 18, 75 n 37, 81, 99, 100 n 8, 101 n 11, 107, 111, 117, 124, 129–33, 136, 138, 142, 144, 155 n 4, 156 n 6, 160 n 13, 188, 200 n 21, 229, 243

Warhol, Andy 11, 13,
Watt, Ian 146, 243
Wedeking, G. 49 n 24, 243
Werness, Hope B. 149 n 12 & n 13,
    150 n 14, 243
Wiggins, David 50 n 27, 67 n 19,
    243
Williams, Emmett 223 n 7, 243
Wittgenstein, Ludwig 12, 13
Wodehouse, P. G. 190, 195, 196
    Bertie Wooster 190, 195–6, 201
Wollheim, Richard 13–14, 58 n 2,
    104 n 16, 142–3, 229 n 12, 243

Wolterstorff, Nicholas xii, 97, 192 n
    7, 194, 244
Wreen, Michael 92 n 30, 244

Yeats, W. B.
    'Sailing to Byzantium' 101

Zangwill, Nick xii, 21 n 24, 71 n 25,
    73 n 31, 75 n 37, 99 n 7, 244
Zemach, Eddy xii, 25 n 33, 49, 58 n
    1, 63 n 11, 72 n 29, 75 n 35 & n
    36, 97, 113 n 31, 244
Zimmerman, D. 66 n 17, 244